RAW FOOD

for

EVERYONE

Essential Techniques and
300 Simple-to-Sophisticated Recipes

ALISSA COHEN

with Leah J. Dubois

AVERY

Published by the Penguin Group
Penguin Group (USA) Inc., 375 Hudson Street, New York, New York 10014, USA • Penguin Group (Canada),
90 Eglinton Avenue East, Suite 700, Toronto, Ontario M4P 2Y3, Canada (a division of Pearson Penguin Canada Inc.) •
Penguin Books Ltd, 80 Strand, London WC2R 0RL, England • Penguin Ireland, 25 St Stephen's Green, Dublin 2, Ireland
(a division of Penguin Books Ltd) • Penguin Group (Australia), 250 Camberwell Road, Camberwell, Victoria 3124, Australia
(a division of Pearson Australia Group Pty Ltd) • Penguin Books India Pvt Ltd, 11 Community Centre, Panchsheel Park,
New Delhi–110 017, India • Penguin Group (NZ), 67 Apollo Drive, Rosedale, North Shore 0632,
New Zealand (a division of Pearson New Zealand Ltd) • Penguin Books (South Africa) (Pty) Ltd,
24 Sturdee Avenue, Rosebank, Johannesburg 2196, South Africa

Penguin Books Ltd, Registered Offices: 80 Strand, London WC2R 0RL, England

First trade paperback edition 2011
Copyright © 2010 by Alissa Cohen
Photographs copyright © 2010 by Tara Donne
Published simultaneously in Canada

Most Avery books are available at special quantity discounts for bulk purchase for sales promotions, premiums, fund-raising,
and educational needs. Special books or book excerpts also can be created to fit specific needs. For details, write
Penguin Group (USA) Inc. Special Markets, 375 Hudson Street, New York, NY 10014.

The Library of Congress has catalogued the hardcover edition as follows:

Cohen, Alissa.
Raw food for everyone : essential techniques and 300 simple-to-sophisticated recipes / Alissa Cohen with Leah J. Dubois.
p.   cm.
Includes index.
ISBN 978-1-58333-403-4
1. Raw foods.   2. Vegetarian cooking.   3. Vegetarianism.   I. Dubois, Leah J.   II. Title.
TX837.C54   2010   2010022714
641.5'636—dc22

Printed in the United States of America
1   3   5   7   9   10   8   6   4   2

ISBN 978-1-58333-437-9 (paperback edition)

Book design by Meighan Cavanaugh

To Dennis,

who makes everything possible

Contents

RECIPES

Acknowledgments

Throughout my life, food has been a constant source of pleasure, health and healing, business, and entertaining. My parents, Mel and Loretta, showed me firsthand that food was truly love at our Jewish deli. My father's joke-telling over the deli counter and my whole family's involvement made the deli not just a business but a second home.

As I got older and explored the properties of food for health and healing, food took on a whole new meaning for me. Not only was food love but it could also be used for optimal health.

My raw foods journey began more than twenty years ago. I spoke about the benefits of raw foods at small, intimate gatherings. There were so many people who believed in me, from my acupuncture and chiropractor friends to the women at the local vitamin shop, who gave me the physical space to talk about raw food and share my message. I want to thank all of those people as well as those who allowed me to be part of their healing journey. I have learned so much from everyone who has come into my life. Every person's story is unique and brings with it a new understanding of how the human body is truly amazing.

There are many people who have been my guides and helpers and continue to teach me more and more about our remarkable bodies and how to keep them healthy. I take little pieces of all these experiences and continue to pass them on to others who need this knowledge. Thank you to the many wise souls for all the lessons.

Creating this book would not have been possible without the help of so many people, but I would like express an enormous thank-you to Harriet Bell, not only for her vast knowledge of the publishing business, food, and cookbooks, but for the direction, advice, creativity, and enthusiasm she shared while I was writing this book. She is the best, and I feel grateful to have had the opportunity to work with her.

And a special thank-you to Mary Ann Naples, Laura Nolan, Tara Donne, Lucia Watson, and the team at Avery.

—Alissa Cohen

RAW FOOD

· *for* ·

EVERYONE

FOREWORD

After attending Alissa Cohen's five-day intensive "non-cooking" raw foods program in Kittery, Maine, and living the past one and a half years on a raw diet, I am convinced this is a superior way to eat and enjoy food.

A raw diet provides all the nutritional food values required, since there's no loss of inherent nutrients as a result of cooking at high temperatures, which destroys much of the beneficial value of foods we eat. Like me, people who become raw food followers notice a significant improvement in how they feel physically and emotionally, as well as a greater sense of overall well-being. Some have even seen dramatic and significant changes in their medical conditions after eating this way. Diabetes disappears. Dramatic weight loss occurs. Blood pressure is under control. Gastrointestinal symptoms are gone. Allergies, sinusitis, and migraines all dissipate. Perhaps if more physicians advocated a raw diet and recommended it to their patients, there would be far fewer chronic illnesses.

Raw foods are also delicious when prepared using Alissa's recipes. You can actually taste the flavors and true textures of fruits, vegetables, nuts, seeds, and grains when they are prepared without traditional cooking. In addition, raw food:

- Adds new excitement to family meals
- Offers new enjoyment when dining out with friends and family
- Brings a new dimension to having dinner parties at home—wait until your friends taste these recipes!
- Guarantees a healthier lifestyle

My guru, Alissa Cohen, has been an excellent and enthusiastic teacher by providing me with a new outlook on nutrition that I never learned in medical school. Try the recipes in *Raw Food for Everyone* and you will see dramatic changes in your health, your body, and your overall well-being.

—Jack Stern, M.D.

INTRODUCTION

When I was in my twenties, doctors couldn't find the causes for my weight gain, fibromyalgia, candida, nerve and joint damage, and other illnesses. I tried every imaginable diet—macrobiotic, vegetarian, vegan—but nothing helped. While working at a health food store I met a woman who introduced me to the benefits of eating only raw and "living" food. So I began to do research on raw food and what it could do for me. I spoke to anyone I could find who had followed a raw foods diet, which wasn't easy because so few people were eating just raw food. I spent some time with the woman I had met in the health food store and picked her brain about going on a raw vegan diet. I decided that since nothing else was working for me, I would experiment for myself. After all, what did I have to lose?

In a matter of weeks my aches and pains disappeared. My eyesight improved so much that I stopped using reading glasses. My mood swings disappeared. My energy levels went through the roof. My hair shined. My skin glowed. My eyes sparkled. I lost seventeen pounds. What was most astonishing was how I felt inside, inside my body and mind. I was calmer, more peaceful, happier, and full of hope and joy for the future. Every morning I would wake up with a profound feeling of gratitude and excited about a new day. Wow! I committed to raw food and have never looked back.

At that time, there were few, if any, cookbooks on the subject, and the Internet was in its infancy, so I had to create my own recipes. More than just bowls of salad, I wanted fresh, hearty, filling food, so I created raw vegan versions of favorites such as pizza with toppings and tortillas wrapped around a medley of fresh vegetables. Light ribbons of zucchini topped with a ladle of creamy nut sauce became my fettuccine Alfredo. Unwilling to give up my sweet tooth, I developed desserts such as chocolate pudding, fudge squares, and apple pie made with raw ingredients including apples, dates, nut butters, and carob.

The more I learned about raw foods, the more I came to believe that they are the most effective way to help people lose weight and achieve optimal health. I began teaching hands-on private classes and speaking at gatherings large and small. No matter how much I talked and raved about how good these dishes tasted, the proof was in the pudding—my raw pudding. When audiences discovered they could eat whenever and however much they wanted without counting calories, fat grams, protein, and carbs, and without weighing and measuring their food, they were hooked.

I was astounded by what happened. People were healing themselves of diseases that were deemed incurable. The weight was just melting off of them and they were literally changing before my eyes into more youthful, more vibrant, more energetic beings!

After endless requests, I gathered my recipes and self-published *Living on Live Food*. The book's success catapulted me into the limelight, and I became internationally known as a raw food authority. My first book was filled with testimonials and simple recipes so that people could easily grasp the concept of this new way of eating.

Since *Living on Live Food* was published, times have certainly changed again. The collective consciousness is more in tune with what a vegetarian diet is and why it is better than the standard American diet. We see ads on TV and in magazines promoting vegetarianism, and people actually know what a vegan is. Something most people had no clue of ten years ago! We are seeing a reemergence of getting back to nature, getting back to a more natural diet and way of living. Everything is about being green, recycling, and taking care of the planet and ourselves with our new food choices. There is so much more information about nutrition that we're finally starting to "get" that what we put into our bodies really does make a difference. Most of us know that fruits and vegetables are good for us. We know that a lot of the sugar-laden, overprocessed junk foods that many of us grew up eating are not something we want to continue eating if we truly want to be healthy.

As a result, the raw food movement has been gaining momentum over the last five to seven years. Years ago if I told people to eat just fruit, vegetables, nuts, and seeds, they would have thought I was crazy! Now, when I tell people this, they inevitably know someone who eats only raw food or have heard stories of how raw food has helped people heal, given them renewed energy, and helped them regain youthfulness.

To further spread the power of raw food, I opened Grezzo (Italian for "raw"), a fine-dining raw food restaurant in Boston in 2008 and hired inventive chef Leah Dubois. Grezzo has garnered rave reviews from restaurant critics who had never eaten a raw food meal before. Grezzo is a high-end establishment with cocktails and a wine list offering biodynamic and organic choices and with knowledgeable servers prepared to answer customers' questions. My goal with Grezzo is not to cater to the raw food crowd, but to show meat-and-potatoes-lovers how good, how healthy, how energizing raw foods can be. They can start with a cocktail like a mojito or a saketini, enjoy wild mushroom fettuccine, lasagna, or papaya steak, and finish with a slice of cheesecake or a few scoops of raw vegan ice cream. By having a raw food experience in an elegant restaurant setting, people can dine on gourmet food that is not only healthy but tastes better than most traditional unhealthy dishes. It allows them to experience how extraordinary the food is rather than just reading about it in a book.

. . .

Because Grezzo was such a success, I opened a second Grezzo in Newburyport, Massachusetts. At both restaurants, people loved that they could go out for a five-star meal and still be eating healthy.

Showcasing the gorgeousness of fine raw food in the restaurants also showed me the need for a new cookbook to give readers the tools to integrate fine raw food cooking into their daily lives, a cookbook with simple *and* sophisticated recipes to make everything from a quick breakfast to an elegant dinner. A book with techniques, ingredients, equipment, and recipes—all in one comprehensive volume.

Because I believe in being able to create a simple, quick meal, it was important to keep this way of eating uncomplicated and easy to do. That's why there are so many basic recipes—ones that I've been making for years, and that have helped keep me raw! In *Raw Food for Everyone*, though, my goal is to change the thinking that a raw food diet is restrictive and lacks food choices. Techniques such as cold smoking and fermenting are used to recreate dishes never thought possible with raw and living food. Given all the available choices, there's no excuse for *not* eating this way.

If you're just starting with raw food, some of the ingredients may be unfamiliar, which is why there are such large sections on ingredients, fruits, and vegetables, and helpful techniques such as soaking and sprouting grains and seeds. I want you to become as familiar with these new foods as you are with your old staples. Whenever embarking on something new, there's always something of a learning curve, and this is true with raw food. The more you use these ingredients and techniques, the sooner they will become second nature to you.

Anyone can learn how to prepare raw foods. And when you do, you'll be amazed at what's in store for you. You'll look and feel better within days, heal yourself of chronic and acute diseases, and lose weight faster than ever before. You'll have more energy and feel and look younger without having to count calories, fat grams, protein, or carbs. Over the past ten years, raw food has gone from underground phenomenon to niche to completely mainstream. But until now, no one has raised raw food to the same level of artful cooking and joyful eating as traditional cooking, with all the information you need to make this amazing food every day. Now that so many more people are discovering the benefits of raw food, I feel strongly that the time is right for another book. One that goes beyond the basics into a whole new realm of what eating raw and living food can actually mean. That's what *Raw Food for Everyone* is all about.

If you are already committed to raw food, *Raw Food for Everyone* will take your cooking to the next level of preparation and the presentation of great flavors. For those of you who are new to or are considering raw food, *Raw Food for Everyone* explains the philosophy and provides instructions as well as tips and techniques. Cooks of all levels will gain the confidence and the knowledge to create their own fabulous recipes. Once you try raw food for yourself and experience its many benefits, you'll be on your way to a better and healthier way of eating and living.

—Alissa Cohen

WHY EAT RAW FOOD
and
HOW TO GET STARTED

Raw and living foods are alkaline-rich foods that contain enzymes. Heating food over 112°F destroys those enzymes. Raw and living foods have significantly higher nutrient values than cooked foods. Raw and living foods are fruits, vegetables, nuts, seeds, and sprouted grains. They're filled with living energy, raw vitality, and unlimited health benefits. With *Raw Food for Everyone*, you'll discover how to reap the benefits of the earth's most powerful healing foods and how to prepare them in innovative ways.

People often ask if there's a difference between raw foods and living foods. Raw and living foods both contain enzymes. Unsprouted nuts, seeds, and grains are considered raw and contain enzymes that are lying dormant. When these foods are soaked and/or sprouted, their dormant enzymes become active, and therefore become living foods. Fruits, vegetables, and sprouts are all living foods. Eating raw food is great, but make sure you're also eating a lot of living food. You can eat raw foods in their natural states—nibble on a handful of nuts or compose a salad. You can prepare simple recipes such as smoothies and soups. You can whip up easy nut pâtés, make hummus, or churn banana ice cream. You can get creative with a dehydrator and turn out crackers, burgers, and breadsticks. You can prepare cheese lasagna, sugar pumpkin ravioli, and apple pie à la mode. You can have dessert for lunch and dinner if you want to. Or even for breakfast. I encourage it because even our most decadent desserts are packed with nutrition and made with raw fruits, vegetables, nuts, and seeds. You can eat anything you want as long as it's raw.

Getting started at something new is often the hardest part. Here's what I suggest:

- **Set a goal.** Make a thirty-, sixty-, or ninety-day commitment to eating raw foods.
- **Go shopping and buy food.** You'll need lots of fresh, raw food—enough to last a week. Having plenty of the right foods in the fridge and pantry is the first step. One bunch of bananas and six oranges won't do the trick. It might seem odd to buy cases of apples, bananas, mangoes, and tomatoes; multiple bunches of greens and herbs; and six jars of raw nut butter, but since raw foods are lighter than cooked foods, you will be eating a lot more when you first start eating this way. Put yourself in a new mind-set when it comes to food. Eating raw foods is not about deprivation, but about savoring the best that nature has to offer. Eat those four bananas. Enjoy smoothies made with six juiced oranges and a couple of puréed mangoes throughout the day. Have three bowls of soup. Feed that sweet tooth some Mexican Chocolate Torte or other dessert.
- **Prepare in advance to make meals simpler.** When you come home with fruits and vegetables, don't just shove them into the refrigerator. Spend an hour preparing them, so they're ready to eat when you're hungry. Make fruit salad. Clean those lettuce greens. Mix salad dressing. If you bought

asparagus, small red onions, or cucumbers, for example, make some quick pickles. It's so much easier to put meals together if everything is ready to go.

- **Experiment with different tastes.** Try different recipes from each chapter: drinks and smoothies, appetizers, entrees, soups, salads, and desserts.

While it may seem that you're eating more food when you first go raw, remember that you're eating more nutritionally dense foods than ever before. You won't have that dull, heavy feeling that comes from eating cooked food. It won't take long for your body to get used to this cleaner, healthier way of eating. You'll quickly notice that you are eating less food, yet are more satisfied. You're getting more nutrients from less food, since raw foods are so nutritionally superior.

Have you ever noticed that when eating cooked food you can eat and eat and sometimes you just never feel full? Or you're eating a lot of food but still craving something more? You may be stuffed after eating a cheese pizza but still want an ice cream cone. Your body is telling you that despite eating all that food with empty calories, chemicals, and preservatives, it craves the vitamins, minerals, and other good things that come from quality food nutrition.

Raw foods eliminate food cravings. You won't have that fear of wanting to eat and then not being able to stop. Raw and living food gives one's body everything it needs to feel perfectly and nutritionally satisfied.

The beauty of eating a raw and living food diet is that there are no rules. Even though the recipes are arranged by categories such as "desserts" and "entrees" and "soups," they're all made up of wholesome, fresh, live foods that you can eat anytime because they are the healthiest, most abundantly nutritious, vitamin-, mineral-, and enzyme-packed foods available.

Not only can you eat as much as you want whenever you want, you'll lose weight and feel better than ever. Eating raw and living foods has helped millions of people feel well and healthy for the first time in their lives. A raw and living foods diet delivers the much-needed vitamins, minerals, enzymes, and other life-giving substances to your body that the heat from cooking destroys.

Raw and living foods are alkaline-rich foods. When your diet is made up of raw fruits, vegetables, sprouted nuts, seeds, and grains, your body shifts from an acid state to a more alkaline state. Sickness and disease occur in acidic bodies. An alkaline body is a healthy body.

Also, raw and living food helps reverse and slow down the aging process because these foods contain high levels of vitamins, minerals, antioxidants, and enzymes. Raw and living foods are extremely beneficial in helping to arrest and in many cases may actually *reverse* aging at the cellular level.

Those starting on the raw food path are often concerned about getting enough protein, calcium, and other nutrients. Foods that we often think of as the best sources of protein—beef, chicken, fish, and eggs—do not create protein in your body. Amino acids create protein in your body. And the best source of amino acids is leafy green vegetables such as spinach, kale, and chard.

When you eat meat, fish, or chicken, you're not getting as much protein as you think you are. Take chicken, for example. Say there are 20 grams of protein in a chicken breast. Once you cook the chicken, half of its protein content is destroyed. Now your body has to process this heavy, dense 10 grams of protein—it can take up to 100 hours to digest and assimilate. How much protein from a cooked chicken breast will you actually get? Maybe a few grams, if you're lucky.

A salad of uncooked greens or sprouts may contain just a few grams of protein, but you can digest and assimilate all of them because the vegetables and sprouts have all of their vitamins, minerals, and enzymes intact, making protein easier to take in and far more useful to your body.

With raw and living foods, you get plenty of protein but without hormones, antibiotics, chemicals, drugs, and other potentially harmful substances found in the feed given to animals. Second, you get a lot more protein while eating a lot less food.

The vitamins, minerals, and other nutrients that are imperative for optimal health are found in abundance in raw and living foods. No other way of eating gives you a broader spectrum of the essential nutrients. Since these nutrients are not lost through cooking and heating, the enzymes remain intact and are better utilized by the body.

Vitamins and minerals must work together synergistically for optimal health. Eating a raw food, plant-based diet assures that you are getting the proper ratio of these essential nutrients without throwing off your nutrient balance by taking individual supplements and guessing at what is needed.

Many people starting to eat raw food are concerned that they'll get fat from eating olives, nuts, seeds, coconuts, and avocados. Well, these foods are packed with the "good" fats and antioxidants our bodies need.

In addition, there's no need to count calories and fat grams because there's a huge difference between cooked fats and raw plant fats. The studies that have been done linking dietary fats to obesity as well as cancer, heart disease, kidney failure, high blood pressure, and all of the other diseases that clog up the blood and the arteries have been done with cooked fats, the majority of which come from animals.

Raw plant fats, on the other hand, have exactly the opposite effect. Raw fats such as avocados, olives, coconuts, nuts, and seeds are imperative in a healthy diet. These fats contain enzymes. They also contain antioxidants and oils that help the joints, nerves, and bones.

Raw plant fats do not cause the body to gain excess weight because raw fats contain lipase, an enzyme necessary for digesting fat. Lipase breaks up the raw plant fats as they are eaten and helps to digest the fats in these foods. On the other hand, cooking fats destroys lipase, along with other important enzymes and minerals. Because raw foods do not contain animal fats and are digested properly, they do not clog arteries or cause chronic and degenerative diseases. Raw fats are not stored as excess weight in the body.

You won't get fat by eating avocados, sprouted nuts and seeds, and other plant fats. (Since they're plants, they contain no cholesterol.) When starting this diet, many people eat two to three avocados a day and lose weight. Even people with just a little bit of weight to lose find that those extra few pounds just melt off because they are eating fats in their whole natural form with all of their enzymes intact.

These enzymes that help digest and assimilate your carbohydrates, protein, and fats (amylase, protease, and lipase) also help in the digestion and absorption of the food that you're eating, and you won't gain weight eating raw and living foods. In fact, you can lose significant amounts of weight, eat whatever you want and however much you want as long as it's raw and never have to count another calorie or fat gram again.

Once you start eating raw foods, your body will go through a detoxification process, which means it is ridding itself of the poisons (or toxins) that have accumulated in your body such as bad food, drugs, caffeine, and alcohol.

As the body begins to detoxify, some people may have headaches, skin rashes, acne breakouts, colds, and fever. Some find themselves fatigued, irritable, and even nauseous. These symptoms may come and go for several weeks, but keep it mind, that it's all part of the process of ridding the body of all those nasty things. This process and the accompanying reactions are normal; it means that the body is cleansing and healing itself.

What I Talk About When I Talk About Raw Food

Pizza. Cheese. Pasta. Ice Cream. Sliders. Cheesecake. They don't sound like raw food, do they? Well, they are, but with a difference. Every recipe in this book is made with raw, live ingredients. Nothing is cooked above 112°F. So why call ribbons of zucchini topped with a puréed cashew–pine nut–garlic sauce fettuccine Alfredo, when there's no pasta or cheese? How can a piece of papaya be compared to a "salmon steak" if there's no salmon? Don't you need chocolate, sugar, and eggs to make "chocolate mousse"?

We use the language of traditional cooking when describing raw food because those words are familiar to everyone and best describe and resemble the textures of each dish. The zucchini is thinly shaved on a mandoline to resemble fettuccine so each ribbon catches the creamy herb sauce, which has the consistency of a traditional Alfredo sauce. Thick slabs of papaya look like salmon fillets when encrusted with a dusting of star anise and Sichuan peppercorns and brushed-on teriyaki glaze. Coconut butter, coconut meat, and coconut water impart a light, airy mousse-like texture to the raw cacao meringue.

Our goal isn't to make everything a mock dish, such as almost-just-like-the-real-thing chicken salad. What's important is to see how a finished dish can be created using healthy, living ingredients and employing food terminology that we're all familiar with. Comparing raw food dishes to cooked dishes imparts a sense of how that particular raw foods dish should taste.

Raw Food for Everyone shows you what raw foods are, how to prepare them, and why they are good for you. Once you start preparing this food yourself, you'll see how creative and nourishing it is. And once you taste it, well, you'll be hooked. And you'll want to stick with it.

(continued)

BECOMING RAW

One of the first things people do when they decide to go raw is clean out their refrigerators, freezers, and pantries of any foods that aren't raw. That's a great way to start, but too often people don't replace discarded foods with enough fruits, vegetables, nuts, grains, seeds, and other raw items.

Those who have just embraced raw foods just don't keep enough food in their kitchens! Eating raw is not about eating sparsely or sparingly. Eating raw is not about starving yourself. Raw food is all about abundance and feeling full. If you're hungry, eat. Eat as much as you want. Raw foods are healthy and good for you.

Stock up on raw condiments and ingredients like agave nectar, olive oil, and dried fruit. Change your food shopping mentality. Instead of buying a bunch of bananas or a head of lettuce, get cases of your favorite fruits and vegetables for juices, smoothies, salads, and other dishes. If you don't have raw food in your house to eat, then you'll be tempted to head to the nearest fast-food place or run to the market for something unhealthy. Pick a handful of recipes to make ahead so you have food for a few days. Nothing's worse than being hungry and staring at an empty fridge.

Eating raw foods means that there will also be a new emotional aspect to your life. Those who eat a raw and living foods diet and begin to heal themselves, lose weight, and feel physically better find that their lives change in other ways, too. Raw food lets people feel healthier, see more clearly, and think straight for the first time in their lives. As a result, there's often a huge shift in all aspects of life. People let go of all the things that no longer work in their lives. They become motivated to leave jobs they hate and follow their dreams. Others end unhealthy friendships or unhappy relationships. Those old behaviors and habits no longer feel good. All that heavy, cooked food was bogging them down in every aspect of life. Becoming raw allows you to experience a new world and a new vision.

STAYING RAW

If you've been eating raw foods and find yourself falling off the wagon, don't panic or beat yourself up. It's okay. Really. You're not going to be punished. (Well, you might feel lousy eating cooked food—that's punishment enough.) Most of us were raised eating cooked foods, so sometimes it's hard to make and stick with such a dramatic change the first time you try.

Eating raw is not about being perfect. It's about being more loving to yourself by feeding your body healthier food choices. The more you do it, the more it will become a habit, and eventually eating raw foods will be the norm. Your taste buds and desires will change, as you will start craving raw food rather than cooked food.

For some this happens quickly; for others it's a longer process. Be gentle with yourself. Creating stress in the body is what we're trying to avoid! Stress creates acid in the body, an unhealthy state, and can be more detrimental to optimal health than eating some unhealthy foods. Give yourself time to adjust. Know that every time you eat raw, whether it's for a few days, several weeks, or six months, you're investing in your body's health and well-being.

THE RAW PANTRY:

INGREDIENTS

The ingredients in this section are those most frequently used in preparing raw foods, particularly the recipes found within these pages. (Fruits and vegetables are in a separate section starting on page 63.) Those who are just starting to eat and live a raw foods lifestyle sometimes find it hard to discern what's raw and what isn't. Use this section as a guideline. Most items can be purchased at health food stores, some supermarkets, and online retailers.

To be 100 percent pure in your consumption of raw foods, read packaging labels carefully and understand what they say. For instance, when buying packaged sea vegetables, the large type might read "Raw Hijiki," but the fine print might say that it has been steamed at a temperature well above 112°F, which is the maximum allowed in raw foods. When ingredients are listed in the recipes, the word "raw" isn't repeated. Instead of "raw almonds" or "raw oats," we list just "almonds" or "oats," assuming that all ingredients are raw.

They're Not Raw. And Here's Why.

Here's a list of common foods and ingredients that might seem to be raw, but are not, because they're often processed at high temperatures or combined with other ingredients that are not raw.

Balsamic vinegar Produced from white grapes that are boiled down to concentrate them before they are fermented and aged.

Bulgur wheat Used in many tabbouleh recipes, bulgur has been cooked and dried.

Couscous Made from cooked wheat.

Frozen fruits and vegetables Most are blanched in boiling water before they are frozen. Even if the label says "organic and raw," contact the company to make sure they truly are raw.

Honey Raw honey is available, but honey is not vegan, since it comes from bees, which are animals.

Juice Even if the label reads "100% fruit juice," if it comes in a can or a glass or plastic bottle, it has been pasteurized and isn't raw. Pass on juices with labels that say "lightly pasteurized," as there's no such thing. That's like being a little pregnant.

Maple syrup Maple tree sap is boiled at a temperature of 219°F until the water evaporates and only the syrup is left. Since it's cooked at such a high temperature, it's not raw.

Rolled oats Even if the label says "raw oats," most are steamed at high temperatures before being rolled. True raw oats are available from online raw food sources.

Soybeans (edamame) Shelled or in-the-shell soybeans are blanched in boiling water. Other soy products—soy cheese, soy mayonnaise, soy ice cream—are either cooked at high temperatures or include ingredients that are not raw. Fresh edamame that have never been cooked or frozen are raw. They can sometimes be found at farmers' markets.

Soy sauce Soy sauce is made from roasted wheat and other grains and fermenting boiled soybeans, and many soy sauces contain artificial flavors and colorings. Tamari is pasteurized, too, and therefore not raw. See Nama Shoyu on page 30 for a raw alternative.

Salt Found in packets and shakers in restaurants and homes everywhere, table salt is refined by heating it to more than 2000°F and important minerals are removed. To make salt free-flowing, an anticaking agent is added, which turns the salt purple. Since no one will buy purple salt, it's bleached, and then glucose, talcum, aluminum silicate, and other ingredients are added. Is there anything else to say about this stuff? Coarse-grained kosher salt is refined just like table salt, allowing it to absorb more moisture than fine-grained salt, although additives such as iodine are not reintroduced. Only pure sea salt or stone salt (Himalayan) is acceptable in raw foods.

Tofu Also known as bean curd, tofu is made from curdled (heated) milk of cooked soybeans.

Agave Nectar (Agave Syrup) A light brown, mild-tasting, natural liquid sweetener; it comes from the same plant from which tequila is made and is used in place of refined sugar, honey, and maple syrup in raw foods. Since it has no aftertaste or its own distinct flavor, agave nectar can be used as a sweetener in smoothies, ice cream, desserts, and sauces.

Agave nectar is extracted from the blue agave plant native to Southern Mexico, then filtered and heated at a low temperature, making it suitable for raw food preparation. Note that "light" agave nectar and "dark" or "amber" agave nectar are available, but only the light variety is truly raw.

Agave nectar is high in fructose, a naturally occurring sugar in some plants, and sweeter than refined sugar. It contains approximately 1.4 times the amount of carbohydrate calories as sugar. Because fructose does not stimulate digestive insulin secretion like other sugars, it doesn't create a "sugar rush," making it an ideal sweetener for diabetics.

It will keep indefinitely at room temperature. To adapt your own recipes, substitute ⅓ cup light agave syrup for 1 cup sugar.

Apple Cider Vinegar   Raw apple cider vinegar, a powerful antioxidant, contains amino acids, along with essential vitamins, minerals, and enzymes. Light brown in color, it helps break down cholesterol formations in the blood vessels and reduces high blood pressure. Apple cider vinegar is promoted to help people lose weight by speeding metabolism and burning fat at a faster rate. Apple cider vinegar improves digestion and helps expel body toxins.

Apple cider vinegar is made by fermenting apples. The resulting liquid is pressed, strained, and bottled. Others such as distilled white, balsamic, rice wine, and most red wine vinegars (see Red Wine Vinegar, page 36) are pasteurized at high temperatures and therefore are not raw.

It can be used in dressings and sauces—in anything that calls for vinegar or where an acid such as lemon juice is used.

Apple cider vinegar can help to restore the body's alkaline-acid balance. One to two teaspoons apple cider vinegar in an 8-ounce glass of water is recommended as a daily health tonic.

Use apple cider vinegar to relieve muscle pain from exercise. Just rub some on your body after a shower as you would moisturizer. It works!

Raw, unfiltered organic apple cider vinegar is available in bottles in many sizes. It will keep indefinitely at room temperature.

Beans   Dried adzukis, chickpeas, and mung beans are used most frequently in raw foods. All of them must be soaked and then sprouted to make them more digestible. Fresh chickpeas have sheaths that can easily be removed and eaten right away. Soak dried chickpeas in water overnight and then sprout for two to three days before using. Black beans and other large beans can be soaked and sprouted, but they still can be hard to digest. Refer to the chart on page 61 for details.

Cacao   Talk about a superfood! Cacao, or raw chocolate, that has not been heated, processed, or sweetened, is packed with antioxidants, essential fatty acids, and other nutrients. It is available as nibs, which are the broken bits of cacao tree seeds, or as a powder. Enjoy cacao nibs sweetened with agave nectar, add them to ice cream and cookies, eat a few out of hand every day, or add them to trail mix. Use cacao powder in smoothies, shakes, and desserts. To store, refrigerate nibs or store at room temperature, and store the powder at room temperature.

Cacao Butter   Not all cacao butters are equal. While it looks like white chocolate, raw cacao butter has not been subjected to high temperatures when processed and it contains no chemicals or solvents. Cacao butter imparts a delicate chocolate aroma. Add a teaspoon when blending smoothies or making desserts, ice cream, or chocolate confections. It is available in chunks; store well-wrapped cacao butter in a cool, dry place. Break off a small piece and try it as a soothing skin moisturizer.

Carob Powder   Ground into a powder from the carob tree pods, also known as St. John's bread, carob is a cocoa powder substitute and rich in vitamin A, B vitamins, and several important minerals, particularly potassium. Try carob powder in desserts and smoothies.

Coconut   We go through cases and cases of coconuts every day at Grezzo, using the water and the meat for many different preparations—drinks, sauces, desserts, and ice cream. We only use Thai, also called young, coconuts, which look like a miniature round, ivory hut with a pointed roof, because their meat is softer and their water is sweeter. Their husks are removed before being shipped to Asian markets, health food stores, and some supermarkets. A Thai coconut yields about ¾ to 1½ cups coconut water.

There are several methods for opening Thai coconuts. Because we go through so many coconuts, we use a small hatchet, but a cleaver or a big knife works just as well. Shave off the pointed spongy end of the coconut with a few quick chops to reveal the hard shell. Use the bottom pointed end of the hatchet or knife to punch a hole in the shell. Shimmy the top point of your tool into the hole to pry open the coconut. Pour the coconut water into a bowl. With one well-aimed chop, cut the coconut in half from top to bottom. Use a spoon to remove the meat.

Confusion abounds when it comes to the many coconut products, so here's a guide:

Coconut Butter is made from coconut meat. This thick, creamy spread can be eaten right from the jar, mixed into fruit smoothies, and used in desserts. When opening a new jar of coconut butter, there will be a layer of coconut oil on top. The firm coconut butter is under the oil. Remove the coconut oil on top. The coconut butter underneath will be thick, like frozen butter.

Coconut Flakes can be added to smoothies and trail mix or used when making macaroons, cookies, and pies. Look for raw flakes that have been slowly dehydrated at below 112°F to preserve their enzymes, vitamins, minerals, and life force. Store in an airtight container in a cool, dry place.

Coconut Milk is made from processing the coconut meat with water in a blender until it has a thin, smooth consistency, similar to 1% dairy milk. See page 108 for making coconut milk. It keeps in the refrigerator for two to three days.

Coconut Oil is processed much like olive oil. The coconut meat is chopped and placed in an expeller press. What differentiates raw coconut oil from others on the market is that during production, the temperature never exceeds 78.8°F (room temperature). Using a large centrifuge, the emulsion is separated into the pure oil. Start the day with a tablespoon of coconut oil to promote healthy, rapid weight loss. Coconut oil has enormous value for people with underactive and overactive thyroid glands. Put coconut oil into smoothies, desserts, salad dressings, and sauces. Massage a bit into your skin as a soothing moisturizer. To soften, place the jar in a bowl of warm water for five minutes, or keep the jar on top of the refrigerator where it's warm and it won't solidify. Stir sea salt into some coconut butter for a real buttery flavor on corn or unroasted vegetables.

Coconut Vinegar Made from fermented coconut water, it is similar in flavor to rice wine vinegar with a sharp, acidic taste.

Coconut Water is the thin, sweet, refreshing liquid inside the coconut. Puncture two holes in a coconut, stick in a straw, and slurp away. Coconut water is also used in smoothies, juice blends, sauces, and desserts.

Flax Seeds Flax seeds, a rich source of omega-3 fatty acids, play an important role in controlling cholesterol and heart disease. They also provide an abundant source of fiber. (Too much flax will have a strong laxative effect.) Raw whole flax seeds are available at many grocery stores and health food stores. They can be soaked in water for four hours or overnight, or ground or milled before using in order to better digest them. Whole seeds will last, but once ground they quickly go rancid. Sprinkle ground flax seeds on salads and cereals. Make crackers, muffins, puddings, pizza crust, and wraps.

Flax oil is also available. Use half flax oil and half olive oil in dressings. Add a tablespoon to smoothies or juices. A tablespoon ingested each day is said to be good for psoriasis and eczema. Packaged in opaque bottles to protect it from light, the oil must be refrigerated and will stay fresh for six weeks after opening. Like other oils, if it smells like motor oil, it should be discarded.

Goji Berries Also called wolfberries, antioxidant- and nutrient-rich goji berries have long been recommended by traditional Chinese medicine practitioners for their many health benefits, especially their effects on inflammatory and skin diseases. There are all kinds of processed goji berry products on the market—juices, candy bars, even face creams—which negate the fruit's power. Avoid them and purchase dried Tibetan goji berries, grown in protected valleys. (Many Chinese goji berries are industrially grown and pesticides are used.)

A goji berry tastes like a cross between a sweet cherry and a tart cranberry. Make your own goji juice by soaking half a cup of berries in four cups of water for six to eight hours. Blend and drink as is, or combine with apples, mangoes, or bananas. Eat them like any dried fruit or add them to smoothies, trail mix, and desserts.

Grains Purchase only whole raw grains, not processed ones such as bulgur and pearled barley. Store whole grains in covered containers at room temperature, marking the date of purchase so you know how long they've been in your pantry.

> **Amaranth** Highly nutritious and sweet-nutty in flavor, amaranth can be sprouted and used as a cereal, used in recipes such as chili, soups, and salads, or ground for crackers. Amaranth contains twice as much calcium as milk. High in protein, it also provides good amounts of lysine and methionine, two essential amino acids that are not frequently found in grains. Amaranth is also high in fiber and contains calcium, iron, potassium, phosphorus, and vitamins A and C.
>
> **Barley** Once sprouted, barley has a chewy texture, much like wheat berries. Sprouted barley is used in breads and stews or ground to make crackers.
>
> **Buckwheat** Once sprouted, gluten-free buckwheat can be used whole or ground. Dehydrate whole sprouted buckwheat to make Buckwheaties (page 199). Serve with almond milk for breakfast and snacks. Make crackers with ground buckwheat or add them to smoothies. Soak and sprout for breadsticks. Blend a banana, coconut water, and buckwheat sprouts for a

nourishing postworkout drink. Although buckwheat is botanically a fruit, it's used like a grain, which is why it's included here.

Corn Cut fresh summer corn off the cob and use in salads, slaws, and corn chips. Toss corn kernels or slather whole ears with coconut oil and sea salt and dehydrate for one hour.

Hemp One of the most nutrient-dense foods available, protein-packed and vitamin E-rich hemp seeds can be eaten out of hand, blended into smoothies and desserts, and sprinkled on salads. Purchase shelled hemp seeds (sometimes called hemp nuts) and store them in the refrigerator or freezer, as they can quickly turn rancid. Hemp protein powder is made from hemp seeds that are finely milled. Adding a tablespoon or two to shakes and smoothies is a good protein booster. Hemp seed oil, which has the lowest amount of saturated fatty acids, at 8 percent, and the highest amount of the polyunsaturated essential fatty acids, at 80 percent, has a nutty, earthy taste, making it ideal for salad dressings. Store in the refrigerator like other seed oils. Combine hemp milk, cacao powder, and dates for the best chocolate milk.

Kamut Kamut berries are similar to wheat berries and can be soaked and used as a substitute for wheat in breads, crackers, and other recipes.

Millet A small gluten-free grain that packs a big dose of iron, millet sprouts in just a day. Mix some with an avocado for a quick lunch. Add to citrus fruit salads. Millet can be ground and used as porridge.

Oats Use raw oat groats that you process yourself or make sure you are buying true raw oats. Steel-cut, quick-cooking, and old-fashioned oats are all steamed; avoid them. Enjoy oats for breakfast with almond or hemp milk. Grind into oat flour and make cookies.

Quinoa A very quick-sprouting, light-tasting grain, quinoa is easy to digest, as it's gluten free. This protein-packed superfood contains more protein than any other grain. Try sprouted quinoa in salads or to make maki rolls, ground into flour for making crackers, or as a morning cereal with fruit and almond milk.

Rye A hearty, earthy grain that takes longer to sprout than most others. Use it to make crackers and breads. We also use rye and wheat berries to make our Rejuvelac (page 133).

Spelt Use spelt berries as you would wheat berries.

Wheat Berries Wheat berries are used in breads, crackers, salads, and rejuvelac for making cheese and growing wheat grass. Hard winter wheat berries are used for breads and crackers; soft winter wheat berries are for making rejuvelac and growing wheat grass.

Wild Rice Wild rice can be sprouted and used in salads or combined with tomato sauce to make a main course that is high in protein and fiber. Brown and white rice will not sprout.

Herbamare Organic Herb Seasoning Salt   A small amount of this sea salt, dried vegetable, and dried herb blend adds a big flavor boost to dips, dressings, burgers, nut loaves, and many other dishes.

Incan Golden Berry   Also called the cape gooseberry or goldenberry, this fruit is reminiscent of Sweet Tarts candy. This dried fruit contains small amounts of vitamin B_{12} and is high in antioxidants. The berries are 16 percent protein, supplying a plant-based, nonfat source of protein.

Kombucha   Kombucha is a fermented drink that has been used by many for medicinal purposes. It's a living culture of beneficial microorganisms. Many people find kombucha good for restoring health, vitality, and balance. Kombucha tea has long been popular in Asia as a health-promoting, detoxifying tonic. Some people do make this themselves at home, but a "mother" culture is necessary to get started. Most health food stores and even some supermarkets now carry many different brands of kombucha. It has a vinegary, bubbly, fizzy texture and taste.

Lentils   Neither a seed nor a grain, lentils are a legume or pulse. They come in an earthy rainbow of colors—red, orange, yellow, and green. High in protein and iron and easy to sprout, they are used in many dishes, such as Buffalo Lentil Tenders (page 239).

Lucuma   Another superfood from the high elevations of South America, lucuma is the edible fruit of the lucuma tree. Once harvested, the fresh fruit doesn't travel well, but it can be dried and ground into a powder and used as a natural sweetener in ice cream and smoothies. Unlike other sweeteners, it has significant amounts of calcium, iron, and other valuable nutrients.

Maca   Rich in amino acids, vitamins, and minerals (magnesium, iron, and calcium— higher than milk), maca, like yacón, is a tuber that grows only in the high Andes plateaus. Used as a food and medicine by indigenous Peruvians and Bolivians, maca is reputed to be good for increasing energy and stamina and balancing hormones in men and women. Raw organic maca is dried at low temperatures and then ground into a powder. It has a malt-like flavor. A little bit of maca powder goes a long way. Add ½ teaspoon to smoothies and juices.

Mesquite Powder   Long used by Native Americans as a sweetener, mesquite powder is made by grinding mesquite tree pods into a fine powder. It's high in protein and rich in minerals with a smoky-woody flavor. Add a small amount to crackers or wraps or try it in Barbecue Sauce (page 307).

Miso   A small amount of miso, also known as bean paste, can be added to soups, dips, marinades, salad dressings, and other dishes to give them a distinct Japanese flavor. Miso comes in many varieties and colors, but most are pasteurized. Look for Miso Master Organic Miso, a fermented soybean paste that is not pasteurized. Although soybeans are first cooked, they are then fermented, making miso a living food because it contains natural digestive enzymes.

Nama Shoyu   This rich, full-bodied soy sauce is the only one that is raw, unpasteurized, and organic. (Supermarket and other types of soy sauce are pasteurized.) Soybeans are first cooked, then fermented. Nama Shoyu is a living food because it contains natural digestive enzymes. Imported from Japan and artisanally made by Ohsawa, a 32-ounce bottle is pricey, but a little bit goes a long way. Use it to make dipping sauces for lettuce wraps and spring rolls. Try it in Asian-style salad dressings. Use as a marinade before dehydrating eggplant, mushrooms, and other vegetables. Float a teaspoon on top of soups made with coconut.

Nuts   What would we do without nuts? They are so versatile and so essential to a raw foods lifestyle, for everything from making cheeses to grinding them into flours and butters. They provide fats (the good kind) and antioxidants. Here are the essentials on using nuts in preparing raw food:

- Buy raw organic nuts from a reliable source with constant turnover.
- Nuts are used and eaten so frequently in raw foods that there's little chance of their spoiling or turning rancid, but once opened, all nuts should be stored well sealed in the refrigerator.
- How do you know if nuts are rancid? If nuts or nut oils smell or taste like motor oil, then they're rancid. Discard them. Your food will only be as good as the ingredients you start with. Nuts with higher fat content like pecans, macadamia nuts, or Brazil nuts tend to become rancid faster than those with lower fat content, such as almonds.

- When making candied or salted nuts, know that the longer they are dehydrated to remove moisture, the crunchier they will be.

Almonds Ever notice how almonds in the shell look like peach pits? Makes sense, as almonds and peaches are in the same botanical family. Almonds are the workhorse nuts of raw foods. Their possibilities are endless. Eat them out of hand. Sprinkle on salads and soups. Grind them finely to make flour for croutons. Grind them further for almond butter. Combine with other ingredients to make sauces and cheeses. Soak, blend, and strain almonds for almond milk. Almost all almonds produced in the United States—largely California—are pasteurized. Make sure that the almonds you buy are truly raw.

A small serving of almonds has more protein than one egg. They contain the highest amount of dietary fiber of any nut. Almonds are loaded with vitamin E, magnesium, fiber, calcium, phosphorus, iron, monounsaturated fat, and potassium. They're also a good source of manganese, copper, and vitamin B_2.

Eat a handful of raw almonds if you have a headache. They contain salicylates, the same pain relief ingredient found in aspirin.

Brazil Nuts Botanically, Brazil nuts are seeds, because they are clustered within pods that look similar to coconuts. Each pod may have a dozen or two seeds, or nuts, with hard-as-nails shells. Once shelled, Brazil nuts can quickly turn rancid, so buy them in their shells if possible. Shave Brazil nuts with a Microplane rasp for an ice cream topping. Brazil nuts have a rich, meaty consistency, almost similar to coconut meat. Brazil nuts make fantastic nut milks and desserts.

Brazil nuts are extremely high in selenium, which has been shown in studies to slow down the aging process and stimulate the immune system.

Selenium is a powerful antioxidant that protects against heart disease and cancers like prostate cancer. Brazil nuts are high in zinc and magnesium and contain substantial amounts of calcium.

Cashews Along with almonds and macadamia nuts, cashews are the go-to nuts for many raw food dishes, especially basics like cream sauces and cheese because of their silky, creamy texture. Used in creamy dips, sauces, and spreads, ice cream, and many desserts, cashews give a velvety texture to many different types of raw food meals. Use to make cashew cheese or as a topping on zucchini and summer squash pasta. Cashews serve as the base for the ice cream recipes in this book. You can substitute macadamia nuts for cashews in many recipes.

Cashews have 5 grams of protein per ounce and high levels of essential minerals such as iron, magnesium, phosphorus, zinc, copper, and manganese. They have a lower fat content than most other nuts, including almonds, walnuts, peanuts, and pecans.

Since cashews contain astringent qualities, they are used to make topical creams and gels. Cashews appear in creams for warts, moles, and other skin growths.

Chestnuts Although peeled chestnuts can be eaten raw, they are best when dried—whole or sliced—and combined with vegetables such as Brussels sprouts, ground into flour, and used as a thickener for soups, stews, and sauces. Purchase new-crop chestnuts in the fall from growers who sell online.

Coconuts Technically they're nuts, but since they're so crucial to raw foods preparation, they have an entry of their own. See page 23.

Hazelnuts Also called filberts or cobnuts, hazelnuts look like acorns in their shells. Use hazelnuts chopped in salads, hazelnut flour to make brownies, and make hazelnut milk for soups and smoothies. Hazelnut butter is a treat. Hazelnuts add complexity to chocolate desserts such as brownies and cheesecake. Combine with some dried fruit in a food processor and blend to make a crust or crumble topping for desserts.

Hazelnuts contain a significant amount of protein, fiber, iron, phosphorus, vitamins B_1, B_2, C, and E, and folate as well as many other essential nutrients. They contain a high proportion of essential oils, and hazelnuts are one of the few nuts with vitamin A.

Macadamia Nuts Buttery, creamy, and rich are words frequently used to describe macadamia nuts. Those same qualities make them perfect for cheeses, sauces, dips, pâtés, and dressings. With their high fat content, they can quickly turn rancid, so buy them as you need them or store in the freezer. Macadamia nuts make a great raw cheese to use in salads, layered in Napoleons, or even plain with breadsticks. Macadamia nut butter is a total indulgence. Look for it in health food stores or make it yourself.

Cashews can be substituted for macadamia nuts in many recipes because of their similar texture in raw food dishes. Macadamia nuts have a heavier consistency, but they are creamy like cashews, especially when soaked.

Macadamia nuts can help reduce cardiovascular disease because they have higher levels of monounsaturated fats, like those found in olive oil, compared with other tree nuts. Oil from the macadamia nut is used in the cosmetics industry.

Peanuts Peanuts aren't true nuts, but rather a legume, which is why raw peanuts taste somewhat like beans. Raw peanuts are always rancid and contain aflatoxins, considered a cancer-causing substance by the FDA and World Health Organization. Avoid them entirely.

Pecans The only true nuts indigenous to North America, pecans are used in sweet and savory dishes. Pecans contain the highest amounts of fats and antioxidants of any nuts. They provide nearly 10 percent of the RDA for zinc, which your body needs to produce testosterone, a key sex hormone. Zinc is helpful in warding off colds and maintaining a healthy immune system.

Pine Nuts Along with almonds, cashews, and macadamia nuts, pine nuts (*pignoli* in Italian) are one of the big four when it comes to nuts and raw foods. Purchase pine nuts imported from Italy and other Mediterranean countries, rather than the less flavorful ones from China. Combine these with other nuts to make cream sauces to use on zucchini noodles or layered between tomatoes for lasagna. Pine nuts add a luscious creaminess to winter squash and root vegetable purées and keep these dishes thick so they don't become watery or separate. Pine nuts have a cheese-like flavor. When ground with sea salt, they can be used as a quick topping on pasta and other dishes.

Pine nuts are high in protein, supply all the amino acids, and provide significant amounts of vitamin A, thiamin, riboflavin, and niacin. They are rich in phosphorus, equivalent to soybeans.

Pistachios Pale green in color and lightly sweet in flavor, pistachios are popular in sweet and savory dishes such as ice cream, trail mix, and granola. Pistachios have more fiber and vitamin B_6 (necessary for protein metabolism and immune system function) than any other nut. They are nutrient-dense with thiamin, copper, manganese, potassium phosphorus, and magnesium, and contain more total polyphenols than any fruit or vegetable on an equal weight basis. Pistachios have more lutein, important for healthy eyes and arteries, than a glass of orange juice or three medium tangerines.

Walnuts Don't walnuts look like little brains, complete with left and right hemispheres, upper cerebrums, and lower cerebellums? They even have wrinkles or folds like the brain does. Traditional Chinese medicine doctors believe that herbs and foods that resemble certain body parts are beneficial to that particular body part. Makes sense, as walnuts have been shown in Western medicine to help develop more than three dozen neurotransmitters for brain function. Packed with vitamin E and antioxidants, walnuts are the only nuts that contain a significant amount of omega-3 fatty acids.

Walnuts are used in brownies and granola and to make walnut cheese. Put them in pitted dates for a quick hors d'oeuvre. Fold candied walnuts into ice cream or use as a topping on desserts.

For instructions on soaking nuts, see page 57.

Nut Butters   Fresh, homemade nut butters contain no added preservatives, additives, or high-fructose corn syrup, just pure nuts. Put one to two cups raw nuts—almonds, cashews, pistachios, hazelnuts, macadamias, pine nuts, Brazil nuts, or a mixture—in a food processor and purée them. Nut butters tend to be chunky. If you want a smoother texture, start by adding one teaspoon olive oil while blending. Add more as necessary. Scoop out the butter into a bowl or lidded jar, cover, and store in the refrigerator for a couple of weeks. (See page 105 for information on seed butters and oils.)

Almond Butter Raw almond butter is available in health food stores and other markets. Make sure it's made from raw—not roasted—nuts. It's easy to make your own by placing one to two cups raw almonds in a food processor. Process, scraping down the sides frequently. First, the nuts will become flour-like in texture, but as you continue scraping and processing, a creamy spread will develop. Taste and add a bit of sea salt if you like. Scrape the almond butter into a container and store in the refrigerator for up to two weeks. Raw nut butters are also available in stores and online.

Nut Flours   Also called nut meals, nut flours are nothing more than nuts finely ground in a food processor. Use them to make sweet and savory crusts, as a binder for Bistro Burgers (page 337), to thicken Breadstick batter (page 382), in Vanilla Macaroons (page 420), and to dust surfaces when rolling out gnocchi or shaping brownies. Store them in airtight containers in the freezer, like other nuts. Many recipes call for almond, cashew, or other nut flours. See page 106.

Nut Milks   These can be enjoyed in smoothies and soups, on cereals, or on their own blended with raw cacao powder and dates for chocolate milk. They're ideal for thinning out cream sauces. Yes, nut milks are available commercially, but they are not raw, as they are pasteurized. It's very easy to make your own. See page 104.

Nut and Seed Oils   These oils are bursting with flavor and can be used in infinite ways. All nut (walnuts, hazelznuts, almonds, and so on) and seed (hemp, flax, sunflower, and sesame) oils should be refrigerated once opened.

Olives   There are several brands and types of olives that are packed in water and spices, but not pasteurized. Use the olives and their brine in salads and cocktails. We also use raw jalapeño-stuffed olives in many of our recipes.

Olive Oil   No, not all olive oils are the same. Look for extra virgin olive oils that are made with ripe olives, stone crushed, cold pressed, and unfiltered. Although there are many fine producers of raw extra virgin olive oil, Bariani, which is deep mossy green in color and has the harvest date and bottling date on each bottle, is a good brand. This California oil is pressed from organic manzanilla and mission olives. Use olive oil as a dip with fresh vegetables accompanied by a dish of sea salt. Drizzle on soups, pastas, and salads.

Red Wine Vinegar   Raw and unpasteurized red wine vinegar is fairly new to the market. It's made from fermented red wine that is fermented again into vinegar. Eden Foods Raw Wine Vinegar is the one most frequently used in raw foods. Use it in salad dressings or to perk up dishes that need a touch of acid.

Rejuvelac   See page 133.

Salt   No synthetic mineral supplement can equal or supply those naturally found in sea salt. Sea salt tastes like salt is supposed to—briny and clean—and a sprinkle enhances food, rather than making it taste "salty." The best ones are farmed by traditional methods with no additives or preservatives. Read the labels or check the producers' websites for details. We like Celtic Sea Brand (France) and Maldon (England). Our favorite is raw Himalayan pink salt, which is a mined in the mountains of Nepal. As mentioned above, avoid table and kosher salts, which are heated so most of their trace minerals are removed, and then processed to put them back in. Sea salt in the recipe ingredients means that you can use either sea salt or Himalayan pink. Purchase a small block of Himalayan pink salt and put it in a designated salt grinder.

At Grezzo, we sprinkle a bit of fleur de sel on some of our dishes as a garnish before sending them out, much like herbs. Fleur de sel, considered the finest because it dissolves so quickly, is taken from the top layer of the salt beds. It can be found in many markets and online.

Sea Vegetables   Sea vegetables sound so much nicer than seaweed. Harvested from marine waters, these beautiful plants are rich in nutrients, vitamins, and minerals—calcium, iron, B vitamins, vitamin K, iodine, magnesium, and so on—so often missing from the human diet. They come in a wide array of vibrant colors—from lime to forest greens, from rich red to eggplant purple—and many different varieties are available from waters all over the world. The ones listed below are used most frequently in raw foods. Buy dried (check the expiration date), which must be rehydrated before using or fresh (the color should be bright, not discolored and pale) sea vegetables from reputable sources. Read labels carefully; they may say they're raw, but if you look closely, many are steamed or heat dried. For instance, to our knowledge, there is no such thing as truly raw hijiki.

Use sea vegetables in place of lettuce on sandwiches. Toss shredded and soaked nori with ribbons of summer squash. Fresh sea vegetables can be dehydrated to make chips.

To rehydrate thin dried sea vegetables such as dulse or wild nori, cover them with water for five minutes. Coarser, thicker ones such as kelp and alaria should be soaked in water for several hours or overnight.

Alaria Like wakame, this brown algae is frequently used in soups.

Arame Sweeter and milder in taste than other sea vegetables, wavy arame is usually available dried and can be reconstituted in just five minutes. Use in soups and salads.

Dulse Available as a leaf for salads or as flakes for dusting on just about anything, deep red dulse has a chewy texture. Soak for five to ten minutes.

Irish Moss/Carrageen Irish moss is used in raw desserts such as mousse and puddings in place of gelatin. Its health benefits include everything from treating eczema and psoriasis to strengthening connective tissues.

Rinse the Irish moss thoroughly in cold running water. If not well rinsed, it can impart a fishy flavor to food. Submerge completely in water, cover, and soak for twelve to twenty-four hours. Do not rinse or change the water or some of the moss's gelling properties will be washed away. Use within twenty-four hours or refrigerate up to one week.

The resulting texture of a mousse or other desserts depends on how much is used, but the standard equivalency is to use 1 ounce of soaked Irish moss for each cup of liquid.

Kelp Light brown to dark green in color, oftentimes available in flake form. Soak kelp overnight in plenty of water. Once pliable, cut into strips with scissors or chop in a food processor for a finer consistency. The soaking water can be used as a stock or in creamy sauces. It makes a soothing tea.

Kombu Sold in strips or sheets and often used as a flavoring for soups. Chop it finely, as it has a chewy texture. Soak for one hour.

Nori Best known of all the sea vegetables, purchase untoasted, wild nori sheets to use for maki and hand rolls. Also available is wild nori, packaged in long strands rather than sheets.

Sea Beans Also known as sea asparagus, glasswort, and drift seeds, sea beans are not sea vegetables, but since they're often sold together, they are included here. These crunchy, sweet, and salty succulents grow in marshy areas and on beaches. Pair them with a horseradish-based dressing.

Wakame Similar to arame and kombu, it's used fresh in Japanese miso soup and dried in the ubiquitous seaweed salad served in Japanese restaurants everywhere.

Seed Oils   Raw pumpkin, sunflower, and sesame oils are available. Just a splash in dressings and sauces adds a nice nutty flavor. Nut oils are intensely flavorful; a little bit goes a long way. We make our own sesame oil by blending one part white sesame seeds to two parts olive oil in a Vita-Mix. It is placed in a glass jar and allowed to sit at room temperature overnight. We then pour it through a nut bag and harvest the fresh sesame oil.

Seeds   Refer to the soaking chart on pages 58–59. Make trail mix with sunflower and pumpkin seeds, raisins, and sea salt. Soaked and ground seeds add texture to burgers and nut loaves. Buy seeds from reputable sources, such as farmers' markets or busy health food stores. If the weather is warm, store seeds in the refrigerator; they can easily turn rancid.

Alfalfa Seeds One teaspoon of alfalfa seeds yields about two pounds of sprouts! Place the sprouts in direct sunlight on the last day of sprouting to "green" them and increase their chlorophyll content.

Alfalfa is high in protein, calcium and other minerals, and vitamins A, B-complex, C, D, E, and K. In herbal medicine, alfalfa is considered helpful for the digestive tract and kidneys and for treating anemia, diabetes, premenstrual syndrome, and many other conditions. Alfalfa is also said to be good for arthritis sufferers.

Chia Seeds As everyone knows from seeing the Chia Pet commercials, chia seeds sprout rapidly and easily absorb liquid. Originally from Central and South America, chia seeds are said to increase endurance and stamina. They are rich in calcium, iron, potassium, and other nutrients, as well as a complete source of protein. Sprinkle a tablespoon on cereal, in juices or smoothies, or use as a flour substitute. When soaked, they become very gelatinous, and are used in sweet and savory puddings.

Clover Seeds Place the sprouts in direct sunlight on the last day of sprouting to increase their chlorophyll content. When sprouted, these spicy seeds are a great addition to salads and sandwiches when you want a little kick.

Flax Seeds See page 25.

Pumpkin Seeds Soak them for eight hours and sprout them for a day, and they're ready to use in pâtés, loaves, and crackers. Pumpkin seeds are used for making butter and milk. Add sprouted seeds to granola or eat them out of hand. They're high in zinc, which is important for bone mineral density, and also known for their anti-inflammatory properties.

Sesame Seeds Purchase white unhulled sesame seeds for making nutty sesame milk, using the same technique as hemp milk. Use black sesame seeds as a garnish or sprinkle them on buns and crackers before dehydrating.

Sunflower Seeds can be eaten raw, but sprouting them increases their nutrient value greatly. Like pumpkin seeds, they sprout quickly and are good in pâtés or sprinkled on salads. They can be ground into flour and made into gnocchi.

Sunflower seeds planted and sprouted produce sunflower greens, which are extremely nutritious. Three and one-half ounces of sunflower greens contain 22.78 grams of protein! (A chicken breast contains 26.25 grams.)

Sunflour, which we often call for, is nothing more than ground up sunflower seeds, and is an essential ingredient in raw food kitchens. Use it for dusting a work surface so dough doesn't stick and in the recipe for Gnocchi Carbonara (page 348). Store Sunflour in a sealed jar or a plastic container for up to two days.

Vegetable Seeds The list is endless, because virtually any seed can be sprouted, from beets and broccoli to peas and peppers.

Sichuan Peppercorns One of the ingredients in five-spice powder, only the husks of these seeds—they're not true peppercorns—are used to impart a warming, rather than fiery, sensation to food. We flavor our coconut soup and star anise for the "au poivre" crust on the papaya steak with these.

Spices Buy whole spices from reputable sources, and then grind them in a designated spice or coffee grinder to bring out their fresh flavors.

Stevia Also known under the brand SweetLeaf, the leaves of the stevia plant are known for their intense sweetness. Use fresh or dried leaves in place of agave nectar; how much depends how much sweetness you want to impart. One tablespoon dried stevia from an herb store equals approximately one cup agave nectar. Avoid powdered stevia; it has a bad aftertaste.

Truffle Oil A few drops of truffle-infused olive oil adds flavors to salads, soups, and sauces. Look for extra virgin olive oil that has been infused with white or black truffles.

Vanilla Beans The seeds in the beans, or pods, are where all the heady vanilla flavor is hidden. To remove the seeds, slice the vanilla bean lengthwise; you'll see lots of little black seeds. Use a knife or teaspoon to scrape them out. Use immediately or they will dry out. Do not discard the pods—they're still packed with vanilla essence! Save them in a covered jar and use in desserts, ice cream, and nut milks.

Water   Since our bodies are made up of at least 70 percent water, it's important to replenish this important nutrient regularly. The good news is that fruits and vegetables contain plenty of water, so by eating or juicing these foods you'll be consuming plenty of that much-needed water. Those who eat raw foods often find that they're not as thirsty as those who eat cooked foods. Much of the water is removed from fruits and vegetables when they're boiled, baked, and so on, creating a desire to drink more water.

Out-of-the-faucet tap water is treated, processed, and disinfected. It is purified with chlorine, and fluoride is often added. Distilled water is water that has been vaporized to remove all the minerals, leaving behind solid residues. Distilled water tastes "dead," with no life force at all. Bottled water can contain toxins that leach into the water from some of the plastic bottles. And it's often nothing more than purified municipal water. Purifying, bottling, and shipping water consumes so many other resources (fossil fuel for trucks that pollute the environment, for instance) that it's just not worth it. Deionized water has had ionized impurities and minerals removed from it but not bacteria or pathogens.

Well water that flows from natural springs and is bottled at the source or mineral water that comes from an underground source is best. These waters have essential minerals and nutrients like magnesium, potassium, and sodium.

Yacón   This South American tuber, similar to jicama but sweeter, is dried, then sliced or ground into a powder or made into a molasses-like syrup. The sugars in yacón can't be absorbed by the body, which means although sweet in taste, it won't quickly elevate blood sugar levels. Yacón also promotes the production of healthy probiotics in the body, which leads to better digestion and colon health.

Use sliced yacón as you would other dried fruit—in salads and cereals or eaten out of hand. Yacón syrup can be used as a sweetener in cookies and other desserts to impart a molasses-like flavor.

What to Buy: Organic and Local

Conventionally grown foods are loaded with herbicides, pesticides, and fungicides. Many pesticides have been proven to cause cancer and other serious diseases in laboratory studies. And if that's not enough, Rutgers University researchers showed that an organic tomato contains 5 times more calcium, 12 times more magnesium, and 1,900 times more iron than a conventionally grown tomato. Organic spinach was found to contain twice as much calcium, three times more potassium, and eighty times more iron than its nonorganic counterpart. The same research found that organic foods contain more than 87 percent more minerals and trace elements than conventionally grown food.

For me, buying locally grown food is even more important. It is fresher than anything in the supermarket, which means it is tastier and more nutritious. It hasn't been trucked across the country wasting fossil fuels. Buying locally is also good for your local economy—buying directly from family farmers helps them stay in business. Support your local farmers.

Because organic certification can take years for farms to achieve, many local farms may not be "certified" organic but may say "transitional," which means they are in the process of getting their certification, but they do follow organic principles.

One of the many joys of raw food is that there's little need for a lot of equipment—no pots and pans, for instance. As explained below, there are times when it makes sense to spend money on top-notch appliances and equipment that will last a long time. A high-speed blender, a dehydrator, a juicer, a food processor, and quality knives are important necessities when it comes to preparing raw food.

Blender   A blender is absolutely essential in the raw kitchen. It's used for smoothies, grinding seeds and nuts, dips, batters, purées, juices, dressings, and soups. While there are many models in many price ranges (from ten to five hundred dollars) available, buy a top-of-the line blender, such as a Vita-Mix or a Blendtec. Their motors don't burn out and they're versatile, easy to clean, powerful, and last forever. The mechanism of a regular blender isn't strong enough to produce the silky, smooth textures necessary for making ice cream and cheese.

Citrus Juicer   If you use a lot of orange, grapefruit, and other citrus juices, then you might want to invest in an electric citrus juicer, though using a citrus reamer works just fine. Roll the citrus fruit on the countertop a couple of times before cutting to loosen the pulp and make juicing easier.

Coffee Grinder   Great for grinding flax or sunflower seeds that will never become fine enough in a food processor or for making spice blends. It's important to get rid of odors, residue, and oils from the grinder if you use it for many things. To clean a coffee grinder, unplug it, add ¼ cup uncooked rice, and grind until the rice becomes a powder. Discard the rice powder. If there's still a smell, repeat the process using a little more rice.

Cutting Boards   With all the fruits and vegetables you'll be chopping, slicing, and dicing, keep several cutting boards on hand. Have on hand a large wooden board and some flexible plastic ones that can be folded, making it easy to pour cut-up food into a blender, food processor, or bowl.

Dehydrator   Meet your new "oven." By blowing warm—not hot—dry air through a dehydrator, water is removed from fruits and vegetables, but their flavors are preserved and their vitamins, minerals, and enzymes are left intact. Dried foods are commercially available everywhere, but they are often treated with preservatives and dried at temperatures well above 112°F.

Dehydration is the best way to keep seasonal fruits and vegetables in the pantry year round. Nibbling on homemade dried peaches, cherries, and apricots with their bright, summery flavors is a real treat come February. Dried fruits, vegetables, and mushrooms can be ground into powders to use in smoothies and other dishes. Dehydrate peppers and then grind them in a coffee mill for homemade paprika. The dehydrator is also used to make nut-vegetable loaves, potato chips, burgers, breads, crackers, and cookies—anything that is traditionally baked in an oven.

While there are many dehydrators on the market, purchase one with a temperature control and removable shelves so taller items, such as nut loaves and breads, have plenty of air circulating around them. Another suggestion is to place an oven thermometer inside the dehydrator to make sure the temperature doesn't go above 112°F.

Buy Teflex sheets when purchasing a dehydrator. These washable, reusable, nonstick liners are essential when drying fruits and vegetables with high water content, drying small nuts and seeds, making fruit leathers, or using a batter to make crackers or cookies. Dehydrators come with mesh screens that allow watery foods or batters to drip on the shelves—and foods—below. Teflex sheets can be trimmed with scissors to fit any dehydrator. Wash them with warm water and soap and then air dry.

Whenever possible, use the mesh screens alone, because they allow a better air flow to surround the food, resulting in lower drying times. If drying tomatoes, for instance, line the mesh screens with Teflex sheets. How long dehydration takes depends on the thickness and water content of each item. One week's tomatoes, peaches, or berries may be juicier than the next batch. The more water a fruit or vegetable contains, the longer dehydration will take.

Remove the shelves from the dehydrator and line them with Teflex. Arrange the food on the shelves, leaving enough space around each item so the dry air can fully circulate. Put the shelves back into the dehydrator and set the thermostat no higher than 112°F. Check the food periodically for desired doneness. Some items, like pizza and wraps, should be chewy and pliable, while crackers and chips should be crisp and firm. Write down how long it takes for each food to be dried to your satisfaction so you'll know the next time you make it.

About halfway through dehydration time, remove each tray and flip the food for even drying. To remove Teflex sheets, place a mesh dehydrator screen on top of the food to be flipped. Place both hands on the sides of the screens, and turn them upside down so the screen with the Teflex sheet is now on top. Remove the mesh screen, and then slowly peel the Teflex sheet off the food. Return the screen to the dehydrator to finish.

Those lucky enough to live in a sunny, hot, dry climate can "sun-dry" tomatoes, apples, herbs, beans, berries, and so on, but will have to buy or rig up drying racks or screens. Lay the cut-up items on a fine-mesh screen from the hardware store. Cover with another piece of screen, making sure that insects can't get in. Set the screens on wooden or cement blocks so air can circulate above and below.

Whether using a dehydrator or the sun, make sure foods are thoroughly dehydrated. If foods are thoroughly dried and crisp, you can leave them out on the counter indefinitely. If any moisture remains, store these foods in the refrigerator to prevent mold.

Food Processor Chopping, blending, shredding, and mixing fruits and vegetables can all be done in the food processor to save time. An expensive model isn't necessary, but get a machine with a 7- to 10-cup capacity.

Glass Jars Glass jars are healthier, more environmentally sound, easier to clean, and more cost-effective than plastic containers. Most of all, there's a sense of satisfaction and abundance that comes from seeing a row of glass jars filled with seeds, nuts, dried fruits, and vegetables lining the pantry. Also known as canning and preserving jars, glass jars and lids are available in hardware stores and supermarkets. Sold individually or in six- or twelve-packs, they come in a number of sizes (half-pint, pint, quart, and half-gallon are most useful). Choose from simple Ball jars to wide-mouth decorative jars with rubber gaskets, glass lids, and wire bail latches to vintage jars found at flea markets and yard sales. Whether new or old, scrub all jars well with soap and hot water or run them through the dishwasher before using. Be sure to label and date every jar once filled.

Hatchet   Yes, really. Investing in a good-quality hatchet makes opening coconuts, cutting pumpkins, and splitting watermelons easy without taking a toll on your kitchen knives.

Ice Cream Machine   Wait until you try the raw ice cream and sorbet recipes in this book! You won't believe how delicious, creamy, and satisfying they are. But you will need to invest in an electric ice cream machine, and there are many good models available.

Ice Cream Scoop   Not just for ice cream and sorbet, ice cream scoops in a variety of sizes allow for accurate portioning of burgers, pizza dough, and sausage patties.

Juicer   Making fresh fruit and vegetable juices is essential for raw foods. You can drink them as meals and as snacks, or use the juices in preparing many of the dishes in this book. Purchase a juicer with twin gears, such as those manufactured by Green Star, because they quickly and effectively juice fruits as well as dark leafy green vegetables. Other juicers, like those made by Juiceman or Breville, have fast, rotating blades that can heat up and destroy nutrients in fruits and vegetables.

Mandoline   For home use, the reasonably priced Benriner Japanese mandoline is ideal. It makes perfectly even slices of fruits and vegetables with its four stainless steel interchangeable blades. The blades can be adjusted for thickness. Always use the finger guard when using the Benriner.

Microplane Rasp   Perforated, lightweight, and super-sharp, these steel rasps (available in houseware stores) are ideal for grating nuts, spices, citrus zests, ginger, horseradish, and garlic and zesting citrus fruit.

Nut Bags   Handy for making nut/seed milks and cheese and for sprouting seeds, nut bags are available in fine nylon mesh or unbleached cotton with drawstrings and can be rinsed and reused. Some people like to use cheesecloth, but the fabric's weave often isn't tight enough and pulp can drip into the nut milk. For nut milks, blend the water and nuts or seeds as directed in the recipe in the blender until puréed. Pour the mixture into a nut-bag-lined measuring cup or bowls, pull the drawstring, and hang the bag well above the bottom of the vessel, so the "milk" can drain to the bottom. Let drain until the pulp is dry. You can also squeeze the pulp. Don't discard the nut pulp; use it for cookies, crusts, and croutons.

For sprouting small amounts of seeds, put the seeds in a nut bag and soak in a large bowl of water overnight or anywhere from eight to fifteen hours. Rinse the bag with the seeds and hang it over the sink or above elsewhere and allow the seeds to sprout.

Spiral Slicer   This inexpensive handheld appliance is essential for making ribbon-like garnishes, slaws, salads, apple rings, onion rings, and angel hair pasta from zucchini and summer squash. Again, there are a number of brands on the market—like Saldacco—in a wide range of prices, and there's no need to spend a lot of money on a spiral slicer. Firm fruits and vegetables such as apples, Asian pears, radishes, daikon, carrots, potatoes, beets, sweet potatoes, and turnips work best.

Sprouting Jars   The ones with mesh tops are great for first-time sprouters. The mesh tops can be made of wire or cloth, but they are essential so the sprouts have some "breathing room." (See Nut Bags, above, for sprouting, too.) Make your own using clean jars and placing small pieces of mesh screen or cheesecloth over the mouth of the jars and securing with a rubber band or a canning ring. Sprouting jars can also be purchased online or in health food stores. See the chart on page 57 for details on sprouting.

Sprouting Trays   Using a sprouting tray is a great way to grow small seeds like clover, alfalfa, or broccoli sprouts. It allows the seeds to lie flat without getting crammed together in a jar or bag. Trays also allow for good air circulation.

What to Do with Those Pots and Pans

One of the many advantages of raw food is that far less kitchen equipment is necessary when preparing food. Less equipment means fewer pots and pans to scrub and more discretionary money in your pocket because you realize you no longer lust after that set of copper pots. If you're like most people who eat raw food, then you probably already have a collection of cookware that you no longer need. Here are some ideas for what to do with those pots and pans.

1. Repurpose them as serving bowls and platters. If you do own high-quality cookware, use that Le Creuset Dutch oven to ladle out bowls of soup or that shiny copper frying pan as a tray for serving soup shots or cocktails.
2. Who says winter socks, a yarn stash, or bills have to be kept in drawers or filing cabinets? Think of those pots and pans as extra storage space, and you don't even have to hide them in a closet. Be sure to label the contents.
3. Sell them at a yard sale. Use the proceeds to buy a dehydrator or high-end blender you covet.
4. Donate the pots and pans to a soup kitchen or other charity.
5. Pots and pans make lovely plant holders. Place a few pots of herbs on a bed of pebbles in a skillet as a centerpiece, or put larger plants in stockpots outside. Leave them outside—rain or shine—and they will take on a new patina.

SOAKING
and
SPROUTING

Remember the experiments in kindergarten when you put some seeds on damp paper towels or in a glass jar, and how they miraculously germinated and grew tails, or sprouts, overnight? The same technique, on a larger scale, is used to sprout legumes and grains for raw foods.

Sprouts are nutritional, tasty, beautiful, and economical. A teaspoon—just one *teaspoon*—of alfalfa seeds yields about two pounds of sprouts. All for just a few pennies.

Sprouting, or germinating, seeds, legumes, and grains is essential to preparing raw foods because

- Textures become softer and more palatable.
- Natural enzyme inhibitors—phytates and oxalates—are removed, allowing

dormant enzymes to become activated. If you don't sprout them, your body has to use its own digestive enzymes to break up these foods. This is taxing to a body that doesn't have enough enzymes. Many people—especially those who are older or sick—don't have enough enzymes to break up these foods. Eating raw foods means eating as many enzyme-rich foods as possible. Sprouting increases the enzymes, vitamins, minerals, and other nutrients found in living foods. When you eat certain foods that are not sprouted, those phytates and oxalates remain, and the body is unable to utilize these foods. Just because certain foods are raw doesn't mean that they can be digested and assimilated into the body. Some foods need a push—sprouting.

- Nutritional values are increased twentyfold. Soaked and sprouted nuts, seeds, grains, and legumes are nutritious, and they produce an amazing amount of nourishment that otherwise would not be available. In sprouted wheat, for instance, vitamins are increased tremendously. Thiamin (vitamin B_1) increases by 30 percent. Niacin increases by 90 percent, vitamin B_2 increases by 200 percent, pantothenic acid increases by 80 percent, and biotin increases by 100 percent! Amino acids increase greatly as well, and because of this predigested state, the body does not have to work as hard to digest this highly concentrated source of protein.

- The enzyme content of these foods is increased. Sprouting activates enzymes that are lying dormant. Again, if you don't sprout them first, your body has to use its own enzymes to break up these foods.

- Their protein content is broken down into amino acids, their starches are changed into simple sugars, and their fats are converted into soluble fatty acids, all of which makes them more digestible.

Why Sprout at All?

Many people are convinced that sprouts are the perfect food . . . and with good reason! Sprouts are packed with vitamins and minerals and bursting with energy from all of the enzymes they contain. And when you sprout seeds, nuts, grains, and legumes, they become more alkaline. (Grains, beans, and legumes must be sprouted before eating them. Sprouting nuts and seeds isn't necessary, unless you prefer them that way.)

Sprouting seeds, legumes, and grains softens them, making their texture more palatable. The easiest sprouts for beginners are alfalfa, sunflower, almonds, lentils, and mung beans.

How to Sprout

There are several ways to sprout seeds, beans, and grains. For home use, buy one-pound bags of mung beans, lentils, buckwheat, alfalfa seeds, and pumpkin seeds. The cost ranges from one to two dollars. With one teaspoon of alfalfa yielding two pounds of sprouts, it's worth the savings to do your own sprouting of seeds, beans, and grains. Buy seeds at farmers' markets, health food stores, and online organic catalogs.

Sprouting can take anywhere from several hours to four or five days depending on what's being sprouted. For instance, buckwheat takes one to two days to sprout, while chickpeas require four days.

There are all kinds of sprouting jars, multilayered clear plastic sprouting trays, and other fancy sprouting equipment, but if you don't want to make a large investment, I find nut milk bags the most convenient. The sprouts can easily be rinsed while in the bags, and the bags can be washed and used repeatedly.

Soak by placing one type of seeds, grains, or legumes in a large bowl. Add enough room-temperature water to cover so that when the seeds expand, they remain under water. Add more water as necessary. Check the chart for the appropriate soaking time (see page 57).

Once soaked, place the seeds, nuts, grains, or beans into the nut milk bag. Rinse and drain the seeds, nuts, grains, or beans for a few days, as indicated. Keep them in the nut bag. Make sure that between rinses, they are kept out of water and drained. Sprouts should be kept moist but well drained.

Place them in a well-ventilated spot, but not in direct sunlight, unless indicated on the chart to increase chlorophyll content.

Most sprouts will keep for five to seven days in the refrigerator. Store them in a closed container without water. Rinse and drain them every other day to keep them fresh.

If you are having trouble getting beans, seeds, or grains to sprout, you may have soaked them for too long. Or they may have been old before you began the sprouting process. Make sure you buy them at a place with a high turnover rate, so that you know they have not been sitting on the shelf for a long time.

Wheat berries and chickpeas tend to mold easily; rinse these more often.

Sprouting in Six Easy Steps

1. Soak.
2. Drain and rinse.
3. Cover with some sort of loose protection such as a nut bag.
4. Set aside to grow.
5. Rinse and drain two or three times a day or water seedlings if using trays.
6. After a few days, check to see if sprouts are done. When they are, rinse, drain, and refrigerate.

SPROUTING CHART

There are many, many types of nuts, seeds, grains, and legumes that you can sprout. This chart illustrates some of the more common types. The figures given are *not* exact; they will vary depending on the seed, climate, and environment. With a little experimentation, you'll get the hang of it in no time.

Nuts	Amount	Soaking Time	Sprouting Time	Yield	Comments and Uses
Almonds	3 cups	24 to 48 hours	_____	4 cups	Only need to soak, not sprout. Once soaked, change water and then refrigerate in water (change daily), and use within 4 to 5 days when a grainier nut is required, as in milk, nut loaves, and dessert crusts.
Brazil nuts Cashews Hazelnuts Macadamias Pecans Walnuts	3 cups	6 to 8 hours	_____	3½ cups	These nuts will not sprout. Soak them for a softer, creamier texture. Soak, then refrigerate in water, and use within 1 to 2 days. Cashews and macadamias for nut milks, soups, smooth sauces, cheese, ice cream, frosting. Walnuts and hazelnuts in meatier dishes like burgers, nut loaves, and pâtés.

Seeds	Amount	Soaking Time	Sprouting Time	Yield	Comments and Uses
Alfalfa	3 table-spoons	8 hours or overnight	4 to 5 days	4 cups	Place sprouts in direct sunlight on the last day of sprouting to increase chlorophyll content.
Chia	1/3 cup	1 to 2 hours		2 cups	Soak (no sprouting) and use in puddings, salads, smoothies, and drinks. Use in place of flax seeds.
Clover	3 table-spoons	8 hours or overnight	5 days	4 cups	Place sprouts in direct sunlight on the last day of sprouting to increase chlorophyll content.
Cruciferous:					Place sprouts in direct sunlight on the last day of sprouting to increase chlorophyll content.
Broccoli	3 table-spoons	6 to 12 hours	3 to 5 days	2 cups	There are as many antioxidants in 1 ounce of broccoli sprouts as in 3 pounds of broccoli.
Cabbage	3 table-spoons	8 to 12 hours	4 to 6 days	2 cups	Cabbage is easy to sprout. Place sprouts in direct sunlight on the last day of sprouting to increase chlorophyll content.
Mustard	3 table-spoons	8 to 12 hours	5 to 6 days	2 cups	A bit difficult to grow, but worth it. Place in sunlight on the last day so leaves open.

Seeds	Amount	Soaking Time	Sprouting Time	Yield	Comments and Uses
Fenugreek	2 table-spoons	6 hours	4 to 5 days	3 cups	The longer they sprout, the more bitter they become.
Flax	1 cup	1 to 2 hours	_____	2 cups	Flax seeds will soak up a large amount of water, so give them enough to absorb. Add more if needed. No need to sprout, just soak.
Radish	3 table-spoons	6 hours	4 to 5 days	4 cups	Place sprouts in direct sunlight on the last day of sprouting to increase chlorophyll content.
Pumpkin	1 cup	6 hours	1 day	2 cups	For salads, garnishes, and sandwiches. These sprout quickly.
Sesame	1 cup	4 hours	1 day	1½ cups	Use unhulled only; hulled won't sprout. Salads, garnishes, and sandwiches. These sprout quickly.
Sunflower	1 cup	6 hours	1 day	2 cups	For salads, garnishes, sandwiches. These sprout quickly.

Grains	Amount	Soaking Time	Sprouting Time	Yield	Comments and Uses
Amaranth	1 cup	8 hours	1 to 2 days	3 cups	Use in salads, soups, and crackers.
Barley	1 cup	8 to 15 hours	3 to 4 days	2 cups	Texture is chewy; perfect in stews and salads.
Buckwheat	1 cup	8 to 15 hours	2 to 3 days	2 cups	For smoothies, cereals, breads, and desserts.
Millet	1 cup	8 hours	12 hours	2 cups	Sprout very quickly. Sprouts are very small. For salads, soups, and crackers.
Quinoa	1 cup	8 hours	1 day	2 cups	For breads and hearty salads.
Rye berries	1 cup	6 hours	2 to 3 days	2 cups	Make rejuvalac; use in rye bread, crackers, and salads.
Spelt	1 cup	8 to 15 hours	2 to 3 days	2 cups	Gluten free; use as regular wheat substitute in breads and crackers.
Teff	1 cup	8 to 15 hours	2 to 3 days	2 cups	For salads, soups, and breads.

Grains	Amount	Soaking Time	Sprouting Time	Yield	Comments and Uses
Wheat berries	1 cup	8 to 15 hours	2 to 3 days	2 cups	To make breads and crackers and grow wheatgrass. Use soft wheat berries for wheatgrass and rejuvelac and hard wheat berries for breads.
Wild rice	1 cup	8 to 15 hours	4 to 5 days	2 cups	Make sure you use *wild* rice, not white or brown rice. For salads, soups, and jambalaya.
Beans and Legumes	Amount	Soaking Time	Sprouting Time	Yield	Comments and Uses
Chickpeas (Garbanzo beans)	1 cup	8 to 15 hours	3 to 4 days	2 cups	Rinse 3 to 4 times each day. For hummus and salads.
Lentils	1 cup	8 to 15 hours	3 days	2 cups	Rinse sprouts under running water to remove hulls.
Mung beans	1 cup	8 to 15 hours	4 to 5 days	2 cups	Rinse sprouts under running water and shake or swirl to remove hulls. Use with sandwiches, salads, soups, and pâtés.
Peas	1 cup	8 to 15 hours	3 days	2 cups	Soups, garnishes, and salads.

There are many fruits and vegetables that you may be familiar with but others you may have never used or even heard of. Here's a guide to some of my favorites—along with some nutritional information—with details on how to purchase and store them. Try those that may be unknown to you and open up your palate to a new world of flavors and textures.

Açaí Berry   Native to the rain forests of Central and South America, dark purple açaí (pronounced ah-*sigh*-ee) berries are packed with antioxidants like their sister fruits, blueberries and cranberries. While açaí berries are highly nutritious, there have been many outlandish claims for their healthful properties. As a result, there are products, many of which are not raw, such as juices, powders, and supplements, that use low-quality berries.

Fresh açaí berries spoil quickly, so they're not shipped to North American markets, but dehydrated berries and frozen pulp are available at some natural food stores and online. Try the former sprinkled on salads, and the latter as an ingredient in smoothies.

Apples   What would we do without apples? They can be eaten out of hand, cut up for salads, dried, and juiced, and they are the base for apple cider vinegar. There are thousands of varieties, so there's no need to buy mediocre, tasteless fruit. Support local growers by visiting orchards or purchasing apples at farmers' markets, where you can ask which apples are best for different purposes. A sweet variety may be best for juicing or eating out of hand, but you may prefer a tarter one for a salad.

The flavonoids in apples help lower asthma risk. Apple skin has been shown to reduce the risk of lung, breast, liver, and colon cancers. Eating two apples a day may reduce cholesterol levels up to 10 percent.

Although a bowl of apples may look lovely on your dining table, apples should always be refrigerated to keep them crisp and juicy. Apples at room temperature quickly deteriorate and become mushy (use them for juicing) because they contain naturally occurring ethylene gas that speeds ripening at room temperature. (You can put this gas to good use when you need to ripen avocados, mangoes, or other fruits by storing them with apples in a paper bag at room temperature.) Wash apples just before using them.

Asian Apples (or Asian Pears)   This crunchy, round fruit tastes like a cross between a pear and an apple. The fruit is crisp and won't soften once picked. It keeps well at room temperature for a few days or in the refrigerator for several weeks. Use them to add texture and a bit of sweetness to salads, sandwiches, and slaws.

Asparagus   The earthy flavor of raw asparagus tastes like spring on a plate. Snap off the tough, woody end of the stem and use only the tender part of the spear. Serve asparagus spears raw with dips or pickled with beverages. Slice them on a mandoline and add the pieces to salads and soups. Asparagus also has diuretic properties, and its juice makes a very cleansing tonic for the urinary tract. Purchase firm, fresh spears with closed, compact tips. Keep fresh asparagus clean, cold, and covered. Trim off about ¼ inch from the stem ends and rinse in warm water several times to remove any sand or dirt, especially around the tips. Pat dry. Wrap a moist paper towel around the stem ends, and place in moisture-proof wrapping. Refrigerate and use within two or three days. For slightly longer storage, if you have the room in your refrigerator, stand them upright in a glass with two inches of cold water, just like a bouquet of flowers.

Avocados   Rich in flavor and almost meaty in texture, avocados contain twenty different vitamins and thirteen essential minerals. The potassium content of an avocado is three times that of a banana. Like olive oil, avocados are high in oleic acid, which may prevent breast cancer. And they have plenty of good, monounsaturated fat that your body needs, so enjoy them. The pebbly, rough-skinned Hass avocados from California, not the large shiny ones from Florida, are preferred.

Once halved and pitted, eat them right from the skin with a drizzle of olive oil, or with a squeeze of lime and some chopped cilantro. As good as avocados are in Japanese-style rolls, guacamole, sandwiches, salads, and soups, they're also an effective skin moisturizer. Turn the skin of an avocado inside out and massage your just-washed face and neck or the rough patches on your elbows and knees with it.

If they are not ripe—slightly soft to the touch when pressed—put them in a brown paper bag (preferably with an apple or banana to release ethylene gas to speed ripening) for a day or two. Buy them in various stages of ripeness—you'll be eating a lot of avocados—and store them at room temperature.

Bananas   A raw food enthusiast's best friend. Available year-round at reasonable prices, a couple of bananas stave off hunger when there's nothing else at hand. They're rich in vitamin B, iron, potassium, and tryptophan, and good for the gastrointestinal tract—they're soothing enough to relieve heartburn as well as high in fiber, which helps constipation.

Bananas are shipped unripe and green; they're one of the few fruits that ripen off the tree. To ripen quickly, seal them in a brown bag. Deep yellow or mottled skins mean they're ripe and ready to eat. If you find yourself with too many overripe bananas, peel them and freeze them in plastic bags. Add frozen ones to smoothies and you won't need any ice. They can be thawed and used in other recipes as well. Bananas can also be added to cheesecake and ice cream and are great sliced and dehydrated.

Beets   Although the garnet red variety of this firm round root vegetable is best known, beets come in a rainbow of colors—yellow, orange, pink, and a candy-striped variety known as Chioggia. Beets are high in folate, manganese, potassium, and antioxidants. Scrub them well with a stiff brush just before use and peel skins when necessary.

Marinate thinly sliced beets in equal parts coconut and olive oil to soften and use as ravioli wrappers; juice them to make beet gnocchi or to use in beverages and pickling solutions. Fresh beet juice is an excellent tonic for cleansing the kidneys and gallbladder. Use beet juice as a sweetener with other juices, or combine it with carrot and/or cucumber juice.

Don't discard those beet greens; they have more vitamin A, potassium, and calcium than the roots and are high in iron. Rinse the greens thoroughly (they are usually very sandy) and use the leaves as wraps for quinoa salad or marinate and use in salads.

To store beets, trim off the greens and use them. Refrigerate the beets without washing (there's no need to put them in a moisture-proof bag), and they should keep for a few weeks.

Berries   Eat your berries. Especially blueberries. Fresh, frozen, or dehydrated. Every day. Peer-reviewed studies have shown that blueberries seem to slow and possibly reverse degenerative diseases associated with aging, and they have high amounts of fiber, vitamins A and C, and antioxidants. Raspberries and blueberries are known fighters against macular degeneration and reduce the release of histamines, which may minimize allergic reactions. Blackberries contain pectin, a soluble fiber, which helps lower cholesterol. Strawberries contain more vitamin C than citrus fruits do. Rub strawberry halves on your gums to eliminate soreness and on teeth to remove stains without harming the enamel.

Look for plump berries—blackberries, blueberries, gooseberries, currants, and strawberries—in season. Eat them fresh or dried out of hand, sprinkle them in salads and on cereals, or blend into smoothies. Always refrigerate berries to stave off molding. For longer storage, freeze them: Spread the berries in a single layer in a sheet pan and freeze until solid (about one hour), then transfer them to a storage container and freeze. Berries can also be dehydrated and kept at room temperature in a lidded container.

Bok Choy   A staple of Asian cuisine, bok choy looks like a cross between celery and chard, with white stalks in a cluster, each stem topped with wide dark green leaves. Some markets now carry baby bok choy, which is no larger than a child's fist. Thinly sliced, boy choy makes excellent slaw, especially with Chinese flavorings like ginger. It can also be used to make kimchee, the firey Korean pickle. Be sure to include it in your raw food diet, because it is the healthiest vegetable in the cabbage family, high in vitamin C, potassium, and calcium and loaded with beta-carotene. Store, without rinsing first, wrapped in damp paper towels in a plastic bag with a few holes poked in it, in the crisper compartment of the refrigerator. Rinse well just before using.

Cabbage   See Cruciferous Vegetables (page 71).

Carrots   Available in a riot of colors from creamy beige and sunny yellow to deep purple and bright orange and in shapes from long and skinny to squat and fat, carrots are rich in dietary fiber, minerals, and antioxidants. No other vegetable has more beta-carotene than carrots. The darker the carrot color, the more beta-carotene it contains, so try some of those beautiful varieties.

Avoid those so-called baby carrots packaged in plastic bags. They're really old carrots with little flavor that are put through a machine to give them a uniform shape. Scrub carrots, rather than peeling them, with a stiff brush; peeling them removes much of their mineral content. Carrot juice is quite sweet, and works well with juices from other fruits and vegetables, such as apples, pears, and kale.

Celery   Crisp, green celery is as versatile as it is tasty. It adds crunch to salads, can be pickled or marinated, served with dips, or juiced. When buying celery, the stalks should be firm with perky leaves—avoid any limp, tired-looking specimens. Rinse the entire head (do not remove the stalks from the head until just before using), wrap in paper towels, and then in a plastic bag and keep in the crisper of your refrigerator.

A blend of celery and green apple juice is said to lower blood pressure and reduce dizziness and aches and pains in the joints. Drink celery juice to relieve the pain from gout attacks. One cup of celery contains folate and vitamins A, C, and K, as well as large amounts of calcium, magnesium, phosphorus, potassium, and sodium and trace amounts of a half dozen other minerals.

Cherimoya   Once you try this custardy fruit with its primitive-looking skin of green armor, you'll agree that its combination of luscious flavors is reminiscent of papaya, banana, mango, passionfruit, lemon, and pineapple.

Choose firm, unripe fruit that are heavy for their size, then place them away from the sun and let ripen at room temperature. Check every day for softness. The fruit should feel as soft as an almost ripe avocado, with a little give but not squishy. The skin may turn brownish as the cherimoya ripens, but that won't affect the flesh. Once ripe, cherimoya can be refrigerated for up to four days, wrapped in a paper towel.

Cut cherimoyas in half lengthwise and scoop out the fruit with a spoon or eat it like a watermelon, scraping the rind with your teeth to get every bit of sweet flesh. Be sure to spit out the black seeds. The fruit can be peeled, cubed, and added to fruit salads or puréed and used as a mousse or pie filling. They're delicious when eaten icy-cold from the freezer.

Chicory   See Salad Greens (page 79).

Chiles   Ranging in size from about a foot long to barely a half inch, and in hotness from mildly warming to incendiary, chiles supply varying levels of spiciness to food. They are an important ingredient in Mexican, Thai, Indian, and Chinese cuisines, among others. Mild chiles, which tend to be larger and can be stuffed with corn and other vegetables, include the dark green poblano and verdant green Anaheim varieties. Hot chiles are used mainly for seasoning. There are dozens of varieties, but here are some of the ones you are most likely to find: The jalapeño is a good all-purpose chile, stubby and about two inches long; the serrano is similar to the jalapeño, but narrower; the cayenne is long, thin, and twisted; the Thai bird chile is only about ½ inch long, and very hot; the habanero looks like a brightly colored little tam o'shanter and is considered the hottest commonly known chile of all. All chiles are high in vitamins A and C and B-complex and cayenne helps to improve circulation. Chiles get their heat from the chemical capsaicin, which is used in some topical pain relief lotions. You are most likely to use fresh chiles to spice up food, especially salsa and guacamole. Buy shiny, firm chiles; red is an indication of ripeness, and jalapeños often have naturally occurring crackles on the skin. To store chiles, refrigerate them, uncovered. Much of the heat is concentrated in the seeds and ribs, so you can cut these out of the chiles if you wish, wearing thin rubber gloves to protect your hands from the capsaicin oils.

Corn   Usually thought of as a vegetable, corn is really a grain, and a powerhouse of nutrition, with large stores of vitamins A, B, C, and E, along with many minerals.

After wheat, corn was responsible for sustaining many civilizations, from Native American to Aztec and Maya. Cut from the cob, the kernels add a touch of sweetness to salads, soups, crackers, tortillas, salsas, and more. To cut the corn from the cob, remove the husks and silks. Cut off the stalk flush with the cob, and stand the cob on the cut end. Using a sharp knife, cut down where the kernels meet the cob, and they will come off in strips. Try to buy corn as soon after picking as possible at a roadside stand or farmers' market rather than the supermarket. The tassels and husks should look moist, not dried. Pull back the husk at one point to check for the worms that love good corn as much as humans do, but don't strip the husks entirely, as they keep the corn fresh. Store the corn, in its husk, in the refrigerator, but try to eat it soon after purchase, because the sugars in the corn start converting to starch almost immediately after picking.

Citrus Fruit   Citrus fruits—oranges, lemons, limes, grapefruit—are very acidic, making them highly detoxifying for the body. Well known as a source of vitamin C, they also contain folate, vitamin B_6, riboflavin, minerals, and other important nutrients. Squeeze half a lemon into a glass of hot water in the morning and drink to aid digestion and elimination. If you can find them, try Meyer lemons—they are more fragrant and slightly less tart than the standard lemons, and can be used in the same ways. In winter months, buy boxes of inexpensive Mandarin and clementine oranges and tangerines and keep them at home, in your car, and on your desk for snacking. Blood orange, grapefruit, tangelo, and ugli fruit segments make bright additions to salads. Combine two or three citrus fruits when juicing—blood oranges with grapefruit, tangerines with oranges. Instead of vinegar, use part or all lemon, lime, or other citrus juices in salad dressings. Use the zest, the colored skin without the white pith, to give foods citrusy flavor without the actual juice. A Microplane zester, which looks like a rasp, does quick work of removing the zest from the rest of the skin. Thinly slice citrus fruit on a mandoline, dehydrate, and chop finely to use as a tangy/chewy sprinkle on salads. Citrus fruit should be brightly colored and firm, without any nicks or bruises, and should be stored, uncovered, in the refrigerator.

Cranberries   A native American fruit, the cranberry is indelibly associated with Thanksgiving. Along with blueberries, raspberries, and strawberries, cranberries are near the top of list of antioxidant-rich foods. To prevent urinary tract infections, drink 7 ounces of fresh cranberry juice daily.

They are much tarter than other berries, so keep that in mind, especially when juicing them. You can macerate cranberries in agave nectar to soak up some needed sweetness. Buy bright, shiny, firm cranberries. They will keep, in their plastic bag package, for a couple of weeks in the refrigerator. Cranberries can also be frozen, but they will lose their bouncy texture when defrosted.

Cruciferous Vegetables   The *Brassica* family of vegetables is huge and incorporates the humble round cabbage and its many relatives. They are all high in fiber, vitamins, and minerals, and contain powerful amounts of antioxidants, which may provide protection against certain cancers and heart disease. They're a good source of calcium. While these vegetables are available everywhere throughout the year, those purchased after the first frost in the fall have a sweeter, more intense flavor. Sprouts of cruciferous vegetables are just as beneficial as fully mature ones. Store them in the refrigerator. Included in this category are the following vegetables:

> **Broccoli and Broccolini** These are packed with more vitamin C than an equal amount of oranges! Toss a few florets (and their stalks) into the juicer the next time you are making a green juice. Of course, they make a great quick salad, and are a dip's best friend. Broccoli is one of the most nutrient-dense foods that exist.
>
> **Brussels Sprouts** Unlike other vegetables, these mini-cabbages are high in

protein. Choose small green, tight heads with no yellow flowers and refrigerate for up to a day or two. It's understandable if you've turned your nose up at Brussels sprouts in the past. When cooked, they give off a noxious sulphur odor. By thinly slicing raw Brussels sprouts on a mandoline or finely chopping them to be used in salads and other dishes, you'll never have to worry about those awful smells again.

Cabbage Green cabbage is a smooth, round, dense orb. The leaves of Savoy cabbage are marked with wavy ridges, and the head isn't as firm as green cabbage. Red cabbage is actually a purple-red magenta color. Pale green with tender leaves, napa cabbage, also called Chinese cabbage, is used in Asian cooking, including kimchee. Use either of these cabbages to make slaw, or add them to more tender greens in a salad. Cabbage juice is used to treat a variety of gastrointestinal illnesses.

Cabbage has a slight laxative effect. Eat cabbage raw or juiced. Drinking cabbage juice is a known remedy for healing peptic ulcers.

Cauliflower Especially high in vitamin C, cauliflower varieties now come in many colors—traditional green, orange, purple, and even lime green (in a space-age-looking variety called Romanesco). Purée raw cauliflower for a side dish or chop it finely to resemble rice. Cauliflower can help relieve the symptoms of rheumatoid arthritis. Grate 3½ ounces of cauliflower and eat it twice daily for a month.

Cucumbers Known for its skin healing properties, cucumber also promotes hair and nail growth. Drink fresh cucumber juice—add mint if you wish—for treating acne and other skin ailments from the inside out. Cucumbers have diuretic properties and provide relief from heartburn and stomach acid. Cucumbers contain silica, an essential component of healthy connective tissue, which includes muscles, tendons, ligaments, and bones. They're a great source of vitamin C and molybdenum, and a good source of vitamin A, potassium, manganese, folic acid, dietary fiber, and magnesium.

You are sure to find two kinds of cucumbers at the supermarket—common cucumber, with its familiar dark green skin, and the longer, thin-peeled seedless (also called English) cucumber. The latter isn't exactly seedless, but the seeds are small enough that they are negligible. You may also find kirby cucumbers (similar to common cucumbers, but smaller) and Persian (elongated, but smaller than the English cucumber). When juicing cucumbers, include the seeds; however, you may want to remove the seeds when using them in salads or other dishes. To do this, cut the cucumber in half lengthwise, then scoop out the seeds with the tip of a teaspoon.

Dates   Many dates are dried and then steamed at a high temperature to make them look plump and moist. Be sure to buy whole dates that are raw, preferably the Medjool variety, a luscious type that tastes like candy. Pit them before using. Dates are a natural sweetener (see Date Paste, page 110) in smoothies (especially date shakes). For a quick, sweet snack, eat them out of hand. Enclose almonds or a bit of raw cheese inside pitted dates and serve with sparkling wine or drinks before dinner.

Rich in natural fibers, dates also contain good-for-you calcium, sulfur, iron, potassium, phosphorous, manganese, copper, and magnesium.

Durian   If you shop at Asian groceries, you may have come across durian, which looks like a spiky soccer ball. Occasionally available fresh in the spring, when it commands extremely high prices, it is usually sold frozen (for only slightly more reasonable prices). Its smell is . . . unmistakable, to be polite, and frankly, the flavor of the fruit can be a love-it-or-leave-it experience.

The shell must be opened to get to the interior fruit. Protecting your hands with a kitchen towel, cut and pry it open by its natural crease to reveal pillows of yellow-fleshed fruit. The taste is unique, much like a combination of banana, caramel, and vanilla with a slight onion-garlic tang. The fruit is made of soft, easily digestible flesh with simple sugars like fructose and sucrose and unsaturated fats to replenish energy and revitalize the body instantly once eaten. Durian is believed to kill parasites in the body.

Serve it freshly defrosted for an easy dessert (spit out the seeds, like watermelon) or blend the seeded pulp with other fruits into a smoothie. If you like the smell, you can refrigerate it, but it will stink up your whole fridge! You can also freeze durian pulp in a very well-sealed container.

Edible Flowers   There are many flowers that can add their beauty and flavor to salads. Always use unsprayed flowers from the garden or a reliable source—some well-stocked produce stores carry them. Use only flowers that have been identified as edible. Some reliable choices include nasturtiums, Johnny jump-ups, roses, chive blossoms, rosemary and basil flowers, and marigolds. Add just a few flowers for color, and don't overpower your dish with handfuls of blossoms.

Eggplant   At first consideration, eggplant might not seem a likely raw food. Dehydrated eggplant makes a crisp "bacon," and it can also be deliciously marinated as a salad or appetizer.

Mediterranean with dark purple skin is the most familiar variety, but other types are showing up more and more at ethnic and farmers' markets. Asian varieties are smaller, with fewer seeds and milder flavor than the large, globe-shaped Mediterranean. Japanese eggplant is lavender and elongated. Thai eggplants can be oval or round, large or small, with skin that comes in a range of colors, including white and green. Graffiti eggplant is light purple with striated skin. No matter what variety you choose, buy firm eggplants without any bruises and glossy, taut skin. Refrigerate uncovered in the crisper.

Eggplant may lower blood cholesterol and help counteract the effects of fatty foods. Eggplant also has antibacterial and diuretic properties.

Fennel   Crunchy like celery, fennel has a slight anise flavor. The entire vegetable—feathery fronds, stalks, bulb, and seeds—is edible. When cutting the fennel bulb, you will come across a hard triangular heart at the base, which can be trimmed out or not, as you wish. Look for bunches of small fennel early in the season; they can be pickled. Larger fennel can be sliced and served with a dish of olive oil and sea salt, or pickled, or juiced. Fennel is packed with powerful antioxidants and can relieve symptoms of digestive disorders and abdominal gas and cramps.

Figs   With delectable honey-sweet juices, a fig is actually a flower inverted into itself, even though it is considered a fruit. Figs have an extremely high mineral content and are an excellent source of fiber. They also contain phenols, which are antioxidants that may help with weight loss and help to protect against cancer and heart disease. Figs are a good sweet addition to tart salads or blended into a smoothie. Their soft texture becomes spreadable when puréed, so they are easily transformed into chutney or cheese.

Cut a fresh fig in half and place the halves under your eyes to get rid of dark circles. Lie down for thirty minutes, then rinse off any fruit on your face with warm water.

Black Mission, Turkish, Calimyrna, and green are the varieties available at various times during fig season, which runs from June to October. They are very perishable—they must be picked ripe and only last for about a week after harvesting—so buy them as close as possible to their source. Refrigerating will prolong their life by a day or two.

Garlic   For thousands of years, pungent garlic has been used as a medicine as well as a food. Long believed to have anti-inflammatory, antifungal, antibacterial, and antiviral properties, garlic provides vitamins B_6 and C, manganese, and selenium.

Squeeze a bulb, and if it feels dry or dusty and is sprouting, don't buy it. Garlic's bitter flavor comes from the germ in the middle of each clove. If you wish to remove it, slice the clove in half and remove the green germ. Grating garlic cloves on a Microplane rasp before adding them to dishes guarantees that no one gets a garlicky surprise from biting into a piece that wasn't finely chopped. It's a technique that we mention in many recipes. Garlic can be used raw, pickled, or dehydrated. Store it at room temperature away from direct sunlight.

Ginger   Always keep a knob of fresh zesty ginger root on hand in the fridge; you'll find many uses for it: ginger lemonade, ginger tea, and ginger salad dressing, to name a few. In addition to its many culinary uses, ginger is best known as a digestive aid for gas pains, stomach cramps, and motion sickness. Put a tablespoon or two of minced fresh ginger in a cup of warm water and let it steep. Add lemon and agave nectar, if you like, and sip.

Before using, peel off the tough skin (you can use the tip of a sturdy teaspoon to scrape it off) and grate on a rasp, mince, peel, or dice as necessary. Buy plump ginger with smooth, unwrinkled skin, and pass over any that are shriveled. Kept uncovered in the refrigerator, it will last for a few weeks.

Grapes   Grapes are another fruit that you should always keep on hand for nibbling when hunger strikes. Freeze them to create a deliciously refreshing snack. Naturally occurring antioxidants in grapes are responsible for the prevention of the accumulation of harmful cholesterol. Grapes contain high levels of caffeic acid, an anticarcinogen.

Seeded or seedless, green or red, there are usually a few different choices for the grape buyer. Seedless grapes, such as Thompson, may be more convenient to eat, but seeded ones (the New England Concord, scuppernongs from the South, and other area-specific varieties) have more complex flavors, which are revealed by juicing. Grapes should have a little grayish bloom on the fruit, with fresh-looking stems. Avoid bunches with small grapes mixed in with the large ones, as the runts will be sour. Store grapes in their perforated bag in the refrigerator, and rinse just before eating.

Green Beans   Ubiquitous green beans are still often called string beans, but most don't have the long fibers that needed to be removed before eating anymore. Look for purple or yellow varieties, too, as they add a splash of attractive color to dishes. For variety, try slim haricots verts; their flavor and nutritional content are the same as the less expensive varieties.

Green beans are one of the best natural sources of vitamin K, which is essential for healthy bones, and they are also filled with vitamin C. For the juiciest beans with the sweetest flavor, buy them as fresh as possible, as their sugars will convert to starch, resulting in tough, starchy beans. Juice them to include in your vegetable beverages, use them with dips, or include them in salads. They can also be dehydrated for a crisp snack. Sort through green beans before buying, and pass over any bruised ones. They should have a crisp snap when broken in two (the reason why some people call them snap beans). Keep unwashed beans in a plastic bag in the refrigerator.

Greens, Dark Leafy   When nutritionists say eat plenty of dark green, leafy vegetables, kale and mustard, turnip, dandelion, and collard greens are at the top of their lists because they're packed with vitamins C and K, beta-carotene, and calcium. Collards, kale, and arugula are actually cabbages that don't form a head, and are members of the *Brassica* family (see Cruciferous Vegetables, page 71), and share their nutritional benefits. Like their cousins, these greens are sweeter in the winter after a dose of frost.

Dark, leafy greens all have a hearty, earthy flavor with a bitter edge. If you like these flavors, then you can serve them on their own. Otherwise, use the greens with complementary ingredients, such as mildly flavored, tender lettuce in a salad, or with sweet juices, such as carrot or apple. All greens should be rinsed well before serving (see Swiss Chard, page 79). Store them, unwashed, in a plastic bag in the crisper.

Arugula The most tender green in this group, peppery arugula is usually served in salads. Look for it in midsummer, as it is quite expensive and sold in very small bunches out of season. Baby arugula, a year-round supermarket staple, is milder than regular arugula. Arugula has great detoxifying properties; put a handful into your juicer with other fruits and vegetables.

Chicory This family of slightly bitter greens has many members. Curly endive is a large green head with frizzy leaves (frisée is a smaller version). Escarole has wider, tougher leaves and a tart flavor. Belgian endive has a distinct conical shape—red Belgian endive is sometimes available along with the more familiar white, yellow-tipped version. Radicchio looks somewhat like a miniature lettuce crossed with a red cabbage, and its bitterness is less pronounced than the other chicories. Some markets carry Treviso radicchio, which has a spear-shaped leaf similar to Belgian endive. Chicory family members are very powerful in fighting disease because of their antioxidant content. They provide a similar antioxidant content to blueberries and spinach.

Collard Greens One cup of collards provides as much calcium as a cup of milk. They are quite sturdy, so cut them into thin shreds before adding to a salad. Collards make good wraps, as they are strong enough to hold fillings and can be wrapped without breaking.

Dandelion Greens A known diuretic, these greens are very cleansing to the liver. Markets carry cultivated greens, which are on the large side. If you gather fresh dandelion greens in the spring, pick only the young, tender small leaves, and be sure that they haven't been sprayed. Dandelion greens are thought to purify the blood and improve liver activity and the flow of bile to the small intestine.

Kale Many varieties of kale are available, from dark green to purple to near black (cavolo nero, also known as Tuscan or dinosaur kale, is showing up at many natural food markets) and with curly or plain leaves. Kale is the best source of calcium available.

Lettuce All lettuce has high levels of vitamins A, C, and K, and lots of fiber, manganese, and folate. Romaine, however, has even larger amounts of these nutrients. There are four distinct categories of lettuce. Crisphead is a firm, round head; iceberg is instantly recognizable as a member of this group. Romaine is a long cluster of dark green, sturdy leaves. Butterhead lettuces, such as Bibb and Boston, are loosely formed heads of very tender leaves. Leaf lettuces have large, somewhat floppy leaves, and you will find both green- and red-leafed varieties.

Mustard Greens These greens are particularly spicy, so keep that in mind when adding to salads or juicing. Mustard greens are ideal for removing heavy metals from the body and because they are so bitter are great for the liver.

Salad Greens These are the tender leafy greens that will certainly form the bulk of your everyday salad making. Happily, there is a huge variety to keep your palate intrigued. When not put into use for salads, they can be juiced. The most flexible greens can be used as wraps for other vegetables and cheeses. Serve small leaves of romaine with dips. In addition to lettuce and chicory, other small-leafed greens add interest to salads. Mâche (also called lamb's lettuce) has a slightly nutty flavor and grows in tight green rosettes that must be washed well to remove sand and grit. Watercress has a mild spiciness. Remove the tough stems before using. Store watercress, like a bouquet, in a glass of water in the refrigerator, covered with a plastic bag, to help keep it fresh.

Buy salad greens with vigorous, sprightly leaves. Wilted greens will always have an off flavor, so don't think you can revive them with a soak in cold water. Refrigerate salad greens in plastic bags to help them retain their moisture.

Swiss Chard With its broad dark green leaves and wide white stalk, Swiss chard is the most common variety, but you may also find red (with green leaves and red ribs), ruby (reddish leaves and stalks), and rainbow (with thinner, multicolored stems) chard. While chard can be juiced, it is really valuable as a replacement for the standard flour tortilla in a raw food wrap—remove the thick stem first, to make rolling easier. Buy chard with supple leaves and crisp stalks. Do not rinse before storing in a plastic bag in the crisper. Chard is usually very sandy and needs to be washed well before using. Rinse the individual chard leaves under cold running water to remove surface dirt. Fill the sink with cold water, add the chard, and agitate to loosen any remaining dirt. Let stand for a few minutes to allow the grit to sink to the bottom of the sink. Carefully lift out the chard, being sure not to disturb the dirt in the sink. Repeat if necessary. Drain and pat dry with paper towels.

Chard is a natural cleanser and helps strengthen bones because of its high sodium, chlorophyll, and calcium content. Chard is high in lutein and zeaxanthin, which are known to help vision.

Turnip Greens Another robustly flavored green, they are usually sold with the roots attached. Cut off the roots before using and storing.

Guava A luscious tropical fruit if there ever was one, with a flavor reminiscent of both strawberries and ripe pears, guava has many varieties. The apple guava is the one most often sold at Latino, Asian, and Indian markets in the United States, although you may occasionally find strawberry guava. Most commercial varieties have red pulp, although yellow guavas abound in the international marketplace. A powerhouse of vitamin C, one apple guava has 165 milligrams, compared to the 69 milligrams in a single orange. Guavas have lots of small seeds, which can be eaten (in fact, they also store lots of nutrients, so eating them is encouraged). Cut guavas into quarters and eat as a snack (eat the rind or not), or juice them and enjoy one of the favorite beverages of the Caribbean. When using in a salad, you can peel guavas or not, according to personal taste—there are a lot of nutrients in guava skin. Choose sweetly fragrant, firm fruit without bruises; they will continue to ripen at room temperature. Try not to refrigerate guavas, as chilling dulls their flavor.

Herbs   Herbs are the aromatic leaves of edible plants used for culinary purposes. We use fresh herbs whenever possible in all of our recipes to add bursts of flavor and pops of color. Fresh herbs are now available at supermarkets year round. If you're lucky enough to have a garden, you know that herbs are the easiest things to grow: Just stomp some seeds into the soil, water appropriately, thin the seedlings, and cut the herbs back during the growing season to make them lush and busy. No garden? Grow some herbs in pots on a sunny windowsill. If you have a bumper crop of herbs, dry them in the dehydrator (see page 46) or tie them together and hang them upside down in a dry area. Once dried, strip leaves from the stems and store in jars in a dark cool place. Infuse olive oil with herbs to make a fragrant condiment.

To store tender herbs with delicate leaves, such as basil, cilantro, and tarragon, stand them in a glass of water like a bouquet, cover with a plastic bag, and put in a cool place outside of direct sunlight. These herbs should not be refrigerated; in fact, refrigeration often wilts the leaves and turns them black. Sturdy herbs, such as rosemary and thyme, can be refrigerated in loosely closed plastic bags. For most uses, remove the leaves from the stems. Here are the herbs we use most frequently:

Basil In Greek, basil means "king," and it is certainly the king of herbs in Mediterranean countries. Lush green and mouthwateringly aromatic, Genovese basil is the most popular cultivated basil, but a trip to the nursery will reveal other varieties, such as opal, purple, and bush. Use one (or a combination) to make pesto. Thai basil, important in Southeast Asian cooking, has more pointed leaves and a slight anise flavor.

Bay Leaves Don't eat bay leaves raw—they are too tough, and the edges of shredded leaves can be sharp and dangerous to swallow. But there is a way to get their robust flavor into raw cooking. Add about twelve fresh bay leaves to a cup of olive oil and let stand overnight. Strain and refrigerate in a jar to use in tomato salads.

Chervil This very delicate herb has a gentle anise flavor, even though its small leaves resemble cilantro. It wilts quickly, so use it soon after harvesting or buying. Try infusing the leaves in water and using the solution as a skin refresher.

Chives The thin green stalks (they look like long blades of grass) require a special storage method. Wrap them in a paper towel, place in a plastic bag, and refrigerate—they should last for a couple of days. Chive blossoms are lovely, and they can be broken up and scattered over salads and dips for a sprinkle of purple color and onion flavor.

Cilantro Also called Chinese parsley, cilantro is used in natural medicine to stimulate digestion. You find it in recipes for Mexican, Asian, and Caribbean cooking, in recipes from salsa to enchiladas to slaws. If you wish, you can chop the tender stems and use them along with the leaves.

Dill Use it to flavor cheese, crackers, and sauces, as well as soups and salads. Dill has a lot of healthful qualities: It has been shown to control bacterial growth and is a powerful antiseptic. The feathery fronds can be finely chopped and used in soups and salads. Dill seeds are often used in pickles. To refresh your breath, chew a few dill seeds.

Lavender These clusters of pale purple blossoms have a distinctive perfume, but they can also be used to flavor food, especially desserts, where their floral scent and taste is especially welcome. The best place to get lavender is from a garden, but be sure that the plants are unsprayed. Beware of dried lavender, as it has usually been dehydrated at high temperatures, and is often shellacked for use in potpourris, and not food. If you can't find fresh, buy "culinary lavender," which is not treated in any way.

Lemongrass This highly aromatic stalk is a must for Southeast Asian cooking.

It is not a leaf, and therefore not really an herb, but because it is always used fresh, it is included in this list. Infuse chopped lemongrass in liquid to release its flavor. Remove the tough outer stalks until you reach the tender interior, then chop as the recipe directs.

Lemon Verbena The citrusy flavor of this leafy herb is wonderful anywhere that you would use lemon, from lemonade to dressings, desserts to dips. It adds lemon's aroma and flavor without its sharpness. You are most likely to find it during the summer at farmers' markets or in a garden, as it isn't widely available commercially.

Lovage These leaves look like celery leaves, and taste similar as well. Try adding chopped lovage to cucumber dishes, a classic combination.

Marjoram Another herb associated with the Mediterranean, marjoram is similar to oregano but somewhat stronger. Use it wherever you want a burst of zesty, herbaceous flavor.

Mint With so many varieties of mint blends available—chocolate, apple orange, banana, and pineapple, for instance—the possibilities for making teas, ice cream, and sorbet are endless. Don't forget the traditional standbys—spearmint and peppermint.

Oregano What would Italian cooking be without oregano? Oregano has many therapeutic uses, for maladies ranging from insomnia and migraines to coughs, colds, and flu. Pizzas love oregano, and so do tomatoes and zucchini.

Parsley One of the most versatile and useful herbs, there are few dishes that wouldn't benefit from a sprinkle of parsley. If that weren't enough, parsley also has strong healing properties. The leaves are rich in vitamins A and C and bone-strengthening minerals. Parsley has three times as much vitamin C as oranges, and its iron content is extremely high. Get in the habit of adding a handful or two to the juicer when making vegetable juices, especially when you want to increase the chlorophyll content of your green juices.

Rosemary Hamlet says, "There's rosemary, that's for remembrance." A contemporary study shows that rosemary, indeed, is an effective memory stimulant. Make it into a tea to aid digestion, or juice it with apples for a nice alternative to the usual beverage. Tiny blue-purple rosemary blossoms are gorgeous as a garnish, sprinkled over salads or what have you.

Sage Sage means "to heal" in Latin and has been used over the centuries to treat many ailments. In addition to the common sage, you might find pineapple, golden, or other varieties named for their aroma or coloration. Dried sage leaves have long been used to make tea to relieve headaches and sore throats.

Shiso Also called perilla, shiso is a large leaf with jagged edges. Green shiso, with a mild anise flavor, is readily available at Japanese grocers and farmers' markets. Red shiso is usually pickled.

Tarragon Another herb with an anise flavor, tarragon is not only wonderful with tomatoes and beets, but also with apples. Use the leaves in salads.

Thyme Gardeners have their choice of growing many different kinds of thyme, from the citrusy lemon thyme to the variegated silver thyme. Most markets only carry common (English) thyme. To easily remove the tender leaves from the tough stems, run the stem through the tines of a fork.

Horseradish For a blast of spicy heat to awaken your senses, use freshly grated horseradish. Unpeeled, it looks unassuming and has no aroma. Peeled and grated, it packs a delicious wallop. First, pare away the dark brown skin. Grate the pale ivory flesh on a Microplane rasp—it is surprisingly hard. Use it immediately after grating, or mix with apple cider vinegar to set its flavor, as it loses it pungency quickly when exposed to air. Look for firm horseradish—don't be concerned if dirt is clinging to the skin. The unpeeled, uncut root can be stored, uncovered, in the refrigerator. After it has been cut, store in a plastic bag and refrigerate.

Jicama   Crunchy in texture, sweet in flavor, and high in vitamin C, jicama is an oval tuber that can be eaten raw, unlike its cousin the sweet potato. Its brown skin must be peeled off, and then it can be cut into slices or matchstick pieces and served with guacamole and other dips. Enjoy jicama sticks with a squeeze of lime and a sprinkle of chili powder. Refrigerate uncut jicama for two weeks. Once cut, wrap well; it will keep for one week.

Kiwi   When ripe, kiwi, or kiwi fruit, tastes like a banana-strawberry combination. Kiwis have five times the vitamin C of oranges, twice the vitamin E of avocados, and a potassium content similar to bananas. A kiwi is ripe when it yields just slightly to the press of your thumb. To ripen, put kiwi in a paper bag with an apple or a banana for a day or two. Peel off the fuzzy, brown covering, chop or slice, and add to dressings, juices, salads, and fruit dishes. Store at room temperature until it is ripe, then refrigerate.

Kohlrabi   Another member of the *Brassica* family, kohlrabi shares a flavor profile with its cousin the turnip. Pare off its thick green skin, cut the crisp, spicy flesh into thin slices, and serve with a dip. Kohlrabi should be firm and smooth, and it should be stored in the refrigerator.

Lychee   In traditional Chinese medicine, the lychee is considered to be a "cooling" food, one that keeps the body calm and collected, and used to relieve pain, shrink swollen glands, and alleviate coughing. Each lychee is the size of a large walnut, covered with a brick red, pebbly skin. Peel off the skin like a tangerine to reveal the white and juicy fruit, and eat away—but watch out for the large central seed. Juice the peeled and seeded fruit (lychee juice is truly nectar), or serve them alone as a snack or dessert.

Before buying, sniff the lychees to check for a sweet fragrance. Store lychees at room temperature or in the refrigerator to prolong their shelf life; refrigeration will turn the skin brown, but that doesn't affect the flavor.

Mango The Sanskrit word for mango is *amra*, meaning "of the people," and in India alone there are more than 350 varieties. During the spring-early summer season on this continent, you will find mangoes from the United States, Mexico, and Haiti, with variations in size and skin color. Mangoes have a very high magnesium content, making them the perfect fruit to replenish nutrients after heavy physical exercise. It is uncommon to find ripe mangoes at the market; you probably will have to ripen them at home. Use the paper bag trick—close the mangoes in a paper bag with apples or bananas. A ripe mango will yield to gentle pressure, and a very ripe one will sport freckles on the skin, too. After ripening at room temperature, refrigerate to keep them longer. Mangoes are as delicious in a salad as they are blended into a smoothie (freeze the mango first and you won't need any ice). Purée mango for an instant dessert sauce. And dehydrated mangoes are candy without sugar.

The most challenging part of dealing with a mango is cutting it. Place the mango on the work surface where it will balance itself. The pit, which is about ½ inch thick, will run east-west through the center of the fruit. Use a sharp knife to cut off the top of the fruit, coming just above the top of the pit. Turn the mango over and cut off the other side of the fruit. Using a large metal serving spoon, scoop the mango flesh from each portion in one piece. The peeled mango can now be chopped or sliced as required. The pit portion can be pared with a small knife, and the flesh nibbled from the pit as the cook's treat.

Melons These large, sweet fruits, which include cantaloupe, Crenshaw melon, honeydew, muskmelon, watermelon, and casaba—are members of the cucumber family. Like cucumbers, they taste clean and refreshing. They're loaded with vitamins A, C, and B_6, and potassium and low in sodium.

In traditional Chinese medicine, sweet cantaloupe, honeydew, and other similar varieties are believed to cool fevers, open the lungs, and stimulate the urinary tract. These melons contain good amounts of beta-carotene and the antioxidant vitamin C, making them good fighters against degenerative diseases such as arteriosclerosis, cancer, and hypertension. They also contain plenty of folic acid, potassium, and dietary fiber.

Red watermelon (not yellow) has more lycopene, a powerful nutrient that has been shown to lower the risk of developing macular degeneration and other diseases related to aging, than tomatoes. Watermelon has diuretic properties; drink a glass or eat a slice to cleanse the kidneys and to stimulate urination. When juicing, use the rind as well as the flesh; most of the vitamins and minerals are found in the rind. Choosing a ripe melon can be hit or miss, though the following suggestions will help: For a watermelon, look for a melon where there's little contrast among the stripes. Thump the fruit. If it sounds hollow, the melon is usually ripe. It there's a pinging sound, put it back. The bottom of the melon should be white where it sat on the ground. For cantaloupes, look for an evenly brown skin without any tinge of green underneath its "netted" outer surface. Cantaloupes and other melons ripen at the end away from the stem first. If that area yields when pressed, the melon is ripe. After ripening, refrigerate all melons to prolong their freshness.

Mushrooms For culinary purposes, mushrooms can be divided into two categories—cultivated and wild. Cultivated mushrooms are grown in controlled environments and include white and brown button, cremini, portobello, shiitake, and oyster mushrooms. Wild mushrooms—black trumpets, chanterelles, hen of the woods, and porcini—are found in forests or can be purchased from foragers. (Never forage for wild mushrooms unless you really know what you're doing.) Cultivated and wild mushrooms can be eaten raw or dehydrated. With shiitakes, remove and freeze the tough stems to use in broths, soups, and tea. Morels can be dehydrated but should not be eaten raw.

Plan to use fresh mushrooms within a few days after purchase. Store them in a brown paper bag in the refrigerator. Many cookbooks tell you to gently scrub mushrooms with a soft brush and very little water to clean them. Our thinking is that since mushrooms grow in damp forests and thrive under rainy conditions, dunking and washing them in water is fine. Spin the clean mushrooms in a salad spinner to remove excess water.

Nopales   The edible pad of the prickly pear cactus (yes, the pods are sold with the spines already removed), the nopale is an unlikely superfood. Eating it, however, will reduce the entire glycemic content of a meal, and it is loaded with vitamins, minerals, and both soluble and insoluble fiber. Nopales are sold at Latino markets. Pare off the skin before cutting up. Mixed with chiles, onions, and garlic, they make a fine salsa, or juice them and mix with sweeter juices. Some people liken their taste and slightly sticky texture to okra. Store them in a plastic bag in the refrigerator.

Okra   One of the many foods that lose many valuable nutrients (vitamins A and C, among others) when cooked, okra makes great pickles. Okra is a love-it-or-leave-it food; some people can't stand its mucilaginous texture, but this quality is lessened by pickling. Buy crisp, unblemished okra. Refrigerate it unwashed in a paper bag, as plastic traps moisture that can make the okra slimy.

Onions   White. Yellow. Red. Cipollini. Ramp. Shallot. Leek. The humble onion, and its siblings and cousins, has a lot going for it. They are so flavorful and versatile that they are often combined with other ingredients to give oomph to a dish, yet they are also appreciated when served by themselves. Nutritionally speaking, onions are a good source of quercetin (twice the amount of tea, and more than three times found in apples), a phytochemical believed to contain antioxidant and anti-inflammatory qualities, and they have antibacterial and antifungal properties as well. You'll find onions in salsas and soups, pastas and salads, chips and breads. Onions with skins should be kept in a cool dark place at room temperature. Do not refrigerate them, as the moisture will encourage sprouting. Onions with green tops, like scallions and leeks, should be refrigerated.

Here are the most common members of the onion family:

Leeks The largest member of the onion family, with vibrant green tops attached to white bases. Unfortunately, the lovely green tops are bitter, and should be cut off where they start to turn pale green. Leeks are almost always sandy, and the white and pale green parts must be washed well to remove any grit. Chop or slice the leek, and place in a bowl of cold water. Agitate well in the water, separating the leek's layers, as that is where the grit lurks. Let stand for a minute or two—the usable parts will float to the top of the water, while the grit will sink to the bottom. Lift the leeks from the water, and use as directed in your recipe.

Onions The standard yellow onion (the larger ones are sometimes called Spanish onions) is sold everywhere, from the fanciest produce stand to the convenience store. White onions are milder, and red onions have a slightly sharper edge. Small boiling onions can be found in all three colors. Cippolini, an Italian variety, are the size of a squat walnut. Sweet onions used to be a local, seasonal crop, usually named after their source (for example, Vidalia, Maui, and Walla Walla). They are now flown in from such far-flung countries as Chile and available year-round. They have a mild but not particularly sweet flavor.

Shallots These resemble small, oval-shaped onions, but with an even more complex, savory flavor. They often grow as two lobes joined at the top; if a recipe calls for a single shallot, use one lobe. The body can digest shallots more easily than onions.

Papaya A large tropical fruit with lush fruit under the skin and dark seeds in the middle. Raw green papaya is used in Southeast Asian salads. Make papaya-ritas by peeling fruit, then blending with lime juice and salt. Place leftover papaya rind on your face for fifteen to twenty minutes; your skin will feel rejuvenated.

Papayas contain papain, a natural digestive aid that breaks down protein and cleans the digestive tract. Papaya is rich in vitamin C, folate, and potassium and is a good source of fiber. The seeds are used as an anti-inflammatory and analgesic.

Unless you buy them at a Latino or Asian market with a large turnover, papayas are difficult to find already ripened. Let them stand at room temperature until they yield to slight pressure. Once ripened, refrigerate them. Slice them in half and take out the seeds or peel with a vegetable peeler before eating. Whether or not you eat the crunchy seeds is up to you—they have a slightly peppery flavor.

Parsley Root Unlike garden variety parsley, which is grown just for its leaves, parsley root develops a thick, edible root. If you like celery and carrots, then you'll love parsley root, as it tastes like a cross between the two. In addition to the expected uses in soups and salads, dehydrate parsley root for a great chip. Parsley root is a diuretic that helps cleanse the urinary tract. Buy slender, firm roots with fresh-looking tops. Store them, wrapped in moist paper towels, in the refrigerator crisper.

Parsnip It is easy to neglect the unassuming parsnip, but don't. This root vegetable is sweeter than a carrot, and makes tasty chips and a filling for nori. It is a good source of fiber and vitamins C and K. Parsnips come in many sizes, from carrot-thin to thicker than a banana. If too large, however, the root develops a hard core, which you should cut out before using. Buy parsnips that look moist, not wizened. Wrap them in moist paper towels and store in the refrigerator.

Passion Fruit A properly ripened passion fruit is wrinkled and not very inspiring to look at. Inside, a bright yellow, seedy pulp with an exotic aroma belies the exterior.

Keep in mind that you will only get about a tablespoon of pulp from each fruit, so you will need a lot of them for most recipes. Like many tropical fruits, this one has many phytochemicals and antioxidants. Store them at room temperature until they exhibit their wrinkles, then refrigerate. You can strain out the seeds, but they are full of fiber, crunch, and flavor.

Pears   If you are a runner looking for a quick energy source, eat pears, as 98 percent of their energy is from carbs. There is a constant supply of pears in the market, but their peak is fall and early winter. Anjou, Bartlett (both yellow- and red-skinned), and Comice are all sweet and juicy and ripen to a tender state. Seckle and Forelle are small pears packed with flavor. Let these pears stand at room temperature until they yield to gentle pressure. Bosc is a somewhat firmer variety, and even when ripe won't be truly soft. Once ripened, pears should be refrigerated.

Peas   A 100-calorie serving of green peas has more protein than ¼ cup of almonds or a tablespoon of peanut butter. Green peas (also known as English peas) have been found to aid energy production, nerve function, and carbohydrate metabolism. The pods are tough and must be removed to get to the peas inside. You will get about one cup of shelled peas from a pound of peas in the pod, so buy accordingly. Snow peas and sugar snap peas are close relatives to the English variety, but they have thin, edible pods. Store all peas in a plastic bag in the refrigerator.

Pea Shoots   You will find these luscious, crisp shoots at Asian markets. They are available year round, but are best from local sources in the spring. Use them in salads and wraps. Store pea shoots in a plastic bag in the refrigerator, but they will only keep for a few days.

Pepper, Bell   Chile peppers and bell peppers belong to the same family, but bell peppers don't have capsaicin, the component that supplies the fiery heat. Green peppers have a slightly bitter edge, while red and yellow bell peppers are milder, with a little sweetness. They are actually fruits, with large stores of vitamins C and A, two antioxidants that work to destroy the free radicals that can attack healthy cells and cause disease. Bell peppers should be bright and shiny. Store them in the refrigerator. Remove the seeds and stems before using.

Here's an easy way to prep a bell pepper: Slice about ½ inch from the top and bottom of the pepper, remove the stem, and set the slices aside. Make a single cut down the side of the pepper and open it up. Cut out the ribs and seeds. You now have three pieces of bell pepper to do with what you will.

Persimmon   This beautiful orange-colored fruit is a cold-weather gift to raw food lovers. Persimmons are packed with vitamins A and C and are a rich source of fiber and potassium. They also have vitamin B_6 and potassium and contain minerals like potassium, manganese, copper, and phosphorus. There are two varieties, and they are quite different. Hachiya persimmons are plump and are a vibrant orange. They must be ripened at room temperature until translucent and very soft to the point of squishy. Underripe Hachiyas are incredibly (and inedibly) tannic. Purée a ripe Hachiya (remove the top calyx and any visible seeds), and you have an instant dessert sauce. Once they're nicely ripened, refrigerate them or freeze the purée. Fuyu persimmons (sometimes called Sharon fruit) are squat, pale orange, and do not need to be ripened until soft. In fact, they can be sliced into wedges and served in salads or nibbled on their own. They keep well at room temperature.

Pineapple   In salads or desserts, or dehydrated for snacking, this sweet Hawaiian fruit is a source good of nutrients like manganese (1 cup of chopped pineapple provides 73 percent of the daily requirement), calcium, potassium, and dietary fiber. Buy fresh pineapple that has a sweet aroma and a green, moist crown. Pineapple can be ripened at room temperature, if needed, then refrigerated. A few hours before you plan to eat the pineapple, cut off the crown and then turn the fruit upside down on a plate and leave it in the fridge. The sweetness of the juice, which is at the bottom of the pineapple, will be nicely distributed throughout the entire fruit when turned over.

To help reduce inflammation, eat pineapple in between meals. If eaten during or after meals, the enzymes will be utilized for digesting food. The protein-digesting enzymes in pineapple help digestion. To get rid of fine wrinkles, rub the core of pineapple on your face and leave it on for ten to fifteen minutes before rinsing off.

Pomegranate   Available in the fall and winter, pomegranates take a little work to get to the juice-filled arils that surround the tiny white seeds, but it is worth the effort. Buy pomegranates that are firm but juicy—if you squeeze one and it emits a small cloud of dust from the central shoot, then the fruit is probably dried out inside. Here's a way to get to the arils without splattering juice all over you and your kitchen. Score the fruit into quarters with a knife. Submerge the pomegranate in a bowl of water, then break it open. Coax the ruby red arils out of the bitter white membrane. The heavy arils sink to the bottom, and any bits of membrane will float to the top. (Some markets sell pomegranate arils already removed from the fruit.) Use them fresh or dried in salads and with grain dishes, or juice them (you will need a juice press for juicing them). Known for their high amounts of antioxidants, studies are being done to show the fruit's effect on heart disease, diabetes, and breast cancer.

Radishes   These spicy root vegetables are considered a very good source of fiber, vitamin A, potassium, and folic acid. Red radishes can be found in every market. Cut off the greens (they are deliciously peppery) before storing, as the tops actually leech nutrients from the roots. A trip to the farmers' market in late spring will reveal unusual varieties, such as the white-tipped breakfast or oblong French radishes. Asian cooking uses black radish and white daikon, both of which are as large, or larger, than baking potatoes. Store all radishes in the refrigerator.

Rhubarb   Rhubarb is the one of the first edible signs of spring. Trim off the leaves (they contain oxalates, which can be poisonous) and cut the rhubarb stems into chunks. Packed in containers, leaving a bit of head space, they can be refrigerated for up to two weeks or frozen for about two months. Rhubarb can also be dehydrated. Tart rhubarb is great in soups, drinks, and ice cream, but it is so puckery it usually is combined with sweeter fruits. It is more versatile than you might expect. Some possibilities include strawberry-rhubarb lemonade and pickled rhubarb.

Rutabaga   See Turnips, page 98.

Spinach   Spinach is loaded with vitamins, especially vitamin A and vitamin K, and has more than thirteen different flavonoid and antioxidant compounds. Spinach is a cool-weather crop, as it bolts easily in the heat of the summer, so even if it is available year-round, it will be best from local sources in spring and fall. There are three distinct spinach varieties: curly-leaf savoy, flat-leaf, and baby. Put any of these three through the juicer, but flat-leaf spinach has the most delicate flavor and texture for salads and other dishes. Buy bright green spinach with sprightly leaves and no signs of sliminess. Store unwashed spinach in a plastic bag in the refrigerator. Spinach is sandy, so separate the stems from the leaves, and wash both well before using (see Swiss Chard, page 79). Even if you buy baby spinach, which may look clean, rinse it first before eating. Dry the leaves in a salad spinner or pat off the water with towels.

Sprouts   See page 53.

Squash Blossoms   The golden blossoms of summer squash can be chopped and turned into soup or stuffed with cheese. You will find them during the height of summer at farmers' markets and some well-stocked produce markets. They are extremely perishable, even when refrigerated, so use them soon after buying. To prep squash blossoms, if the flower is closed, make a slit down its side (bees love to hide inside, so be careful), and remove the pistil through the slit to make more room for the stuffing. If the flower is open, just remove the pistil.

Stone Fruits   This group of fruits, members of the *Prunus* family, share the trait of a hard pit (or stone) in the center of each fruit. Finding stone fruit that has been handled properly can be a problem, as not all of them will ripen after picking, and shipping can damage ripe fruit. Buy them from local sources whenever possible. The fruit should be firm but yield a little when pressed gently and free from damage. Refrigerate ripe fruit without washing it before storing.

> **Apricots** The seed of the apricot is really a nut that is rich in protein and vitamin B_{17}. Apricots are high in minerals, including beta-carotene, potassium, boron, iron, and silica. They are one of the best natural sources of vitamin A, especially when dried. When you dry an apricot, its nutritional value multiplies. Do not buy hard apricots or those with greenish skin, as they will not ripen sufficiently.
>
> **Cherries** There are few fruits more delicious than cherries and few more healthful. They are packed with beta-carotene, and are one of the few food sources of melatonin, a chemical compound that regulates sleeping patterns and some people find helps alleviate jet lag. Every supermarket carries Bing cherries during their late spring to midsummer season, and you may be lucky enough to find golden Royal Ann cherries, too. Fresh sour cherries are very tart, and while they have high levels of antioxidants, you may find that they need lots of sweetening. Eat cherries by the handful. If you put them through the juicer (and you should, as the juice is amazingly tasty), be sure to pit them first.
>
> Cherries help inhibit enzymes that are associated with inflammation,

because the compounds in cherries have similar activity as aspirin. Drinking 1 ounce of concentrated tart cherry juice every day can help alleviate arthritis pain.

Look for shiny, plump, smooth cherries without any sign of mold. Store cherries, unrinsed and uncovered, in the refrigerator. If mold does appear, remove the offending ones immediately from the rest of the cherries.

Peaches Packed with potassium, antioxidants, vitamins A and C, and beta-carotene, peaches contain more than 80 percent water and are a good source of dietary fiber. In early summer, cling peaches (with fruit that adheres tightly to the pit but can be cut away) show up in the markets. Midsummer is the time for freestone peaches, with a pit that comes easily away from the flesh. White peaches are also a midsummer fruit, and their flavor is more delicate and perfumed than the yellow-fleshed cling and freestone varieties. Look for doughnut peaches, so called because they're somewhat flat and indented in the center like a doughnut hole. Nectarines are similar to peaches, with thinner skin and a slightly more acidic flavor.

Plums Plums are a great source of vitamins A, K, and C and are well known as a digestive aid. Red Santa Rosa plums are among the first plums to arrive in the summer. These are followed by purple Italian prune plums, which last into early fall. Prunes, or dried plums, are a chewy, tasty snack, especially when they come from your own dehydrator, without the preservatives found in the commercially produced ones.

Summer Squash Squash is technically a fruit, because it contains the plant's seeds, but it is treated like a vegetable. Zucchini is green and straight; yellow straight-neck squash is a close relation. The curve in a crookneck squash gives it away as such, and a pattypan squash is round and squat with scalloped edges and can be pale green, yellow, or even striated. Shredded, sliced, or chopped, summer squash adds texture and flavor to many dishes, and it can be juiced. Purchase firm, unblemished summer squash, and store it in the refrigerator. Scrub it under cold running water before using to remove any clinging dirt, which may not be readily visible.

Sweet Potatoes/Yams   For most Americans, the terms sweet potato and yam are interchangeable. In truth, the two are from different species. Sweet potatoes have light skin with interiors ranging from pale yellow to dark orange flesh. True yams can be found in Latino markets. Sweet potatoes/yams may be sold in room-temperature bins at the market, but refrigerate them when you get home to keep them fresh longer.

Tomatillos   They may look like a green tomato, but tomatillos are actually related to the gooseberry, which also has a papery outer husk. Filled with vitamin C, they are an important ingredient in Mexican cooking, and have a slightly acidic flavor that works well in salsa. Buy firm tomatillos with dry husks, with bright green, unblemished fruit underneath; softness is an indication of deterioration, not ripeness. After removing the husk, rinse away the naturally occurring sticky surface, and cut as needed. Store in a paper bag in the refrigerator.

Tomatoes   While tomatoes are sold year-round, it is worth waiting for their summer season when they are at their most flavorful. But not only are seasonal tomatoes utterly delicious, they also provide lycopene, a powerful antioxidant that has been shown to prevent certain types of cancer and other diseases, as well as a cornucopia of valuable vitamins and minerals. A rainbow of tomatoes is available (yellow, orange, striped, green, and even purple in addition to the standard red), and even many supermarkets now carry the beautiful heirloom varieties—with unique names like Green Zebra, Mortgage Lifter, and Cherokee Purple—from original, not hybridized, seeds. They all share the same nutritional benefits, but it is interesting to note the flavor differences (for example, yellow tomatoes are less acidic than other colors). Juice them, dehydrate them, turn them into salsas or salads, but eat them often. For the most part, buy tomatoes that are evenly colored and give off a vegetal aroma. Tomatoes should be firm and plump with unblemished skin. Refrigeration turns tomatoes mealy, so store them out on the counter.

Turnips   Turnips are usually overcooked, which destroys their crispness, one of their best qualities. Peel, slice thinly on a mandoline, and soak in ice water to increase their crunchiness. Drain and fill with cheese to make ravioli. For a change of pace, use turnip's larger cousin, rutabaga. Turnips should be firm, without any sign of softness. Choose the smallest, youngest ones in the bins, as they will be more tender with the thinnest skins. They are usually displayed without their green tops, which are sold separately, and are equally healthful. Peel or don't peel the turnips, as you wish. Store the turnips, unwashed, in a closed plastic bag in the refrigerator crisper. The plastic bag is important, as it will retain the turnips' moisture, and also keep their strong aroma from seeping into the other food in the fridge.

Wheat Grass   Grow this verdant green grass, which is nothing more than blades of common wheat, at home to add to the juicer. Wheat grass juice is an excellent source of chlorophyll, active enzymes, and amino acids, but to get its full benefit, it must be consumed soon after juicing. One ounce of wheat grass is said to have the nutritional equivalent of 2½ pounds of vegetables. Buy house-size "plots" of wheat grass at natural food stores or online.

Winter Squash   Tender-skinned squash harvested in the summer are (obviously) called summer squash. Other varieties that develop thick, tough skin and are traditionally harvested in cool weather are winter squash. Winter squash has large stores of vitamin A and beta-carotene. If you plan on juicing them, buy large squash with a good proportion of flesh to seeds, such as butternut, hubbard, or pumpkin, as the thinner-skin varieties (for example, delicata, turban, and acorn) will require more squash per serving of juice. Peel off slices with a vegetable peeler and add to salads. When buying winter squash, look for hard skin without any nicks. They can be stored in a cool, dark place. Dehydrate the seeds and salt them for snacking.

RECIPES

From nut milks to spice blends, here are the basic recipes that you'll use again and again when preparing recipes from this book or creating your own. Easy to prepare, these milks, butters, condiments, and seasoning blends can all be made ahead and will last as indicated in each recipe. And when you're ready to start cooking, you'll be one step ahead.

· · · · · · · · · · · · · · · ·

NUT OR SEED MILK

Nut and seed milks are one of the many workhorses of the raw foods kitchen. Refreshing and easy to make, these beverages can be enjoyed as is or in other drinks, sauces, and soups. And here's where you'll get to use that stash of leftover vanilla bean pods you've been saving from the other recipes in the book.

To make sweeter nut milk, increase the amount of dates to your liking.

• • • Makes 6 cups • • •

2 cups nuts (such as almonds, cashews, or Brazil nuts) *or* **2 cups seeds (hemp or sesame)**
5 pitted dates
5 vanilla bean pods

1. Put the nuts or seeds and 6 cups fresh water in a Vita-Mix. Blend until smooth, 1 to 2 minutes.
2. Pour the mixture through a fine-mesh strainer or into a nut bag over a bowl. Press on the strainer with a wooden spoon or squeeze the nut bag to remove all the milk.
3. Rinse out the blender so no nut or seed residue remains. Return the milk to the blender, add the dates, and blend. Transfer the milk to a pitcher or glass jar, add the vanilla pods, and cover. Infuse for 6 to 10 hours in the refrigerator. Refrigerate for up to 2 days.

NUT OR SEED BUTTER

Although raw nut and seed butters can be purchased in markets and online, homemade is less expensive, tastier, and fresher than store-bought. Use almonds, hazelnuts, cashews, macadamias, pistachios, or pine nuts. Walnuts can be bitter. Any seed can be made into butter.

A homogenizing, twin-gear juicer, such as Champion or Green Star brand, makes the best nut butters. Place all of the ingredients in the chute and press down firmly with the plunger. The creamy nut butter will be extruded where the juice pulp comes out.

Nut butters can also be made in a food processor. If you prefer creamy nut butters, it may take a while for the machine to blend the nuts to a smooth consistency.

Smear nut butter on crackers, apples, and celery or add a big spoonful to a smoothie.

* * * Makes 1 cup * * *

2 cups nuts

3 tablespoons extra virgin olive oil

1 teaspoon sea salt

1. Put the nuts, oil, and salt through a juicer or process in a food processor.
2. Transfer the nut butter to a covered container and store in the refrigerator for up to 2 weeks.

NUT FLOUR

Almost any nut can be ground into nut flour. (Pine nuts won't work; they immediately become butter.) Put whole nuts into a food processor or Vita-Mix and pulse in short bursts until they are finely chopped. Stop the machine to check the texture. Too much blending will quickly result in nut oil or nut butter. If not using the nut flour immediately, freeze it in an airtight container to prevent rancidity. One cup whole nuts makes approximately 1½ cups nut flour.

SEASONED ALMOND FLOUR

A seasoned breading for Onion Rings (page 236) and Avocado Skins (page 232).

* * * Makes 1 cup * * *

1 cup almond flour (page 106)

2 teaspoons paprika

½ teaspoon cayenne pepper

1 tablespoon chopped mixed fresh herbs, such as parsley, dill, and/or thyme

Dash of sea salt

A few grinds of black pepper

1. Toss together all the ingredients in a bowl.
2. Store in a covered container in the refrigerator for up to 2 weeks.

COCONUT MILK

Coconut milk is used in many recipes—from smoothies to soups.

• • • Makes 4 cups • • •

3 cups dried coconut flakes

1. Combine the coconut and 5 cups water in a Vita-Mix. Blend for 1 to 2 minutes.
2. Pour the mixture through a fine-mesh strainer or into a nut bag over a bowl. Press on the strainer with a wooden spoon or squeeze the nut bag to remove all the milk.
3. Cover and refrigerate for up to 3 days.

CHOCOLATE HEMP SEED MILK

Rich and creamy, this milk is perfect for kids of all ages. One of our favorites is a half-and-half combination of chocolate hemp seed milk and almond milk (page 104).

• • • Makes 8 cups • • •

1 cup hemp seeds

1 cup cacao powder

1 cup pitted dates

1. Blend the hemp seeds with 6 cups water in a Vita-Mix. The mixture will be rather thin.
2. Strain the mixture through a fine-mesh strainer or pour into a nut bag over a bowl. Press on the strainer with a wooden spoon or squeeze the nut bag to remove all the liquid.
3. Rinse out the blender after Step 2 to remove all seed residue and pour the milk back into the Vita-Mix. Add the cacao powder and dates and blend until well combined.
4. Cover and store in the refrigerator for up to 3 days.

DATE PASTE

Date paste provides a less pronounced sweetness than agave nectar. Keep a container of date paste on hand to add a touch of sweetness to smoothies and desserts.

• • • Makes 2 cups • • •

2 cups pitted dates

1. Soak the dates in 1 cup water for 8 hours in the refrigerator.
2. Purée the soaked dates and water in a Vita-Mix until smooth, starting and stopping the machine as necessary so the paste doesn't become too hot.
3. Store in a sealed container for up to 1 week in the refrigerator.

PURÉED CHILES

This is just what it says: puréed chiles. Choose chiles with some heat—habaneros or jalalpeños—and purée them in a food processor or Vita-Mix. Transfer to a plastic container and freeze for up to 6 months. Scoop out the purée as needed. Or freeze the purée in a mini-ice cube tray and pop out cubes as needed. Remember, these chiles are hot; wear gloves when working with them.

CHILE OIL

Red jalapeños turn this oil an attractive hue. If only green ones are available, use them with green bell peppers for a different flavor and color.

• • • Makes 2½ cups • • •

2 cups extra virgin olive oil

3 red jalapeño chiles

2 red bell peppers, quartered and seeded

3 garlic cloves

1. Combine all the ingredients in a Vita-Mix, stopping the machine to scrape down the sides as necessary.
2. Strain the mixture through a nut bag or a fine-mesh strainer into a lidded glass jar. Store in the refrigerator for up to 5 days. Allow the oil to come to room temperature before using.

HERB OIL

1 bunch scallions, green and white parts, halved

1 cup fresh flat-leaf parsley leaves

1 cup spinach leaves

½ cup fresh tarragon leaves

2 cups extra virgin olive oil

1. Put the scallions, parsley, spinach, and tarragon in a food processor and coarsely chop. With the machine on, slowly drizzle in the olive oil through the hole in the top until well combined with the herbs.
2. Pour into a jar, cover, and refrigerate for up to 1 week. Allow the oil to come to room temperature before using.

GARLIC OIL

1 cup extra virgin olive oil

5 garlic cloves, grated on a Microplane rasp

1. Combine the oil and garlic in a glass jar. Cover the jar and give it a good shake.
2. Use immediately or store in the refrigerator for up to 1 week. Let the oil come to room temperature before using.

EGGPLANT BACON

This crispy treat can be tossed in salads, added to sandwiches, and served for breakfast. At Grezzo, eggplant bacon accompanies Gnocchi Carbonara (page 348).

• • • Makes about 40 strips • • •

½ **cup Nama Shoyu**

2 tablespoons agave nectar

1 teaspoon cayenne pepper

3 large eggplants

1. Whisk together the Nama Shoyu, agave, and cayenne in a large bowl and set aside.
2. Peel and discard the eggplant skin. Continue peeling the eggplant and make 1-inch-wide long strips, rotating the eggplant and peeling until the seedy core is reached. Discard the core. Arrange the eggplant strips in a shallow dish and marinate in the shoyu-agave mixture for 1 hour.
3. Once marinated, lay the strips flat on mesh dehydrator racks and dehydrate for at least 12 hours, until crisp. Once dehydrated, keep the eggplant strips in the dehydrator for optimum crispness or put them in a plastic container and cover. They will keep indefinitely at room temperature or in the dehydrator.

UNROASTED PEPPERS

These are nothing more than stemmed, seeded, and halved peppers that are dehydrated for a few hours to concentrate their flavor. Marinate them in olive oil, garlic, and herbs for an antipasto. This is the amount of bell peppers required to make our Breadsticks (page 382), but feel free to double or triple the recipe using poblano or Anaheim chiles for some spice in salads, soups, sandwiches, and as a pizza topping.

· · · Makes 6 peppers · · ·

2 *each* red, green, and yellow bell peppers, stemmed, halved, and seeded

1. Arrange the pepper halves on Teflex-lined dehydrator racks. Dehydrate for 3 to 5 hours, until soft and tender.
2. Cover and refrigerate for up to 2 to 3 days.

Making Unroasted Vegetables

Unroasting vegetables in the dehydrator softens them, allowing their flavors to intensify and become almost sweet.

Almost any vegetable takes well to unroasting. Try diagonally cut carrots, green beans, halved Brussels sprouts, sugar snap peas, corn kernels shaved from the cob, broccoli, cauliflower, sliced garlic, onions, and shallots. Toss the vegetables with enough extra virgin olive oil to coat, or use coconut oil for a more buttery taste, and season with salt and pepper, adding some grated garlic or other seasonings as you wish. Arrange the vegetables on Teflex-lined dehydrator racks and dehydrate for 3 to 5 hours.

Unroast a rack or two of vegetables whenever you're running the dehydrator so you'll always have some on hand for nibbling or creating a meal.

24-HOUR TOMATOES

These tomatoes are similar in texture to chewy, oven-roasted tomatoes with a caramelized sweetness. Be sure to keep a batch on hand. Purée them for a quick tomato sauce or add them to soups and salads. Before dehydrating, rub them with any one of the seasoning mixtures on pages 120–126.

• • • Makes 40 tomatoes • • •

20 plum tomatoes, halved

½ cup extra virgin olive oil

¼ chopped fresh flat-leaf parsley or basil

½ tablespoon sea salt

1. Combine all the ingredients in a bowl and toss.
2. Arrange the tomatoes in a single layer on Teflex-lined dehydrator racks.
3. Dehydrate for 24 hours. Cover and refrigerate for up to 3 days.

Seasoning Blends

Making your own spice blends in a designated coffee or spice mill guarantees that blends are fresh. While it's best to grind spices at the last minute, who has time for that? Keep spice mixes on hand. Store these blends in glass jars away from sunlight and heat to keep them fresh. Write the date they were made on each one to know how long they've been around. Once ground, spices quickly lose their potency; use them within a few weeks.

Creating your seasonings allows you to tailor the flavors to your own taste. Try the blends below, then add more or less of certain herbs and spices as you wish.

. . . .

CAJUN SEASONING

Sprinkle a dusting over papaya, add a pinch to any fruit salsa, or sprinkle on chips or vegetables before dehydrating.

• • • Makes ½ cup • • •

2 tablespoons cumin seeds

2 tablespoons coriander seeds

2 tablespoons mustard seeds

2 tablespoons fennel seeds

¼ teaspoon ground cinnamon

2 teaspoons cayenne pepper

1. Put the cumin, coriander, mustard, and fennel seeds in a spice or coffee mill. Grind the spices.
2. Transfer the ground spices to a glass jar, add the cinnamon and cayenne, and shake well. Store at room temperature.

GARAM MASALA

Add a tablespoon or so to cheese for an Indian-inspired flavor.

• • • Makes ½ cup • • •

2 tablespoons cardamom pods

1 cinnamon stick, broken in half

2 tablespoons whole cloves

2 whole nutmegs

5 star anise

2 tablespoons fennel seeds

1. Put all the ingredients in a spice or coffee mill. Grind the spices.
2. Transfer the ground spices to a glass jar. Shake until the spices are combined. Store at room temperature.

SEA VEGETABLE SALT

Sprinkle on nori rolls or in soups. Add 2 tablespoons unhulled sesame seeds to the mixture before dehydrating if you like.

• • • Makes ½ cup • • •

2 cups dulse

¼ cup sea salt

1. Dehydrate the dried dulse for 8 to 10 hours, until crisp.
2. Put the dehydrated dulse in a Vita-Mix. Blend for 30 seconds to create a powder.
3. Transfer the dulse to a glass jar, add the salt, and shake to combine. Store at room temperature.

MUSHROOM SEASONING

Any mushroom dish takes well to this blend of spices.

• • • Makes ½ cup • • •

1 teaspoon cardamom pods

1 teaspoon allspice

2 tablespoons mustard seeds

2 tablespoons coriander seeds

2 tablespoons anise seeds

1. Put all the ingredients in a spice or coffee mill. Grind the spices.
2. Transfer the ground spices to a glass jar. Shake until the spices are combined. Store at room temperature.

SALAD SEASONING

• • • Makes ½ cup • • •

6 tablespoons celery seeds

6 tablespoons cumin seeds

1 tablespoon crushed red pepper flakes

1. Put all the ingredients in a spice or coffee mill. Grind the spices.
2. Transfer the ground spices to a glass jar. Shake until the spices are combined. Store at room temperature.

SLIDER SEASONING

A seasoning that adds flavor to Sliders (page 240) and burgers of any kind.

• • • Makes ½ cup • • •

8 cardamom pods

4 teaspoons mustard seeds

4 teaspoons coriander seeds

4 teaspoons fennel seeds

2 tablespoon cumin seeds

1. Put all the ingredients in a spice or coffee mill. Grind the spices.
2. Transfer the ground spices to a glass jar. Shake until the spices are combined. Store at room temperature.

ZAATAR

Zaatar refers to the wild thyme that grows throughout the Middle East and to a particular fragrant spice blend from that region. Sprinkle zaatar in tahini vinaigrette, hummus, or unroasted vegetables. Add a teaspoon to salad dressings for a Mediterranean flavor, or fold some into any bread or cracker batter.

• • • Makes ½ cup • • •

Zest of 2 lemons

15 sprigs fresh thyme

¼ cup white unhulled sesame seeds

2 tablespoons caraway seeds

1 teaspoon sea salt

1. Arrange the zest and thyme on Teflex-lined dehydrator racks. Dehydrate for 8 hours. Remove the thyme leaves from the stems.
2. Put the sesame and caraway seeds in a spice or coffee grinder. Grind the spices. Transfer the ground spices to a glass jar. Add the zest, thyme, and salt, cover, and shake to combine. Store at room temperature.

CHEESE:
QUICK AND CULTURED

Of all the things that raw food folks seem to miss the most, cheese is at the top of their list. So we developed recipes using nuts and other ingredients to mimic the consistency and flavor of certain cheeses. Our ricotta cheese is smooth and neutral in flavor so herbs and other seasonings can be added. Quick Cheese has the consistency and taste of mozzarella, making it ideal to use on pizza and in lasagna. Grezzo Cheese is thick, creamy, and spreadable, and can be used in endless ways—in Land and Sea (page 350), ravioli, and cheesecake, or as part of a fruit and cracker platter.

Grezzo Cheese is not hard to make, but it requires several steps and time to ferment. Make a few batches, freeze them, and they'll always be on hand. For instant cheese gratification, there are a number of quick cheeses that can be made without fermenting and can be substituted in any recipe that calls for Grezzo Cheese.

Here are some guidelines for making raw cheeses:

- For savory cheeses, use macadamia nuts and flavor with garlic, herbs, and spices. Cashews work best when a slightly sweeter flavor is desired, as in the Miso-Cashew Cheese (page 143). When making quick cheeses, we prefer equal parts cashews and macadamias. For Grezzo Cheese (page 132), use a combination of the two or just one type of nut.
- Using a Vita-Mix produces cheeses with airy, smooth texture. The texture will be rich and creamy, and the ingredients will be well blended. Some cheeses, such as feta, are made in a food processor to achieve a coarser, slightly crumbly texture.
- The more you press with weights on cheeses made with rejuvelac, the firmer the cheeses will be.
- Quick Cheese (page 129) and Grezzo Cheese (page 132) can be used interchangeably in recipes.
- Once frozen cheese is defrosted, do not refreeze it.

QUICK CHEESE

Add herbs, spices, or finely chopped vegetables or other ingredients to this basic cheese. It is similar to mozzarella in taste and texture and is perfect for pizza and lasagna. Try the Nacho Cheese variation (page 136) in Mexican dishes.

• • • Makes 2 cups • • •

1 cup macadamia nuts

1 cup cashews

2 tablespoons Nama Shoyu

1½ tablespoons freshly squeezed lemon juice

1. Combine all the ingredients in a food processor. Turn on the machine and slowly add ¼ cup water through the hole in the top. Add more water as necessary, up to another ¼ cup, until the mixture is smooth, thick, and creamy.
2. If not using immediately, cover and store in the refrigerator for up to 3 to 4 days.

SAVORY CHEESE

A combination of nuts gives this cheese lots of flavor. Use it when making ravioli or Land and Sea (page 350).

• • • Makes 2½ cups • • •

1 cup pine nuts

1 cup macadamia nuts or cashews

1 cup walnuts

1 cup chopped fresh parsley

2½ tablespoons freshly squeezed lemon juice

2 tablespoons Nama Shoyu

2 garlic cloves

1. Put all the ingredients in a food processor. Blend well, until creamy.
2. Cover and store in refrigerator for up to 3 to 4 days.

QUICK RICOTTA

Like dairy ricotta, this cheese is somewhat bland in flavor and takes well to add-ins. Use this recipe and the Grezzo Ricotta (page 146) interchangeably.

• • • Makes 1½ cups • • •

1 cup macadamia nuts

1 cup almonds

Juice of ½ lemon

¼ cup freshly squeezed orange juice

1. Put the nuts, lemon and orange juices, and ¼ cup water into a food processor. Blend until creamy.
2. Use immediately or transfer to a bowl, cover, and store in the refrigerator for up to 3 to 4 days.

GREZZO CHEESE

Those who taste this cheese simply can't believe that it's a dairy-free, soy-free raw vegan cheese. Once it's made, endless flavorings can be added. Stir in herbs and garlic for a Boursin-like cheese, black olives and basil for Mediterranean flavors, or cilantro and habaneros to go with Mexican food. It's so popular that we ship it, along with our ice cream, all over the country.

Making this cheese takes several days, but most of the work doesn't require your attention. First, wheat berries and rye berries are soaked for one day, then sprouted in a nut bag and rinsed with water 3 to 5 times a day for up to 3 days, until ⅛-inch to ¼-inch tails appear. Second, transfer the sprouts to a large jar filled with fresh water and let them sit at room temperature for 12 to 14 hours. The fermented liquid is called rejuvelac. Strain the rejuvelac into a clean container and discard the sprouted berries. Raw nuts are then puréed with rejuvelac and the mixture is allowed to sit and ripen for one day. The result is Grezzo cheese. It remains fresh for 5 to 7 days in the refrigerator or frozen for up to a couple of months. A couple of notes: Read the instructions carefully. Use spring or filtered, not distilled, water for soaking the berries and making the rejuvelac. Cool water from the tap can be used to rinse the berries. You will need a 24-ounce jar with a vented lid and a one-gallon jar with a lid to make the rejuvelac. For making the cheese, have cheesecloth or a few nut bags on hand.

When making rejuvelac, if the room temperature is between 70°F and 80°F, the process takes about 3 days. If the room temperature is between 60°F to 65°F, the process may need as many as 5.

When making cheese, use raw nuts—macadamia nuts, cashews, walnuts, hazelnuts—of your choosing. Hazelnuts work if you want a sweet cheese.

Four cups of nuts and two cups of rejuvelac will yield about three cups cheese, but this process is time-consuming, so the recipe can be doubled.

Grezzo cheese made in a Vita-Mix will have just the right creamy, smooth texture. Any flavorings—herbs, vegetables, spices—should be added in a food processor or folded in by hand for the best consistency.

• • • Makes 3 cups • • •

REJUVELAC

½ cup wheat berries

½ cup rye berries

4 cups nuts of your choosing, preferably cashews and/or macadamia nuts

1. Day 1: Combine the wheat berries and rye berries in a 24-ounce jar with a vented lid. Add 3 cups water. Put the jar in a warm spot and let sit at room temperature.

2. Day 2: Discard the liquid. Transfer the berries to a nut bag and put the bag in a bowl.

3. Days 2 to 4: Rinse the berries under cooling running water 3 to 5 times a day.

4. Day 5: When the berries have tiny tails, that means they have sprouted. Rinse the sprouted berries once more. Put the berries in a one-gallon glass jar with a lid. Fill the jar completely with spring water and let sit overnight in a warm spot.

5. Day 6: The sprouted berries will produce one gallon of a fermented liquid called rejuvelac. Strain and discard the berries, but save the liquid, which is the rejuvelac. The liquid will be pale yellow, and cloudy, and smell quite pungent. Refrigerate for up to 1 month.

TO MAKE CHEESE:

1. Put the nuts and 2 cups rejuvelac in a Vita-Mix. Blend for 1 minute, stop the machine for 30 seconds, then blend again for 1 minute. Stopping the machine keeps the cheese from becoming warmer than 112°F. While the Vita-Mix is on, remove the lid, and use a paddle motion with your spatula to keep the cheese moving. It is essential to keep the cheese mixture in constant motion. Lowering the spatula just 2 inches into the cheese will help make sure you don't knick the blade. Continue starting, paddling, and stopping in 1-minute increments until the mixture is a smooth purée. If the cheese is too thick and won't turn over in the machine, add ¼ to ½ cup rejuvelac as needed. The mixture needs to be as smooth as possible. (When doubling the recipe, do this in two steps without washing out the Vita-Mix.)

2. Pour the mixture into a cheesecloth-lined sieve over a bowl to drain. Fold the cheesecloth so it's tucked in and weight the top for excess liquid to strain out. (Use jars filled with water as weights.) Cover and let the cheese ripen at room temperature overnight.

3. The next day, remove the weights, uncover the cheese, and in one motion, flip the cheese into a large bowl or onto a large piece of parchment paper. Transfer to clean, dry plastic containers. Cover, label with the name and date, and store the cheese in the refrigerator for 5 to 7 days or in the freezer for a couple of months. Enjoy as is, try one of the variations below, or create one of your own.

Rejuvelac

Rejuvelac is a fermented liquid made from wheat and rye berries and filtered water. The grains are soaked and sprouted, and then strained from the liquid and discarded.

In addition to making cheese, rejuvelac can be consumed as a digestive aid and a detoxifier. Rejuvelac contains eight of the B vitamins, vitamin K, and a variety of beneficial proteins, dextrines, carbohydrates, phosphates, saccharine, and amylases. It is rich in enzymes that assist digestion and the growth of friendly bacteria, such as lactobacillus bifidus, which produces a lactic acid that helps the colon maintain its natural environment. Lactobacillus bifidus also helps cleanse the lower intestinal tract.

Once made, rejuvelac can be kept in the refrigerator for up to a month. Drink as is or add lemon juice for a refreshing lemonade.

NACHO CHEESE

You can also dehydrate this cheese to make nachos. Thinly spread the cheese mixture on Teflex-lined dehydrator racks and dehydrate for 7 to 10 hours. Remove the racks, peel off the Teflex, flip the cheese, and dehydrate for another 5 to 6 hours. When done, break up the cheese into small pieces and top with guacamole and salsa. For some heat, add a jalapeño with the other ingredients.

• • • Makes 2 cups • • •

2 cups macadamia nuts

1½ cups seeded and chopped red bell pepper

Segments from 1 large navel orange

4 garlic cloves

Juice of 1 lemon

2 tablespoons Nama Shoyu

1. Put all the ingredients in a food processor. Blend until smooth and creamy.
2. Cover and store in the refrigerator for up to 3 to 4 days.

FETA CHEESE

For a cheese with more texture, try this feta. Accompany with some olive oil and oregano, or roll into balls like mozzarella and add to a Greek salad with tomatoes, peppers, red onions, and cucumbers. For a refreshing summer salad, combine feta, watermelon, and some mint leaves.

• • • Makes 2 cups • • •

2 cups macadamia nuts

1 cup Rejuvelac (page 133)

1 shallot

1 teaspoon sea salt

1. Soak the nuts in the rejuvelac for 8 hours.
2. Process the shallot in a food processor until finely minced. Add the soaked nuts, any remaining soaking liquid, and salt. Blend until combined. The texture should be slightly coarse and chunky like feta.
3. Pour the mixture into a cheesecloth-lined sieve over a bowl to drain. Fold the cheesecloth so it's tucked in and weight the top so excess liquid can strain out. (Use jars filled with water as weights.) Let the cheese ripen at room temperature for 8 hours.
4. After 8 hours, remove the weights, uncover the cheese, and in one motion, flip the cheese into a large bowl or onto a large piece of parchment paper. Transfer to a clean, dry plastic container. Cover, label with name and date, and store the cheese in the refrigerator for up to 5 to 7 days.

HERB-GARLIC CHEESE

Pair this cheese with Unroasted Peppers (page 116) or as a filling for hollowed-out cherry tomatoes, mushroom caps, or celery sticks, or as a spread with crackers (pages 375–380).

• • • Makes 3 cups • • •

3 cups Grezzo Cheese (page 132), made with macadamia nuts

7 garlic cloves, finely grated on a Microplane rasp

½ cup chopped mixed herbs, such as parsley, thyme, rosemary, tarragon, dill, and/or chervil

1½ teaspoons sea salt

1½ teaspoons freshly ground black pepper

1. Combine all the ingredients in a bowl and mix well by hand using a spatula.
2. Scrape the cheese into a serving bowl, cover, and refrigerate for up to 5 to 7 days.

GREEN OLIVE–JALAPEÑO CHEESE

If you can't find savory or chervil, use parsley or lemon thyme or other herbs of your choosing. Accompany with sliced peaches and rye bread for breakfast. Make this only with Grezzo Cheese (page 132).

• • • Makes 2 cups • • •

12 green olives, pitted

1 small jalapeño chile

2 cups Grezzo Cheese (page 132), made with macadamia nuts

¼ cup chopped fresh savory or chervil

3 garlic cloves, grated on a Microplane rasp

1 teaspoon fleur de sel

1 teaspoon freshly ground black pepper

1. Coarsely chop the olives and jalapeño in a food professor.
2. Add the cheese, herbs, salt, and pepper and blend until well incorporated.
3. Scrape the cheese into a serving bowl, cover, and refrigerate for up to 5 to 7 days.

HABANERO-CILANTRO CHEESE

Any Tex-Mex-style dishes—avocado salad or nachos—go well with this spicy and piquant cheese. Add more Puréed Chiles if you want a spicier cheese. Make this only with Grezzo Cheese (page 132).

• • • Makes 3 cups • • •

3 cups Grezzo Cheese (page 132), made with macadamia nuts

1 garlic clove, grated on a Microplane rasp

½ cup chopped fresh cilantro

1½ teaspoons Puréed Chiles (page 111)

1½ teaspoons fleur de sel

1½ teaspoons freshly ground black pepper

1. Combine all the ingredients in a food processor. Blend until smooth.
2. Scrape the cheese into a serving bowl, cover, and refrigerate for up to 5 days.

DILL-SCALLION CHEESE

Serve with Rye Rounds (page 384) for brunch and a salad of sliced tomatoes and red onions, Cold Smoked Papaya (page 206), or as an accompaniment to Breadsticks (page 382). A scoop of this cheese makes a nice addition to any salad. Make this only with Grezzo Cheese (page 132).

• • • Makes 2 cups • • •

2 cups Grezzo Cheese (page 132), made with macadamia nuts

2 garlic cloves, grated on a Microplane rasp

¼ cup chopped fresh dill

6 scallions, halved

1 teaspoon sea salt

1 teaspoon freshly ground black pepper

1. Combine all the ingredients in a food processor. Blend until thoroughly combined, stopping the machine to scrape down the sides as necessary.
2. Scrape the cheese into a serving bowl, cover, and refrigerate for up to 5 days.

CURRY-CASHEW CHEESE

Serve with an antipasto platter, an arugula-radicchio salad, and some Breadsticks (page 382). Make this only with Grezzo Cheese (page 132).

• • • Makes 2 cups • • •

2 cups Grezzo Cheese (page 132), made with cashews

2 garlic cloves, grated on a Microplane rasp

1½ tablespoons freshly grated ginger

1½ teaspoons ground turmeric

¼ teaspoon ground cloves

¼ teaspoon ground coriander

¼ teaspoon Garam Masala (page 121)

1 teaspoon fleur de sel

1 teaspoon freshly ground black pepper

1. Combine all the ingredients in food processor and blend until well incorporated.
2. Scrape the cheese into a serving bowl, cover, and refrigerate for up to 5 days.

MISO-CASHEW CHEESE

Spread this Asian-inspired cheese on sheets of nori and cut up into hand rolls. Accompany with a seaweed salad. Make this only with Grezzo Cheese (page 132).

• • • Makes 2 cups • • •

2 cups Grezzo Cheese (page 132), made with cashews

1½ teaspoons miso paste

1½ tablespoons Nama Shoyu

6 scallions, green and white parts, coarsely chopped

1. Put all the ingredients in a food processor. Blend well.
2. Scrape the cheese into a serving bowl, cover, and refrigerate for up to 5 days.

SAGE, SHISO, AND MUSTARD CHEESE

Spread dark leafy greens like collards or chard with this cheese to make roll-ups, or serve with apples and figs in the fall. Make this only with Grezzo Cheese (page 132).

• • • Makes 3 cups • • •

3 cups Grezzo Cheese (page 132), made with cashews

10 fresh sage leaves

10 fresh shiso leaves *or* a combination of mint and basil

1 tablespoon freshly ground mustard seeds

1½ teaspoons sea salt

1½ teaspoons freshly ground black pepper

1. Put all of the ingredients in a food processor and blend thoroughly.
2. Scrape the cheese into a serving bowl, cover, and refrigerate for up to 5 days.

FRENCH ONION CHEESE

Dehydrated onion and tomato, herbs, and garlic give this cheese a sweet and savory flavor. Serve with crudités or Salt and Vinegar Potato Chips (page 370). Make this only with Grezzo Cheese (page 132).

• • • Makes 2 cups • • •

1 yellow onion, thinly sliced and dehydrated overnight

1 small tomato, thinly sliced and dehydrated overnight

2 cups Grezzo Cheese (page 132), made with macadamia nuts

1 garlic clove, grated on a Microplane rasp

½ tablespoon mixed herbs (such as parsley, thyme, and/or basil)

1 teaspoon fleur de sel

1 teaspoon freshly ground black pepper

1. Put the onion and tomato in a food processor. Blend until finely chopped.
2. Add the cheese, garlic, herbs, salt, and pepper and process until combined, but do not overprocess. Stop the machine to scrape down the sides.
3. Scrape the cheese into a serving bowl and refrigerate for up to 3 to 4 days.

GREZZO RICOTTA

The whipped texture of this cheese, along with the essence of lemon and fresh mint, imparts a fresh, slightly sweet flavor reminiscent of ricotta cheese. We use it with Land and Sea (page 350), and it's perfect for stuffing mushrooms, serving on antipasto platters, and topping Pepperoni Pizzas (page 334).

• • • Makes 2 cups • • •

**2 cups Grezzo Cheese (page 132), 1 cup made with cashews and 1 cup made
with macadamia nuts**

Zest of 1 lemon

½ small red onion, finely diced

2 tablespoons chopped fresh dill

2 tablespoons chopped fresh mint

2 tablespoons chopped fresh thyme

1½ teaspoons sea salt

1½ teaspoons freshly ground black pepper

1. Put the cheese, zest, onion, herbs, salt, and pepper in a bowl. Mix well by hand using a spatula.
2. Scrape the cheese into a serving bowl, cover, and refrigerate for up to 5 days.

PINE NUT ROMANO

Once the cheese is dehydrated, break it into shards and use it to garnish salads and pasta dishes.

• • • Makes 2 sheets • • •

2 cups pine nuts

1 cup Rejuvelac (page 133)

3 garlic cloves

¼ cup freshly squeezed lemon juice

1 teaspoon sea salt

1 teaspoon freshly ground black pepper

1. Soak the pine nuts in the rejuvelac for 8 hours.
2. Put the soaked pine nuts and any remaining soaking liquid, the garlic, lemon juice, salt, and pepper in a Vita-Mix until smooth. Stop the machine and scrape down the sides with a spatula as necessary.
3. Spread the mixture ⅛ to ¼ inch thick on Teflex-lined dehydrator racks. Dehydrate for 8 hours, or until the cheese is crisp.
4. Break cheese into shards just before serving. Store in the dehydrator for up to 2 weeks.

PICKLES and OTHER CONDIMENTS: PUTTING FOOD BY

Pickling is a method of preserving food by fermentation. Marinating tenderizes and flavors fruits and vegetables. Macerating usually refers to soaking fruit in a liquid. All of these techniques make fruits and vegetables softer, flavorful, and easier to digest. Eating pickled and fermented foods on a regular basis aids in digestion.

Glass jars are ideal for all of these recipes. If giving pickles, vinegars, or fruits as gifts, beautiful glass jars and bottles abound. Be sure to run them through the dishwasher or wash them in hot water to make sure they're scrupulously clean.

While all of these make great accompaniments to many of the dishes in this book, our favorite way to serve them is in a variety of bowls as an antipasto.

PICKLED PINK ONIONS

When submerged in a brine of vinegar, beet juice, vanilla pods, and bay leaves, red onions become an even brighter pink. These quick pickles are sweet and mild with none of that raw onion taste. Use them as a bright garnish on salads, as an accompaniment for Sliders (page 240), or on cheese plates.

• • • Makes 4 cups • • •

2 bay leaves

2 vanilla bean pods

3 large red onions, thinly sliced

1 cup apple cider vinegar

1 large red beet, juiced

1. In a bowl or plastic container, place the bay leaves and vanilla pods on the bottom, then cover with the onions. Add the vinegar, beet juice, and 1 cup water, adding more water as necessary to submerge the ingredients.
2. Cover the bowl and refrigerate overnight before using. Transfer to a clean jar with a lid. The onions will keep for several weeks.

PICKLED PINE NUTS AND CURRANTS

A unique garnish to salads, Ajo Blanco (page 313), and zucchini noodles with carbonara sauce.

• • • Makes 2 cups • • •

1 cup coconut vinegar

1 cup pine nuts

½ cup currants

1 tablespoon coriander seeds

1. Put the vinegar, ½ cup water, the pine nuts, currants, and coriander seeds in a clean pint-size jar.
2. Cover and let sit overnight in the refrigerator before using.
3. Refrigerate and use within 1 month.

PICKLED CAULIFLOWER

The turmeric turns the cauliflower bright yellow. For an added flavor boost, add 2 tablespoons freshly grated ginger and 1 peeled and bashed lemongrass stalk.

• • • Makes 4 cups • • •

1½ cups apple cider vinegar

2 tablespoons ground turmeric

1 teaspoon cardamom pods, crushed

1 teaspoon fennel seeds

1 teaspoon mustard seeds

1 teaspoon coriander seeds

1 small head cauliflower, broken into small florets

4 garlic cloves, smashed

1. Put the vinegar, ½ cup water, and turmeric in a bowl and whisk to create the brine. Set aside.
2. Tie the crushed cardamom, fennel and mustards seeds, and coriander pods in a square of cheesecloth to make a sachet. Drop the sachet into a clean quart-size jar. Add the cauliflower and garlic and cover with brine.
3. Cover and refrigerate for 3 days before using. These pickles will keep for up to 1 month in the refrigerator.

PICKLED GINGER

• • • Makes ½ pint • • •

4 ounces fresh ginger, peeled and thinly sliced on a mandoline

2 whole star anise

¼ teaspoon whole black peppercorns

1 cup apple cider vinegar

1. Put sliced ginger, star anise, peppercorns, ½ cup water, and vinegar in a clean half-pint mason jar.

2. Allow to pickle for 2 days in refrigerator before enjoying. Will stay fresh for up to 1 month covered in refrigerator.

SAUERKRAUT

Shred the cabbage with a knife, rather than in a food processor, so the cabbage comes out shredded rather than diced. Sauerkraut makes a great addition to wraps and other sandwiches. If you want less heat, reduce the amount of jalapeño. No water is necessary in this fermenting process because of the high moisture content of cabbage and the use of salt in this recipe. Warmer weather will expedite the process. It's ready when the cabbage has softened and there's a slightly fizzy, slightly sour taste.

• • • Makes 8 cups • • •

3 cups apple cider vinegar

1 to 2 jalapeño chiles, stemmed

1½ tablespoons coriander seeds

½ head napa cabbage, shredded

½ head purple cabbage, shredded

2 teaspoons sea salt

1 teaspoon freshly ground black pepper

1. Put the vinegar, jalapeños, and coriander seeds in a Vita-Mix and blend to create the brine. Set aside.
2. Combine the cabbage, salt, and pepper and thoroughly toss with the brine. Place in a ceramic bowl or large crock. Store at room temperature on the countertop for 5 days, stirring at least once a day.
3. Transfer the sauerkraut to clean quart-size jars, cover, and refrigerate for up to 3 weeks.

KIMCHEE

No Korean meal would be complete without this complex pickled vegetable dish.

• • • Makes 6 cups • • •

½ **head napa cabbage, thinly sliced**

½ **head bok choy, thinly sliced**

1 **small daikon, peeled, cut into matchstick pieces**

1 **bunch scallions, green and white parts, chopped**

½ **cup apple cider vinegar**

¼ **cup Nama Shoyu**

2 **tablespoons agave nectar**

3 **garlic cloves, grated on a Microplane rasp**

2 **tablespoons freshly grated ginger**

1 **tablespoon crushed red pepper flakes**

1 **teaspoon sea salt**

1 **tablespoon unhulled sesame seeds**

1. Put the cabbage, bok choy, daikon, and scallions in a large ceramic or glass bowl. Toss well and set aside.

2. Whisk together the vinegar, Nama Shoyu, agave, garlic, ginger, red pepper flakes, salt, and sesame seeds. Pour the vinegar mixture over the cabbage and toss thoroughly.

3. Cover and let sit on countertop for 5 days to ferment. Stir daily. When the kimchee is to your liking in texture and flavor, cover and store in the refrigerator for up to 2 weeks.

PICKLED CUCUMBERS

A good pickle has crunch. Use the following spice blend or create your own. Choose a large wide-mouth glass container. This brine has so much flavor that it can be re-used for another batch of pickles. Taste and enhance with more spices or vinegar as necessary.

• • • Makes 12 • • •

12 pickling (kirby) cucumbers, washed

2 jalapeño chiles, halved, seeds intact

8 large garlic cloves, smashed

5 bay leaves

3½ cups apple cider vinegar

¼ cup whole black peppercorns

2 tablespoons fennel seeds

2 tablespoons coriander seeds

1 tablespoon allspice berries

1 tablespoon whole cloves

1. Pack the cucumbers in a large, clean jar, nestling the jalapeños, garlic, and bay leaves in between.
2. Whisk together the vinegar, 1½ cups water, the peppercorns, fennel and coriander seeds, allspice berries, and cloves in a bowl to make the brine.
3. Pour the brine over the cucumbers, making sure all the pickles are covered. Cover and store in the refrigerator. Let the cucumbers pickle for 1 week before using. They will keep in the refrigerator for up to 1 month.

BREAD-AND-BUTTER PICKLES

A sweeter pickle and the classic accompaniment to sandwiches.

• • • Makes 12 • • •

12 pickling (kirby) cucumbers, washed

2 cinnamon sticks, cracked in half

3 cups apple cider vinegar

1 cup agave nectar

1. In a large jar, stack the pickling cucumbers. Nestle the cinnamon sticks among the pickles.
2. Whisk together the vinegar, 1 cup water, and the agave. Pour this brine over the cucumbers. Top with a piece of wax paper or parchment paper to keep the pickles submerged.
3. Refrigerate for 7 days before using. The pickles will keep for up to 1 month.

SWEET PICKLED ASPARAGUS

Either skinny or thick asparagus will work. A combination of green and white asparagus is a nice touch. The figs, added for sweetness, are delicious, too.

• • • Makes 3 pounds • • •

3 pounds asparagus, woody stems trimmed

6 to 8 fresh figs, quartered

5 garlic cloves, smashed

4 cups apple cider vinegar

1 teaspoon whole cloves

1 teaspoon allspice berries

1. Arrange the asparagus in a shallow glass dish. Scatter the figs and garlic over the asparagus.
2. Whisk together the vinegar, 2 cups water, the cloves, and allspice in a bowl to make a brine.
3. Pour the brine over the asparagus. Cover with parchment paper to make sure all the asparagus is submerged. Refrigerate for 2 days before using. The pickles will keep for up to 2 weeks in the refrigerator.

LAVENDER PICKLED MUSHROOMS

Use these mushrooms on pizza or to garnish Land and Sea (page 350) or Wild Mushroom Fettuccine (page 355).

• • • Makes 4 cups • • •

4 cups assorted firm mushrooms, such as button, shiitake, or cremini

3 lavender sprigs *or* ½ teaspoon culinary lavender

1 garlic clove, crushed

1 cinnamon stick, cracked in half

1 tablespoon whole fennel seeds

1 cup apple cider vinegar

½ cup agave nectar

1. Pack the mushrooms in a clean, quart-size jar, nestling the lavender, garlic, cinnamon, and fennel seeds in between.
2. Whisk together the vinegar, 1/2 cup water, and the agave in a bowl to make a brine.
3. Pour the brine over the mushrooms, making sure the brine covers all the mushrooms. Cover and refrigerate for 2 days before enjoying. The mushrooms will keep for up to 3 weeks in the refrigerator.

PICKLED GARLIC

Shave pickled garlic cloves onto pasta dishes and salads.

• • • Makes 2 cups • • •

2 cups garlic cloves

⅔ cup apple cider vinegar

2 sprigs rosemary

1 teaspoon black peppercorns

1. Put all the ingredients and ⅓ cup water in a clean pint-size jar.
2. Cover and let pickle for 3 days in the refrigerator before using. Store in the refrigerator for up to 3 weeks.

PICKLED FRENCH CARROTS

These carrots go with salads and burgers. Use slender, young carrots. If you can find small carrots in early spring, use them whole. The onions are delicious, too.

• • • Makes 4 cups • • •

6 to 7 carrots, quartered lengthwise and sliced into 2-inch pieces

¼ cup sliced white onions

1 cup apple cider vinegar

¼ cup agave nectar

1½ teaspoons salt

1 teaspoon freshly ground black pepper

1. Pack the carrots and onions in a clean, quart-size jar.
2. Whisk together the vinegar, 1 cup water, the agave, salt, and pepper in a bowl to make a brine. Pour the brine over the carrots, making sure the brine covers the carrots.
3. Cover and refrigerate for 3 days before using. The carrots will keep for up to 1 month in the refrigerator.

MARINATED RED BEETS

Use this recipe as a blueprint for other ingredient combinations—mustard seeds and blood oranges, and grapefruit and thyme, to name a couple.

• • • Makes 2 cups • • •

3 large red beets, peeled and thinly sliced on a mandoline

Zest and juice of 1 orange

1 teaspoon ground cumin

⅓ cup extra virgin olive oil

3 tablespoons apple cider vinegar

½ teaspoon sea salt

½ teaspoon freshly ground black pepper

1. Combine all the ingredients in large bowl. Toss well to combine, making sure all the beets are coated. Let the beets sit for 15 minutes before serving.
2. Transfer the beets to a clean pint-size jar, cover, and refrigerate for up to 1 week.

MARINATED GOLDEN BEETS

Golden beets become even brighter when marinated in turmeric and mustard.

• • • Makes 2 cups • • •

3 large golden beets, peeled and thinly sliced on a mandoline

1 tablespoon ground turmeric

1 teaspoon ground mustard seeds

6 tablespoons apple cider vinegar

6 tablespoons extra virgin olive oil

½ teaspoon sea salt

1. Put all the ingredients in a bowl. Toss well to combine, making sure all the beets are coated. Let the beets sit for 15 minutes before serving.
2. Transfer the beets to a clean pint-size jar, cover, and refrigerate for up to 1 week.

MARINATED GREENS

Any combination of dark leafy greens can be used, including collards, mustard, kale, or spinach. These make a great pizza topping, too.

• • • Makes 3 to 4 cups • • •

⅓ cup extra virgin olive oil

1 tablespoon freshly squeezed lemon juice

2 tablespoons apple cider vinegar

2 garlic cloves, grated on a Microplane rasp

½ teaspoon cayenne pepper

1 teaspoon sea salt

2 cups dandelion greens

2 cups Swiss chard leaves

1. Whisk the olive oil, lemon juice, vinegar, garlic, cayenne, and salt together in a large bowl. Add the greens and toss well to combine.
2. Cover and let the greens marinate at room temperature for 2 hours before serving. Transfer to a clean quart-size jar, cover, and refrigerate for up to 3 days.

MARINATED WATERMELON RADISHES

While this recipe works with any radishes—red, white, daikon, or icicle—search out stunningly colorful watermelon radishes. They look like turnips, but once sliced, they have a creamy white-green edge and a bright magenta center. We use them to garnish salads and as the "pepperoni" on pizzas.

• • • Makes about 2 cups • • •

3 large watermelon radishes, peeled and sliced on a mandoline

1 tablespoon ground anise seeds

1 tablespoon ground fennel seeds

2 teaspoons crushed red pepper flakes

Juice of 1 lemon

2 tablespoons apple cider vinegar

¼ cup extra virgin olive oil

½ teaspoon sea salt

½ teaspoon ground black pepper

1. Put all the ingredients in a large bowl. Toss well to combine, making sure all the radishes are coated. Let the radishes marinate for 15 minutes before serving.
2. Transfer the radishes to a clean pint-size jar, cover, and refrigerate for up to 1 week.

RASPBERRY MIGNONETTE

Any berries—blueberries, strawberries, or cranberries—can be used to make home-made vinegar. Vary the herbs as well, trying rosemary, lemon thyme, or lavender. Put some in a decorative bottle for gift-giving.

• • • Makes 4 cups • • •

3 cups apple cider vinegar

1 cup fresh raspberries

1 large shallot, minced

3 sprigs fresh thyme

1. Combine all the ingredients in a clean quart-size jar.
2. Cover and let the berries macerate in the refrigerator for 1 week before using.
3. Store in the refrigerator for up to 3 weeks.

MACERATED FENNEL COINS

A unique garnish for desserts or with a salad of bitter green lettuce.

• • • Makes 1 cup • • •

Stalks of 1 large fennel bulb, peeled and sliced into ¼-inch rounds

Zest and juice of 1 orange

¼ cup agave nectar

½ teaspoon black peppercorns

1. Combine all the ingredients in a clean pint-size mason jar.
2. Cover, give a good shake, and allow to macerate in the refrigerator for 1 day before using.
3. Store in the refrigerator, covered, for up to 1 week.

MACERATED CRANBERRIES

Toss these sweet and tangy cranberries on salads or to garnish your brownie sundaes.

• • • Makes 2 cups • • •

1½ cups dried cranberries

¼ cup freshly squeezed lime juice

Zest of 1 lime

¼ cup agave nectar

1. Put the cranberries in a clean pint-size jar. Add the lime juice and zest, agave, and ¼ cup water. Cover and give the jar a few good shakes. Let sit overnight before using.
2. Refrigerate for up to 1 week.

MACERATED SUPER BERRIES

Any combination of dried fruit works here, but we like this colorful combination.

• • • Makes 1 cup • • •

⅓ **cup goji berries**

⅓ **cup Incan golden berries**

⅓ **cup dried currants**

½ **cup apple cider vinegar**

1. Combine the berries in a clean jar. Add the vinegar, cover, and give the jar a few good shakes. Let sit for 1 day before using.
2. Refrigerate for up to 1 month.

FIGS IN ORANGE JUICE

Use these as an ice cream topping, or purée to make jam.

• • • Makes 2 cups • • •

1 cup dried figs, halved

½ cup freshly squeezed orange juice

¼ teaspoon ground cloves

1. Pack the figs in a clean half-pint jar. Add the orange juice, ½ cup water, and cloves, cover, and give the jar a few good shakes. Let sit for 1 day before using.
2. Refrigerate for up to 1 week.

SMOOTHIES, JUICES, *and* OTHER BEVERAGES: NOURISHING DRINKS

The difference between a juice and a smoothie? A juice uses a juice extractor to release just the juice from fruits and vegetables. The fiber and pulp are left behind. A smoothie is made in a blender or Vita-Mix and has a thicker, creamier texture and contains fiber, as the whole fruits and vegetables are used. With juices, you don't have to worry about coring apples, as all those bits are left behind in the juicer.

Most people don't get enough greens in their diets. Making a smoothie out of half a bunch of kale, collards, and Swiss chard with an apple and a beet thrown in delivers the nutrition of more greens than most people eat in a week. Imagine how many vitamins, minerals, and enzymes are packed into one glass of juice! A smoothie for lunch or in between meals helps keep you going. If you're going to be on the road, take a travel blender with you so you can mix up a quick and healthy smoothie anytime.

Think of these recipes as suggestions and guidelines. If you're out of kale, just add more of some other ingredients. If you don't like mint, substitute parsley or chervil. Keep trying and testing until you find combinations that suit your tastes.

Once your smoothie or juice is made, drink it right away when it's fresh and tastes best. Smoothies and juices will begin to oxidize and lose valuable nutrients the longer they stand. They also tend to separate if left for too long.

The following recipes make approximately 16-ounce drinks. Just put the ingredients in a Vita-Mix or blender!

. . . .

BURDOCK-SHILAJIT LATTE

Burdock root tea is a powerful anti-inflammatory herbal tea. A mildly bitter herb, it also stimulates the release of gastric juices and aids digestion. Shilajit is considered the king herb of Ayurveda, the traditional Indian system of medicine. Shilajit contains at least 85 minerals in ionic form. *Shilajit* is a Sanskrit word meaning "conqueror of mountains and destroyer of weakness." It is a mineral-rich humus (soil) that emanates from the crevices of the Himalayan mountains. Shilajit is truly a remarkable substance with a long history of human usage for healing, building, and rejuvenation. Combine burdock tea and shilajit powder with these other ingredients to take the place of your morning coffee.

1 cup brewed burdock tea

1 cup almond milk (page 104)

1 teaspoon shilajit powder

1 tablespoon agave nectar

MUIRA PUAMA CAPPUCCINO

This is our version of a cappuccino. Muira puama is another Ayurvedic herb used to enhance libido and sexual function and ease the symptoms of menstrual cramps and premenstrual symptoms. Powdered muira puama can be purchased online or at health food stores.

¾ **cup burdock tea**

¾ **cup almond milk (page 104)**

1 **teaspoon muira puama**

½ **teaspoon cacao powder**

1 **tablespoon agave nectar**

VITALITY WATER

The electrolytes from the coconut water, vitamins and minerals from the green powder, and protein from the hemp powder make this a powerhouse of nutrition. It's much thinner than the usual smoothie. There are many green powders available online and in stores. Read the label carefully to make sure the one you choose is raw.

2 cups coconut water

1 tablespoon hemp powder

1 tablespoon green powder

Seeds from ½ vanilla bean

2 bananas

CHOCOLATE-BANANA SHAKE

This is a rich, thick 32-ounce shake, and with the addition of hemp protein, maca, almonds, and coconut, it makes the perfect pre- or post-workout "meal."

2 bananas

1 tablespoon maca

2 tablespoons hemp protein powder

½ cup cacao powder

¼ cup agave nectar

⅓ cup almonds, preferably sprouted

1 tablespoon coconut oil

3 cups water

8 to 10 ice cubes

MUDSLIDE

Sweet, rich, and filling, this is like dessert in a glass!

½ **cup ice**

1 **cup water**

1 **banana**

⅓ **cup almonds**

4 **pitted dates**

CHOCOLATE MALT

Better than any old-fashioned malt you've ever had.

1 **cup coconut water**

2 **cups Chocolate Ice Cream (page 452)**

2 **tablespoons hemp protein**

½ **tablespoon maca**

BERRY REALITY

This deep purple smoothie is bursting with berry flavor.

1 cup ice

1½ cups blueberries

1½ cups strawberries

½ cup cashews

2 tablespoons agave nectar

GOJI JULIUS

Packed with antioxidants and very refreshing.

½ cup ice

2 cups strawberries

2 oranges, peeled

2 tablespoons goji berries, soaked in water for 10 minutes

NEROLI BLOSSOM

Neroli hydrosol is made from bitter orange blossoms. Look for it in health food stores. Pineapple, coconut, and banana make a great combination; neroli gives this a unique flavor. Don't use more than a teaspoon.

¼ **cup ice**

¾ **cup coconut water**

1 cup pineapple chunks

1 teaspoon chopped fresh mint

1 banana

1 teaspoon neroli hydrosol

Fifty Smoothies: Sweet and Savory

Since smoothies are thicker than juices, add water, coconut water, or nut milk to thin to desired consistency. Nuts add thickness. A bit of agave nectar, stevia, or date paste can be included for a sweeter flavor if you like.

Almond butter–banana-date

Apricot-strawberry-pineapple

Banana-date–almond milk

Banana-orange-strawberry

Banana-apple-raspberry

Banana-strawberry-kiwi

Banana-spinach-celery

Banana-cacao-date

Blackberry-raspberry-tangerine

Blueberry-mango-banana

Blueberry-raspberry-banana

Brazil nut–water-date

Sprouted buckwheat–banana-date

Cashew-banana-strawberry

Cashew-strawberry–coconut meat

Coconut water–kale-banana

Coconut meat–cherry-mango

Cucumber-banana-celery

Cucumber–hemp seed–banana

Grape-kiwi-banana

Grape-pineapple-orange

Guava–almond milk–pineapple

Guava-raspberry–coconut water

Hemp seed–almond milk–strawberry

Hemp seed–cacao-date

Kale-orange-kiwi

Kale-strawberry-peach

Kiwi-banana-celery

Lettuce-strawberry-pineapple

Macadamia-blueberry-banana

Mango-orange-blueberry

Mango-papaya–coconut water

Mango-lettuce-mint

Mango-strawberry-banana

Orange-strawberry-mint

Orange-pineapple–goji berry

Papaya-mango-kale

Peach-plum-cherry

Pear-kale-mint

Pineapple-spinach-kiwi

Pineapple-strawberry-banana

Pineapple–coconut water–banana

Pineapple-mint-banana

Pomegranate juice–orange–goji berry

Plum-apricot-banana

Plum-orange-banana

Spinach-banana-kale

Spinach-cashew-apricot

Spinach-pear-banana

Swiss chard–banana-strawberry

VERDE GRANDE

Black grapes and kale are loaded with vitamins and minerals, although all you'll taste is how sweet and delicious this is.

¼ **cup water**

½ **cup seedless black grapes**

1 **orange**

1 **banana**

1 **pear**

½ **cup packed kale leaves**

POPEYE

You won't believe how delicious these two ingredients are together.

3 **cups packed spinach leaves**

3 **bananas**

1 **cup ice**

Easy Juicing

For best results when making juices, put smaller items like pieces of ginger and garlic cloves into the extractor first. The larger fruits and vegetables that are put in next will help push through the smaller ones. All of the following recipes make an approximately 16-ounce drink. Put the ingredients into a twin-gear juicer for best results or a centrifugal juicer if necessary.

EVERYDAY GREEN JUICE

A basic green drink and a quick and easy way to get a lot of greens into your diet.

   2 cups packed kale leaves

   4 collard green leaves

   2 Swiss chard leaves

   ½ cucumber

   2 celery stalks

   1 apple

CUCUMBER COOLER

Simple and refreshing.

2 small garlic cloves

1 tablespoon freshly grated ginger

3 celery stalks

½ cucumber

1 apple

GRAPE CURE

If you can't find black grapes, use another color.

2 cups black grapes

1 green pear

1 red apple

BROMELAIN BREW

Pineapple contains natural bromelain, an enzyme that helps relieve pain.

2 cups pineapple chunks

13 carrots

1 orange

GOOD MORNING, MARY

Our morning version of the classic cocktail.

1 small garlic clove

5 tomatoes

2 celery stalks

2 scallions

1 carrot

1 handful kale leaves

Garnish the juice with ½ teaspoon Puréed Chiles (page 111) and ½ teaspoon grated horseradish.

AUTUMN CRISP

Reminiscent of autumn but delicious anytime.

1 apple

1 pear

Juice and then stir in ½ cup almond milk and top with ground cinnamon.

LIMONCELLO

Our zippy version of lemonade.

½ lemon

¼-inch slice fresh ginger

3 apples

2 carrots

RED DANDELION

Juiced dandelion leaves, parsley, and beet make a great liver tonic.

¼-inch slice fresh ginger

1 medium beet

½ cup packed dandelion leaves

1 medium cucumber

½ cup fresh flat-leaf parsley

2 celery stalks

Pinch of sea salt

Fifty Juices: Sweet and Savory

Although we offer some recipes for fruit, vegetable, and fruit-and-vegetable juices, the possibilities are endless. Here are some ideas based on what's commonly found in many refrigerators. If blood oranges, persimmons, currants, Clementines, or other seasonal fruits are available, then, by all means, try them. Amounts aren't important here; try more of one vegetable and less of a fruit or the like until you have a blend that satisfies you. Don't forget fresh herbs—parsley, mint, lemon verbena, cilantro, chives, basil, and so on, for an extra burst of flavor.

Swiss chard–spinach-apple
Tomato-celery-scallion
Apple-lemon-carrot
Apple-carrot-ginger
Apple-beet-carrot
Apple-beet-kale
Apple-strawberry-lemon
Beet-carrot-kale
Beet-orange-carrot
Beet-spinach-kale
Beet-spinach-lemon
Beet-spinach-ginger
Blackberry-pomegranate-lemon
Blueberry-pineapple-strawberry
Blueberry-pineapple-lemon
Carrot-beet-spinach
Carrot-celery-spinach
Carrot-pineapple-orange
Carrot-spinach–dandelion leaves
Carrot-strawberry-orange

Celery-scallion-beet

Coconut water–blueberries-spinach

Dandelion leaves–beet-ginger

Dandelion leaves–carrot-ginger

Garlic-ginger-beet

Grape-apple-strawberry

Grape-apple-pear

Grapefruit-orange-pomegranate

Green bean–spinach-apple

Green grape–green apple–lemon

Kale-cucumber-beet

Kiwi-grape-strawberry

Lettuce-apple-ginger

Parsley–green apple–ginger

Parsley-apple-kale

Pear-kale-apple

Pineapple-beet-dandelion

Pineapple–Swiss chard–carrot

Pineapple-strawberry-carrot

Pineapple-kale-strawberry

Pineapple–Swiss chard–celery

Raspberry-blueberry-strawberry

Red bell pepper–kale-cucumber

Spinach-tomato-scallion

Spinach-cucumber-tomato

Strawberry-pineapple-spinach

Strawberry-kale-carrot

Swiss chard–spinach-carrot

Tomato-celery-scallion

Watermelon-honeydew-cantaloupe

LEMON-LIMEADE

Light and refreshing, rather than super-tart and cloyingly sweet. Serve in tall glasses over ice.

• • • Makes ½ gallon • • •

½ cup freshly squeezed lemon juice

½ cup freshly squeezed lime juice

Zest of 1 lemon

Zest of 1 lime

½ cup agave nectar

Combine all the ingredients and 6½ cups water in a pitcher. Stir well and chill until ready to use.

STRAWBERRY-VANILLA LEMON-LIMEADE • Add ½ cup Strawberry-Vanilla Sauce (page 443) to each quart.

Herbal Teas

To make teas, fill a reusable cloth or disposable paper tea bag with one tablespoon of your favorite combination of dried or fresh herbs. Put the tea bag in a glass pitcher, fill with sixteen ounces of cool—never boiled or heated—water, and let the tea steep for several hours.

Tea blends can be made with fresh or dried herbs. When using dried herbs, make sure they come from a reliable source with a high turnover. Teas made from musty, old herbs taste old and musty. Mountainroseherbs.com and frontiercoop.com are reliable online sources for dried herbs and spices and essential oils.

Herbal tea combinations are as infinite as your imagination, but here are some of our favorites. Make your own blend in large batches and store them away from sunlight.

. . . .

PEACEFUL EVENING TEA

Drink a cup or two of this soothing tea before bedtime.

2 cups dried chrysanthemum flowers

1 cup dried lemon balm

1 cup dried chamomile

½ cup oats

1 cup dried red roses

½ cup dried lavender flowers

¼ cup dried stevia

MINT TEA

Enjoy anytime, but especially to appease an upset stomach.

2 cups dried spearmint

2 cups dried peppermint

2 cups dried lemon balm

HAVE-A-HEART TEA

Hawthorn has been shown to have heart-healthy benefits.

- **1 cup dried hawthorn leaf and berries**
- **1 cup oat tops**
- **1 cup ginkgo leaf**
- **1 cup nettle leaf**
- **1 cup motherwort**
- **1 cup dried hibiscus flowers**

BREAKFAST: NEW WAYS

to

START THE DAY

t's best to eat lightly in the morning and give your digestive system time to wake up, so fruit or vegetable juices, a smoothie, or some fruit are best. Having said that, many people like having a large breakfast or perhaps they're just transitioning to eating more raw food. So if you need something more in the morning, here are some suggestions.

ON-THE-GO MIX

Stash small bags of this berry-nut-cacao combination in your backpack, desk, or car for snacking throughout the day. Add nuts as desired.

· · · Makes 4 cups · · ·

1 cup goji berries

1 cup Incan golden berries

1 cup golden raisins

1 cup cacao nibs

1. Toss all the ingredients together in a bowl. Divide among plastic bags.
2. Store at room temperature for up to 3 weeks.

YOGURT

Rejuvelac gives this yogurt that tangy, fermented flavor and smooth texture found in dairy milk yogurt. Enjoy with fruit or Buckwheaties (page 199) for breakfast or make it savory by adding Zaatar (page 126) or other seasoning blends.

• • • Makes 1 cup • • •

1 cup tightly packed coconut meat

¼ cup Rejuvelac (page 133)

1. Put the coconut and rejuvelac in a Vita-Mix. Blend until completely smooth.
2. Serve immediately or cover and store in the refrigerator for up to 2 days.

GRANOLA

Note that the buckwheat has to be sprouted and dehydrated to make this granola.

• • • Makes about 4½ cups • • •

⅔ **cup agave nectar**

½ **cup pitted dates**

⅛ **teaspoon sea salt**

Seeds from 1 vanilla bean

1 cup raw oats

½ **cups pecans**

½ **cup dried coconut**

1 cup chopped dried fruit, such as raisins, apricots, cranberries,

   and/or goji berries

¾ **cup buckwheat, sprouted, then dehydrated for 12 hours**

1. Combine the agave, dates, salt, and vanilla seeds in a food processor. Blend to a smooth paste. Transfer to a bowl and set aside.
2. Fold in the oats, pecans, coconut, dried fruit, and sprouted buckwheat.
3. Spread the batter onto a Teflex-lined dehydrator rack to ½-inch thickness. Dehydrate for 12 hours. Break up the granola into pieces. Cover and store at room temperature for up to 1 month.

BUCKWHEATIES

Buckwheat is sprouted and then dehydrated for a crunchy breakfast cereal. Make a big batch so there's always some on hand. Add fresh or dried fruit of your choice and some almond milk (page 104) or Yogurt (page 197) to start the day.

• • • Makes 4 servings • • •

4 cups sprouted buckwheat

1. Spread the sprouted buckwheat on Teflex-lined dehydrator racks. Dehydrate for 12 hours, or until crunchy.
2. Store in an airtight container for up to 3 weeks.

OAT GROAT PORRIDGE

This is great on a nippy winter day. Try experimenting with buckwheat and other grains as well as other fruit.

• • • Makes 2 servings • • •

2 cups oat groats, soaked in water overnight and drained

1 apple, cored

6 dates, pitted and soaked in water for 20 minutes

Seeds from ½ vanilla bean

⅛ teaspoon ground cinnamon

¼ cup raisins

1 banana, sliced

1. Put the oats, apple, dates, vanilla seeds, and cinnamon in a food processor. Process until smooth. If necessary, add a tablespoon or so of water, but the mixture should be very thick.
2. Divide between 2 bowls and stir in the raisins and banana. Serve immediately.

REALLY RAW ROLLED OATS

Make sure the oats you buy are truly raw. Add dried or fresh fruit of your choosing.

• • • Makes 2 servings • • •

3 cups rolled oats

2 tablespoons coconut butter, melted

1 tablespoon agave nectar

1 teaspoon ground cinnamon

Pinch of sea salt

1. Put the oats in a bowl and add 1 cup water. Soak for 20 minutes to 10 hours. The longer the oats soak, the creamier their texture.
2. Drain the oats through a fine-mesh strainer and put them in a bowl. Add the coconut butter, agave, cinnamon, and salt. Serve immediately.

CHIA PUDDING

Chia seeds are filling, packed with energy, and act as a natural thickener. Start your day with a bowl of this tapioca-like pudding and some fresh or dried fruit stirred in. If you prefer a thicker pudding, use less water. This can be made with unsprouted almonds, but if you have sprouted ones, use them.

• • • Makes 2 to 4 servings • • •

1 cup almonds

½ cup chia seeds

2 tablespoons agave nectar

Dash ground cinnamon

1. Put the almonds and 3 cups water in a Vita-Mix. Blend until creamy and smooth. Add the chia seeds, agave, and cinnamon and pulse the blender several times just to mix. If it's not sweet enough, add a little more agave.
2. Pour the mixture into a bowl and chill for 1 hour or longer to thicken. Store in the refrigerator for up to 2 days.

MORNING, NOON, AND NIGHT PANCAKES

When you want pancakes for breakfast or dinner, try these. These pancakes are the real deal. They have a maple-pecan flavor and the fluffy texture of real pancakes. Since they're dehydrated ahead of time, keep some on hand for a quick breakfast or dinner.

• • • Makes about 20 pancakes • • •

2 cups pecans, soaked for 8 hours	Seeds from 2 vanilla beans
2 cups pine nuts	1 teaspoon sea salt
2 ripe bananas	2 cups blueberries, muddled
1 cup agave nectar	A dollop of Coconut Cream (page 441)

1. Put the soaked pecans, pine nuts, bananas, agave, vanilla seeds, and salt in a Vita-Mix. While the machine is running, carefully remove the lid, and using a rubber spatula, stir the mixture along to make sure it is continuously turning over. Add a tablespoon of water if necessary. Blend until smooth. Using a spatula, fold in the muddled blueberries.

2. With a ladle, drop ¼-cup measures of the batter onto Teflex-line dehydrator racks, leaving at least ½ inch between the pancakes. They should be thick like pancakes, about ½ inch thick, not thin like crêpes. Dehydrate for 8 hours. Flip the pancakes onto clean Teflex sheets and dehydrate for 8 more hours. These should be soft and fluffy and have the consistency of a pancake. Don't dehydrate them for too long; they shouldn't be hard.

3. Cover and refrigerate for up to 3 days. Garnish with blueberries and Coconut Cream.

BANANA-ROSEMARY CRÊPES WITH LAVENDER COCONUT CREAM

For an added touch, drizzle on some Cinnamon Agave Sauce (page 436).

• • • Makes 8 to 10 crêpes • • •

5 ripe bananas

¼ cup chopped fresh rosemary leaves

¾ cup agave nectar

3 cups tightly packed coconut meat

¾ cup coconut water

2 fresh lavender stems *or*

½ teaspoon culinary lavender

2 cups berries or cut-up fruit

Ground cinnamon

1. Put the bananas, rosemary, and ½ cup of the agave in a Vita-Mix. Blend until liquefied, using the tamper as necessary to push down the bananas. Once blended, immediately (or the starch in the bananas will cause the batter to clump) ladle ¼-cup measures batter into thin crêpes onto Teflex-lined dehydrator racks. Dehydrate the crêpes for 8 to 10 hours. Remove and flip the dehydrator racks over and gently peel away the Teflex sheets. If the crêpes are sticky, dehydrate for another hour. The crêpes can be made ahead and stored in the refrigerator up to 4 days.

2. Put the coconut meat and coconut water, lavender, and the remaining ¼ cup of agave in a Vita-Mix. Blend until smooth and creamy, about 2 minutes. Transfer the coconut cream to a bowl. Using a spatula, fold the berries or chopped fruit into the coconut cream.

3. Arrange a crêpe on a plate. Spoon some of the coconut cream in the center, then fold and roll the crêpe like a burrito. Continue with the remaining crêpes. Top with some more coconut cream and sprinkle with ground cinnamon before serving.

LOBSTER MUSHROOMS BENEDICT

We make this with lobster mushrooms, but any variety can be substituted. When rehydrated, 1 ounce of lobster mushrooms will make 3 cups.

• • • Makes 4 servings • • •

1 ounce dried lobster mushrooms, rehydrated

1 cup Saffron Sauce (page 300)

1 teaspoon sea salt

1 teaspoon freshly ground black pepper

4 cups baby spinach leaves

1 garlic clove, grated on a Microplane rasp

2 tablespoons extra virgin olive oil

4 Rye Rounds (page 384)

1. Put the mushrooms and Saffron Sauce in a bowl. Toss with half of the salt and pepper. Set the mushrooms aside to marinate while preparing the rest of the dish.

2. Put the spinach, garlic, olive oil, and the remaining salt and pepper in a bowl. Toss to combine.

3. Arrange 1 rye round on each of 4 plates. Top with the spinach, followed by the mushrooms. Serve immediately.

COLD SMOKED PAPAYA

When this dish is presented, no one will believe it's actually papaya. Once the fruit is carved, dusted with seasonings, cold smoked, and sliced, it looks like smoked salmon! We serve this with Caraway Crackers (page 380), Dill-Scallion Cheese (page 141), paper-thin slices of red onions, and a selection of homemade pickles. This is our raw version of lox and bagels.

Sweet as well as musky Maradol is the papaya variety we prefer. Select ripe papayas that are beginning to turn yellow-orange. The flesh should be salmon colored and the seeds should be dark and crunchy. Peel the thick skin with a knife; a vegetable peeler won't work.

· · · Makes 8 servings · · ·

1 ripe papaya, halved, seeded, and skinned

2 tablespoons Cajun Seasoning (page 120)

1. Using a knife, make ¼-inch-deep crisscross marks over the entire outer surface of both papaya halves. There are no rules here—just make them decorative to resemble grill or sear marks.
2. Dust the papaya steaks with Cajun Seasoning.
3. Cold smoke the papaya halves for 30 minutes as directed on page 207.
4. Slice the papaya as thin as possible to resemble smoked salmon and serve as suggested.

Cold Smoking

Smoking foods at a low temperature—not higher than 110°F—is a technique that brings new flavor dimension to fruits and vegetables. Papaya, garlic, plums, peppers—you name it—can easily be smoked. Here's how:

You need a large metal mixing bowl, a metal colander, aluminum foil, and an instant-read thermometer. We suggest that you do this outdoors, not in your home.

Line the bowl with foil. Add a few sheets of newspaper and cardboard and light a fire. You don't want big flames, just a delicate smolder.

Once the fire has died down, place the colander inside the bowl. Using tongs, add the ingredients you want to smoke to the colander and cover the whole thing with foil. Poke a few holes in the foil with a knife to let some smoke escape. Insert the thermometer into the foil to be sure the temperature does not exceed 110°F. If the temperature is higher, remove the foil and let it cool down a bit.

Let the food smoke for 30 minutes. The smoke will stop after 10 minutes, but the smoky flavor will continue to permeate the food until the foil is removed.

Using tongs, remove the food and let sit for 10 minutes before proceeding with a recipe. Smoked foods can be covered and refrigerated for up to 3 days.

SAUSAGE PATTIES

The spices and fennel give these nut-and-mushroom–based patties the scent of Italian sausage. Serve with breakfast pancakes, or crumbled into pasta, pizza, or Brazilian Stew (page 347). They can also be shaped into links before dehydrating.

• • • Makes 6 • • •

1 cup cashews

5 portobello mushroom caps

½ cup chopped fennel

2 tablespoons extra virgin olive oil

½ cup mixed chopped fresh herbs, such as parsley, oregano, basil, and/or sage

2 garlic cloves, grated on a Microplane rasp

1 tablespoon Nama Shoyu

1 tablespoon coarsely ground fennel seeds

¼ teaspoon cayenne pepper

¼ teaspoon crushed red pepper flakes

1. Put the cashews in a food processor and grind into flour. Transfer to a large bowl.
2. Put the mushrooms, fennel, olive oil, herbs, garlic, Nama Shoyu, fennel seeds, cayenne, and red pepper in the food processor and blend until smooth in consistency. Return the cashew flour to the food processor and pulse just until incorporated.
3. Using wet hands, divide the batter and shape into patties on a Teflex-lined dehydrator rack. Dehydrate for 8 hours, or until the sausage patties are crisp on the outside and moist in the middle. Turn and dehydrate for longer if necessary.
4. Cover and refrigerate for up to 5 days.

Making Fruit Leather

Fruit leather is *so* easy to make. The secret is to use ripe fruit. Below are instructions for apple-prune, banana, and pear leathers, but try experimenting with other fruits—apricots, cherries, plums—and fruit combinations—orange-cranberry, blueberry-raspberry, ginger-peach. They're great for snacking and brown bag lunches.

Dried and fresh fruits are puréed. Add agave nectar or date paste to taste if a sweeter leather is desired. One cup of the purée is evenly spread on a Teflex-lined dehydrator rack, leaving a border around the edge to make it easy to peel off the fruit leather. Dehydrate until pliable but not sticky. You'll know the fruit leather is ready when it easily peels off.

Store the leather by rolling each piece up in wax paper or plastic wrap at room temperature for up to one month.

APPLE-PRUNE LEATHER

• • • Makes 2 sheets • • •

2 apples, cored and diced

6 pitted prunes, soaked in water for 15 minutes

1. Put the apples and prunes in a food processor. Blend until smooth.
2. Remove from the processor and spread onto Teflex-lined dehydrator racks. Dehydrate for 24 hours.

BANANA LEATHER

• • • Makes 2 sheets • • •

6 ripe bananas

1. Place the bananas in a food processor. Blend until smooth.
2. Using a knife or an offset spatula, spread the bananas as thinly as possible onto Teflex-lined dehydrator racks. Dehydrate for 10 to 12 hours. Turn the leather over, peel off the Teflex sheets, and dehydrate for another 10 to 12 hours.

PEAR LEATHER

• • • Makes 2 sheets • • •

6 ripe pears, cored

1. Place the pears in a food processor. Blend until smooth.
2. Using a knife or an offset spatula, spread the pears as thinly as possible onto Teflex-lined dehydrator racks. Dehydrate for 12 hours. Turn the leather over, peel off the Teflex sheets, and dehydrate for another 12 hours.

STRAWBERRY FRUIT ROLL-UPS

Speckled with black pepper, strawberry roll-ups are good for breakfast or snacking.

• • • Makes 4 sheets • • •

2 pounds (about 8 cups) strawberries, hulled

¾ cup agave nectar

¼ teaspoon sea salt

¼ teaspoon freshly ground black pepper

1. Put all the ingredients in a Vita-Mix. Blend until puréed. Do not overprocess.
2. Spread the strawberry mixture onto 3 or 4 Teflex-lined dehydrator racks. Dehydrate for 24 hours.

APPETIZERS: SMALL BITES *for* MEALS AND MUNCHING

Dips, spreads, stuffed vegetables, dumplings, nori rolls, and other small bites can be enjoyed as morsels to perk up the palate for the rest of the meal to come, as snacks to nibble on throughout the day, or as an entire meal put together from a selection of these appetizers.

Keeping a few dips, some chips, a batch of sliders, avocado skins, and other dishes on hand ensures that you can put a meal on the table within minutes of walking through the door.

When entertaining, think big. Large platters of stuffed vegetables. Baskets of corn chips. Colorful dips in bowls. Nori rolls on bamboo trays. And go beyond this chapter for other ideas: An array of raw cheeses. A selection of pickled vegetables. Mini-burgers with all the trimmings. Piles of cookies. A dessert bar with several ice cream flavors and a choice of toppings.

CANDIED NUTS

Keep a tin of candied nuts on hand for making pie and other dessert crusts, garnishing salads, or nibbling with a glass of wine. Since these require two days in the dehydrator, you might want to double the recipe.

• • • Makes 2 cups • • •

2 cups nuts, such as walnuts or pecans, soaked in water for 8 hours and then
    dehydrated overnight
¼ cup agave nectar
1 teaspoon cayenne pepper
1 teaspoon coarse sea salt

1. Put the nuts in a bowl and toss with the agave, cayenne, and salt. Arrange the spiced nuts on Teflex-lined dehydrator racks and dehydrate for 24 hours.
2. Store the nuts in a sealed container until ready to use.

> **CANDIED BRAZIL NUTS** • Substitute 1 teaspoon curry powder for the cayenne and salt.
>
> **CANDIED MACADAMIA NUTS** • Add ¼ cup grated lime zest and 1 cup dried coconut and omit the cayenne.
>
> **CANDIED PINE NUTS** • Add 1 tablespoon ground cinnamon; omit the salt and cayenne.

RAWCONA ALMONDS

Marcona almonds, known as "the Queen of Almonds," come from Spain. They are shorter and flatter than California almonds, almost heart-shaped, and have a softer texture. Marcona almonds are often fried at high temperatures in olive oil, then salted before packaging.

Raw Marcona almonds are difficult to locate. Instead, use our technique for making dehydrated Rawcona Almonds. Yes, they do require three days in the dehydrator to make them crisp, but they're worth it. Serve with cocktails, sprinkled on salads, or make a salty almond crust for pastries.

• • • Makes 2 cups • • •

2 cups almonds, soaked and sprouted and then dehydrated overnight
½ cup extra virgin olive oil
2 teaspoons sea salt

1. Toss the almonds and olive oil in a bowl to coat.
2. Arrange the nuts in a single layer on a Teflex-lined dehydrator rack. Sprinkle on the salt and dehydrate for 1 to 3 days. Store in a covered container for up to 1 week.

CASHEW SHRIMP

By themselves or added to Brazilian Stew (page 347), you won't be able to stop eating these nuts.

2 cups cashews

2 garlic cloves, grated on a Microplane rasp

1 tablespoon freshly squeezed lemon juice

1 tablespoon paprika

1 tablespoon chopped fresh herbs (such as basil, parsley, and/or mint)

1 teaspoon sea salt

3 tablespoons extra virgin olive oil

1. Put the cashews, garlic, lemon juice, paprika, herbs, salt, and olive oil in a bowl. Toss to combine.
2. Put the nuts on Teflex-lined dehydrator racks and dehydrate for 24 hours. Store in a covered container at room temperature for up to 1 week.

CALAMARI

Just like fried calamari. Serve with Sauce Rémoulade (page 303) and some greens.

• • • Makes 2 cups • • •

2 tablespoons freshly squeezed lemon juice

2 tablespoons extra virgin olive oil

½ pound oyster mushrooms

Pinch of sea salt

Pinch of black pepper

1 cup Seasoned Almond Flour (page 107)

Lemon wedges

Sauce Rémoulade (page 303)

1. Whisk together the lemon juice, olive oil, and 2 tablespoons water in a bowl. Set aside.
2. Slice the mushrooms into ¼-inch-thick rings. Use a 1-inch ring to punch out smaller circles to create rings.
3. Soak the mushroom rings and circles in the olive oil mixture. Remove and season with salt and pepper.
4. Dredge the soaked mushrooms in the seasoned almond flour.
5. Dehydrate on mesh dehydrating racks for 8 hours, until crisp. Serve immediately with lemon wedges and Sauce Rémoulade.

MUSHROOM PÂTÉ

This mushroom-nut spread can be put together in minutes. Serve with crackers or fresh vegetables.

• • • Makes 2½ cups • • •

1 cup chopped button mushrooms

3 cups chopped portobello mushrooms

1 cup pecans

1 cup walnuts

1 teaspoon chopped fresh sage leaves

½ teaspoon chopped fresh rosemary leaves

½ cup diced onions

1 garlic clove

1 teaspoon freshly squeezed lemon juice

1 tablespoon extra virgin olive oil

1½ teaspoons sea salt

1. Put all the ingredients in a food processor. Blend until combined. The mixture should be smooth with some texture, but not soupy.
2. Pack the pâté into a decorative mold or dish. Chill for 1 hour before serving. Store in the refrigerator for up to 2 days.

ROOT VEGETABLE PURÉE

Perfect for any winter holiday table.

• • • Makes 4 cups • • •

½ cup pine nuts

2 large parsnips, peeled, cored, and coarsely chopped

2 carrots, coarsely chopped

1 cup chopped pumpkin or butternut squash

1 small turnip, peeled and coarsely chopped

1 yellow beet, peeled and coarsely chopped

3 garlic cloves

½ cup almond milk (page 104)

2 teaspoons sea salt

2 teaspoons freshly ground black pepper

1. Put the pine nuts, parsnips, carrots, pumpkin, turnip, beet, garlic, and almond milk in a Vita-Mix. Using the tamper, blend the ingredients into a satiny, smooth purée, like mashed potatoes.
2. Transfer the purée to a bowl and stir in the salt and pepper. Adjust the seasonings as necessary. This is best served immediately, but it can be covered and left at room temperature for up to 3 hours.

WHIPPED PARSNIPS

A creamy replacement for mashed potatoes, especially on holiday tables. Serve with Mushroom Gravy (page 308).

• • • Makes 4 cups • • •

1½ pounds parsnips (about 4 large), peeled and chopped

½ cup cashews

1 cup pine nuts

1 garlic clove

1 tablespoon coconut oil

1 tablespoon extra virgin olive oil

1 teaspoon sea salt

A few grinds of black pepper

1. Put all the ingredients and ½ cup water into a food processor. Blend until the mixture is creamy and has the consistency of mashed potatoes.
2. Serve immediately or store in the refrigerator for up to 2 days.

TOMATO SALSA

Our all-purpose tomato salsa can be served with Corn Chips (page 373), Guacamole (page 226), or Enchiladas (page 362). Use more or less jalapeño as desired.

• • • Makes 2 cups • • •

1½ cups (about 3) diced tomatoes

1 small jalapeño chile, minced

¼ cup chopped fresh cilantro leaves

½ red onion, minced

Pinch of sea salt

A few grinds of black pepper

1. Combine all the ingredients in a serving bowl and lightly mash with a wooden spoon to release some of the tomato juices. The salsa should remain chunky.
2. Use immediately or store in a covered container for up to 1 day.

AVOCADO-CORN SALSA

Serve a scoop of this salsa with a big green salad or as an accompaniment to Enchiladas (page 362).

• • • Makes 3 cups • • •

1 cup corn kernels and milk from cobs (about 2 cobs)

1 red bell pepper, seeded and diced

½ red onion, diced

1 avocado, peeled, pitted, and diced

½ cup chopped fresh cilantro

2 tablespoons extra virgin olive oil

2 tablespoons freshly squeezed lime juice

1 garlic clove, grated on a Microplane rasp

1 teaspoon ground mustard seeds

1. Put all the ingredients in a large bowl. Toss to combine.
2. Serve immediately or cover and refrigerate for up to 3 days.

TROPICAL FRUIT SALSA

Fruit salsa makes a lovely accompaniment to many dishes, and the combinations are endless. They don't require oil or any other dressing, so just combine the ingredients and toss.

• • • Makes 2 cups • • •

1 ripe mango, peeled, pitted, and diced

1 red bell pepper, seeded and diced

½ cup diced pineapple

½ cup diced coconut meat

Pinch of sea salt

5 to 6 torn basil leaves

1. Put the mango, bell pepper, pineapple, coconut, and salt in a bowl and toss. Let sit at room temperature for 1 hour before serving.
2. Just before serving, toss again with the basil. Cover and refrigerate for up to 3 days.

GUACAMOLE

Traditionally served as a dip with chips and vegetables, you can also add a generous spoonful to Tomato-Basil Bisque with Gremolata (page 324) or other soups.

• • • Makes about 2 cups • • •

3 avocados, peeled and pitted

1 small jalapeño chile, minced, *or* 2 tablespoons Chile Oil
   (page 112), optional

1 teaspoon ground cumin

2 tablespoons freshly squeezed lemon juice

Sea salt and freshly ground black pepper

1 tablespoon chopped fresh cilantro

1. Put the avocados, pepper, cumin, and lemon juice in a serving bowl and mash with a fork until creamy but some chunky texture remains. You don't want a smooth purée. Add salt and pepper to taste. Stir in cilantro.
2. Guacamole is best served immediately after it's made, but if you need to prepare it a few hours ahead of time, press a lettuce leaf on the surface to keep it from oxidizing and store in the refrigerator.

HUMMUS

Change the flavor of this basic hummus by adding a handful of chopped vegetables such as red peppers or carrots. And, yes, the recipe is correct: a lemon, but no garlic. Raw tahini is available in health food stores, or make your own by blending unhulled white sesame seeds and a little olive oil together in a Vita-Mix.

• • • Makes 6 cups • • •

4 cups sprouted chickpeas

1 cup Tahini Dressing (page 296)

1 medium onion, coarsely chopped

1 cup extra virgin olive oil

1 lemon, peeled and quartered

½ cup chopped fresh parsley

1 tablespoon Nama Shoyu

⅛ teaspoon sea salt

1. Put all the ingredients in a food processor. Blend until smooth.
2. Transfer to a bowl and serve. Cover and refrigerate for up to 2 days.

SPINACH DIP

This easy dip should be put together at the last moment and served immediately, since it doesn't keep well.

• • • Makes 2 cups • • •

4 cups packed spinach leaves

1 large avocado, peeled, pitted, and coarsely chopped

½ tablespoon freshly squeezed lemon juice

½ teaspoon Herbamare Organic Herb Seasoning Salt

1. Put all the ingredients in a food processor and process until smooth. Taste for seasoning and add more seasoning salt, if necessary.
2. Transfer the dip to a bowl and serve immediately.

CURRY SPINACH DIP • Follow the directions above, adding ½ garlic clove, ¼ teaspoon curry powder, ⅛ teaspoon freshly grated ginger, and a dash of cumin when blending the other ingredients.

CREAM CHEESE DIP

Serve this easy-to-make dip with crackers and vegetables (endive and radicchio leaves or celery sticks). Soaking cashews for just an hour makes them easier to blend into cheese. Substitute other fresh herbs as desired.

• • • Makes 1½ cups • • •

1 cup cashews

½ to 1 cup chopped fresh dill

½ teaspoon Herbamare Organic Herb Seasoning Salt

1. Soak the cashews in 1 cup water for 2 to 4 hours. Drain the water, but do not discard.
2. Put the nuts, soaking water, dill, and seasoning salt in a Vita-mix and blend until the mixture is smooth, thick, and creamy. If necessary, add another tablespoon or so of water for desired thickness.
3. Scrape the cheese into a bowl. Cover and store in the refrigerator for up to 3 or 4 days.

NOPALES NACHOS

Nopales are the pads of the nopal, or prickly pear, cactus. They are used in endless ways in Mexican cooking. Look for them in Latino markets, where they're sold with the spines removed. Nopales have a vegetal flavor, much like green beans. We use them to make this cheese and serve them with Corn Chips (page 373), Guacamole (page 226), and Tomato Salsa (page 223).

• • • Makes 2 cups • • •

2 large nopale leaves, diced

1 garlic clove, grated on a Microplane rasp

1 teaspoon ground cumin

2 tablespoons fresh cilantro leaves

Juice of 1 lime

1 teaspoon sea salt

Pinch of cayenne pepper

2 cups Quick Cheese (page 129) *or* Grezzo Cheese (page 132),
    made with macadamia nuts

Corn Chips (page 373)

1. Put the nopales, garlic, cumin, cilantro, lime juice, salt, cayenne, and cheese in a food processor. Blend until smooth.
2. Serve immediately with chips or transfer to a bowl, cover, and refrigerate for up to 5 days.

ONION DIP

Remember onion dip made with sour cream and a package of onion soup mix? Serve this party classic with crudités or Salt and Vinegar Potato Chips (page 370). The success of this dip depends on folding in the onions by hand.

· · · Makes 2 cups · · ·

2 cups macadamia nuts

1 teaspoon sea salt

1 cup diced onions

1. Put half the macadamia nuts, ½ cup water, and the salt in a Vita-Mix or food processor. Blend until the mixture is thick and creamy. Slowly add the remaining nuts until combined. If the dip is too thick, add an additional tablespoon of water.
2. Transfer the dip to a bowl and, using a spatula, fold in the onions. Cover and chill.

AVOCADO SKINS

A raw spin on a bar food staple—avocado halves breaded and dehydrated, then topped with broccoli, sour cream, and bacon, much like potato skins. These are wildly popular at our Newburyport restaurant; we suggest you double or triple the recipe. The avocados are halved, the pits taken out, and the fruit is carefully removed in one piece from its skin, which is discarded.

• • • Makes 4 skins • • •

3 tablespoons extra virgin olive oil

1 garlic clove, grated on a Microplane rasp

Salt and freshly ground black pepper

1½ cups chopped broccoli florets

1 cup Quick Cheese (page 129) *or* Grezzo Cheese (page 132)

2 tablespoons apple cider vinegar

2 ripe avocados, halved, pitted, and gently scooped out of their skins

1 cup Seasoned Almond Flour (page 107)

8 strips Eggplant Bacon (page 115), crumbled

1. Whisk together the olive oil, garlic, dash of salt, and a few grinds of pepper in a bowl. Add the broccoli and toss well to cover. Arrange the broccoli on Teflex-lined dehydrator racks and dehydrate for 2 hours.

2. Whisk together the cheese, vinegar, dash of salt, and a few grinds of pepper in a bowl until the mixture is similar to sour cream. If it doesn't have that sour cream tartness, stir in another teaspoon of vinegar.

3. Sprinkle each avocado half with salt and pepper, then dredge each one in the almond flour mixture to coat completely. Place on a dehydrator rack and dehydrate for 2 hours along with the broccoli.

4. Arrange the avocado halves on a platter. Spread each one with a quarter of the sour cream and broccoli. Top with crumbled eggplant bacon and serve.

· · · · · · · · · · · · · · · · ·

CANDY BEET RAVIOLI WITH FIGS AND COCONUT CREAM

A filling of dried figs and exotic spices is nestled between two thin slices of beets and then each one is topped with a dollop of coconut cream. When marinated overnight in vanilla, coconut oil, and olive oil, the beets become soft, like pasta. Use Chioggia beets, also known as candy-striped beets, for their swirly kaleidoscope-like pink-and-white interiors. Red beets will bleed; yellow ones won't hold their color.

These ravioli look stunning on the plate, especially when garnished with some black sesame seeds, salad greens, or a dusting of Garam Masala (page 121).

· · · Makes 4 servings (6 ravioli per person) · · ·

3 vanilla bean pods

¼ cup coconut oil

¼ cup extra virgin olive oil

2 large Chioggia beets, peeled and thinly sliced on a mandoline
   to give 24 slices

1 tart apple, such as Granny Smith, cored, seeded, and grated

Juice of 2 oranges

1 teaspoon curry powder

½ teaspoon ground star anise

½ teaspoon ground cardamom

½ teaspoon ground cinnamon

1 pound dried Mission or Calimyrna figs, stemmed

Coconut Cream (page 441)

1. Put the vanilla pods and oils in a glass jar. Shake well to combine. (This can be made ahead and kept for several weeks.)
2. Brush a baking sheet with the vanilla-oil mixture and arrange the beet slices in a single layer. Brush each slice generously with the oil mixture. Cover and refrigerate for 8 hours or overnight.
3. Put the apple, juice, spices, and figs in a bowl, cover, and refrigerate for 8 hours. Blend in a Vita-Mix until smooth and creamy.
4. Arrange 6 beet slices on each of 4 plates. Top each beet slice with 1 teaspoon of the fig mixture. Place another beet slice on top. Top each ravioli with ½ teaspoon more of the coconut cream. Garnish as desired and serve.

. . . .

ONION RINGS

Accompany with a dip, add to an antipasto platter, or top off salads.

• • • Makes 24 to 30 rings • • •

2 large onions, sliced ⅛ inch thick

1 cup Seasoned Almond Flour (page 107)

1. Separate the onion rings and soak them in a bowl of cool water for 10 minutes.
2. Remove the onion rings from the water and dredge them in the almond flour.
3. Arrange the onion rings on Teflex-lined dehydrator racks and dehydrate for 4 to 6 hours, until crisp. Serve immediately or cover and store at room temperature. They won't last long.

PESTO-STUFFED MUSHROOMS

These are best when served warm just out of the dehydrator. The pesto can also be tossed with zucchini noodles or used as a condiment with burgers.

• • • Makes 14 stuffed mushrooms • • •

**14 button mushrooms, stemmed (save the stems for Mushroom Tea,
   page 310)**

1 cup walnuts

½ cup pine nuts

2 cups fresh basil leaves

½ cup extra virgin olive oil

3 garlic cloves

½ teaspoon sea salt

1. Place the mushroom caps top side down on a plate.
2. Put the walnuts, pine nuts, basil, olive oil, garlic, and salt in a food processor. Blend until smooth.
3. Fill each mushroom cap with a spoonful of pesto.
4. Arrange the mushrooms on a dehydrator rack and dehydrate for 6 to 8 hours. Serve immediately or store in the refrigerator for up to 2 days. Any leftover pesto can be frozen for other uses.

ASPARAGUS WRAPPED IN EGGPLANT BACON

A lovely appetizer to pass around before dinner or to add to an antipasto plate. For this recipe, the eggplant bacon shouldn't be too crisp so it will wrap around the asparagus.

• • • Makes 24 spears • • •

24 asparagus spears

2 garlic cloves, grated on a Microplane rasp

¼ cup extra virgin olive oil

Sea salt

Freshly ground black pepper

48 strips Eggplant Bacon (page 115)

1. Snap off the tough bottom 2 inches of the asparagus. Using a knife, slice a little bit off the bottom of each one to make a diagonal point.
2. Toss the asparagus with the garlic, olive oil, and salt and pepper to taste.
3. Wrap 2 bacon strips around each asparagus spear and dehydrate for 2 hours. Serve or cover and store at room temperature for up to 1 day.

BUFFALO LENTIL TENDERS

Accompany with creamy Blue Cheese Dressing (page 279), Chile Oil (page 112), and celery sticks.

• • • Makes 12 tenders • • •

2 cups coarsely chopped carrots

1 small shallot

2 cups sprouted red lentils

2 teaspoons cayenne pepper

1 teaspoon pink salt

¼ cup apple cider vinegar

2 tablespoons extra virgin olive oil

1. Put the carrots and shallot in a food processor. Process until finely ground. Add the lentils, cayenne, salt, vinegar, and olive oil and process until a batter forms. Stop the machine and scrape down the sides as necessary.

2. Divide and shape the mixture into "tenders" approximately ½ inch thick by 3 inches long and 1½ inches wide. Place the tenders on Teflex-lined dehydrator racks and dehydrate for 4 hours. Carefully flip the tenders over so the other side has an opportunity to dehydrate. Return the racks to the dehydrator and dehydrate for another 2 hours. The tenders should be firm and moist, not dried out. Enjoy immediately or cover and store in the refrigerator for up to 3 days.

SLIDERS

We serve our sliders between tomato slices as "buns," garnished with sesame seeds, pickled cucumbers and onions, and watercress with a blue cheese dressing. Note that the nuts and seeds are ground separately, then measured. These are small burgers—slider size. Cut the recipe in half if you wish.

• • • Makes 20 to 25 sliders • • •

6 large carrots, chopped

4 garlic cloves, chopped

1 bunch scallions, chopped

1 medium tomato, chopped

3 celery stalks, coarsely chopped

1 red bell pepper, quartered and seeded

1 jalapeño chile, quartered

¼ cup pine nut butter

2 cups cashew flour (page 106), plus more if needed

2 cups Sunflour (page 41), plus more if needed

1½ tablespoons Slider Seasoning (page 125)

¼ cup Nama Shoyu

1 teaspoon sea salt

8 thick tomato slices

Pickled Cucumbers (page 156)

Watercress

Blue Cheese Dressing (page 279)

1. Put the carrots in a food processor and grind to a fine pulp. Transfer to a large bowl.
2. Add the garlic, scallions, tomato, celery, bell pepper, and jalapeño to the food processor. Process the vegetables until finely chopped like a salsa. Transfer to the bowl with the carrots.
3. Add the pine nut butter, cashew flour, Sunflour, slider seasoning, and Nama Shoyu to the vegetables. Add the salt. Mix together with a large wooden spoon to incorporate all of the ingredients. If the mixture is too wet and won't hold together, add up to 1 cup Sunflour and/or cashew flour as necessary.
4. Brush mesh dehydrator racks with olive oil. Scoop and flatten the mixture into ½-cup patties. Dehydrate for 15 hours, or until they are firm.
5. Assemble the sliders between tomato slices and layer with pickles and watercress tossed with blue cheese dressing.

. . . .

CALIFORNIA MAKI

Sprouted quinoa takes the place of cooked short-grain rice and traditional crab salad in these rolls. Ground kelp gives the filling a briny flavor usually imparted by sushi. Cucumber and avocado finish off these tasty rolls. Accompany with a bowl of Spicy Mayonnaise (page 294). Multiply the recipe as needed and arrange the slices on a large platter for a party.

• • • Makes 24 pieces • • •

1 cup sprouted quinoa

½ cup ground kelp, rehydrated for 2 hours

½ cup finely diced mixed vegetables, such as carrots, onion, celery, and/or red bell pepper

½ cup Rawmesan (page 292)

1 tablespoon apple cider vinegar

1 tablespoon agave nectar

Pinch of sea salt and freshly ground salt pepper

Pinch of chopped fresh herbs, such as parsley or thyme

4 sheets nori

1 cucumber, sliced lengthwise, seeded, and cut into long, thin matchstick pieces

1 avocado, peeled, pitted, and sliced into thin strips

Spicy Mayonnaise (page 294)

1. Toss the sprouted quinoa, kelp, vegetables, Rawmesan, vinegar, agave, salt and pepper, and herbs together in a bowl to combine.

2. Place 1 nori sheet on a work surface and spread one quarter of the quinoa mixture down the middle. Arrange one quarter of the cucumber and avocado pieces on top of the quinoa. Roll up the nori and then moisten the last inch of the inside of the nori with water to seal the roll. Continue with the remaining nori, filling, cucumbers, and avocado.
3. Slice each roll into 6 pieces and arrange cut side up on a platter. Top each piece with a dollop of spicy mayonnaise or serve the sauce in a separate bowl. Serve immediately or chill for a few hours in the refrigerator.

NOTSTICKERS

Best when eaten right out of the dehydrator, these crisp-on-the-outside, chewy-on-the-inside snacks can be served at parties or as part of an Asian-inspired meal.

• • • Makes 20 notstickers • • •

2 cups Quick Cheese (page 129) *or* Grezzo Cheese (page 132)

2 leeks, coarsely chopped

2 cups shredded napa cabbage

1 garlic clove, grated on a Microplane rasp

1 tablespoon freshly grated ginger

1 teaspoon sea salt

1 large turnip, thinly sliced on a mandoline

Barbecue Sauce (page 307), optional

1. Put the cheese, leeks, cabbage, garlic, and salt in a food processor. Blend until the ingredients are thick and creamy.
2. Arrange half of the turnip slices on Teflex-lined dehydrator racks. Drop a tablespoon of the cheese mixture on each slice, then cover with another turnip slice like a sandwich. Dehydrate for 6 to 8 hours, until crisp. Serve with the barbecue sauce.

Antipasto

Morning, Noon, and Night Pancakes

Autumn Napoleon Salad

Avocado Skins

Sliders

Wild Mushroom Maki

Maroon Carrot Bisque

Bacon-Lettuce-Tomato-Avocado Wraps

VEGETABLE NORI ROLLS

The "rice" in these rolls is actually made of finely chopped parsnips, cauliflower, and nuts. Serve with bowls of Nama Shoyu on the side.

• • • Makes 4 servings • • •

2 medium parsnips, peeled
  and coarsely chopped

½ cup pine nuts

½ cup cashews

Florets from ½ head
  cauliflower, broken up

1 teaspoon sea salt

½ teaspoon Nama Shoyu

4 sheets nori

1 avocado, peeled, pitted, and thinly sliced

½ cup shredded carrots

1 cucumber, quartered, seeded, and thinly
  sliced horizontally

½ cup sprouted mung beans

1. Put the parsnips, pine nuts, cashews, cauliflower, salt, and Nama Shoyu in a food processor. Pulse until the mixture looks like sticky rice; it shouldn't be too smooth.

2. Place 1 sheet of nori on a work surface and spread one quarter of the cauliflower mixture down the middle. Arrange some of the avocado, carrots, cucumber, and mung beans on top of the cauliflower. Don't pile up the vegetables or you won't be able to roll up the nori. Roll up the nori and then moisten the last inch of the inside of the nori with water to seal the roll. Continue with the remaining nori, cauliflower mixture, and vegetables.

3. Slice the rolls into 6 pieces. Put the rolls, cut side up, on a serving plate. Accompany with a small bowl of Nama Shoyu or Asian Dipping Sauce (page 290).

WILD MUSHROOM MAKI

A mixture of cultivated fresh mushrooms is what makes these rolls unique. Wipe the mushrooms with a damp paper towel before using.

• • • Makes 24 pieces • • •

2 cups finely chopped mixed fresh mushrooms, such chanterelle, hedgehog,
  maitake, oyster, hen of the woods, shiitake, and/or honshimeji
¼ cup extra virgin olive oil
2 tablespoons freshly squeezed lemon juice
½ teaspoon sea salt
1 cup Quick Cheese (page 129)
2 teaspoons miso
2 scallions, green and white parts, finely minced
4 sheets nori
8 spears Sweet Pickled Asparagus (page 158)
Nama Shoyu

1. Put the mushrooms in a bowl and toss with the olive oil, lemon juice, and salt. Marinate the mushrooms for 10 minutes, stirring constantly.
2. Whisk together the cheese, miso, and scallions in a small bowl.
3. Place 1 sheet of nori on a work surface and thinly spread with one quarter of the cheese-miso mixture, leaving a 1-inch area at top. Put 2 asparagus spears horizontally in the middle of the nori, then spoon one quarter of the mushroom mixture

on top. Roll up the nori and then moisten the last inch of the inside of the nori with water to seal the roll. Continue with the remaining nori, cheese, asparagus, and mushrooms.

4. Slice into 6 equal-size pieces. Put the rolls, cut side up, on a serving plate. Accompany with a small bowl of Nama Shoyu.

. . . .

CABBAGE WRAPS

Easy to put together at the last minute, these wraps can be enjoyed at meals or as an appetizer on a large platter with a bowl of Asian Dipping Sauce (page 290).

• • • Makes 4 wraps • • •

1 cup mung bean sprouts

1 cup snow peas, trimmed

½ cucumber, cut into matchstick pieces

6 button mushrooms, thinly sliced

4 napa cabbage leaves

Asian Dipping Sauce (page 290)

1. Divide the sprouts, snow peas, cucumber, and mushrooms among the cabbage leaves. Roll up dumpling style, tucking in the ends.
2. Serve with the dipping sauce. The wraps can be made a few hours ahead and stored in the refrigerator.

SALADS: MORE THAN JUST GREENS

When Grezzo first opened, there were no salads on the menu, to prove to customers that raw food is so much more than just "rabbit food." But people wanted salads, so we added them. Lots of them.

Green salads with vinaigrette quickly get boring. A salad of raw beet chunks, big slices of red onion, and orange quarters isn't as appealing to the palate or to the eye as one with long, thin ribbons of colorful beets, red onions sliced so thin you can see through them, and blood orange segments tossed with dressing. Here's where those kitchen tools—spiral slicer, mandoline, and knives—are put to work to make raw foods even more visually tantalizing. A spiral slicer quickly makes soft filaments of beets, carrots, celeriac, turnips, daikon, and other firm vegetables. A mandoline slices vegetables such as radishes and mushrooms and fruits such as lemons and apples into the thinnest of slivers. A knife makes short work of finely chopping broccoli and cauliflower or shredding kale and other dark, leafy greens. A vegetable peeler produces thin asparagus or zucchini shavings for pasta-like strands.

From slaws to sea vegetable mélanges to innovative ideas using fruit, you'll find some intriguing salad combinations to keep you satisfied.

Fifty Salad Combinations:
Good Things Come in Threes

Sometimes it's hard to get out of the lettuce-cucumber-tomato salad rut, so here are some fruit-and-vegetable threesomes that you may not have considered. The success of these recipes depends on the freshness of the fruits and vegetables as well as their individual textures.

Once you have your fruit and vegetable combinations, think about other additions—edible flowers, sprouts, herbs, nuts, seeds, a scoop of cheese, croutons, other types of lettuce, pickled fruits and vegetables, and an appropriate dressing.

Apple-fennel-date
Apricot (dried)-walnut–Belgian endive
Arame-cabbage-scallion
Artichoke-mushroom–lemon zest
Arugula-grapefruit-avocado
Arugula-beet-orange
Asparagus-scallion-radish
Avocado-spinach-orange
Baby greens–walnut-beet

Beet-watercress-grapefruit

Broccoli–Unroasted Peppers–olive

Brussels sprouts–cranberry-walnut

Cabbage-carrot-pineapple

Carrot-dulse-scallion

Cauliflower-carrot-raisin

Celery-cucumber-carrot

Chickpea-mint-parsley

Corn–red pepper–tomato

Daikon radish–watercress-scallions

Escarole-cucumber-olive

Fennel-celery–Belgian endive

Fig (fresh)-almond-orange

Grapefruit–green leaf lettuce–sprouted almond

Green bean–grape tomato–shallot

Green papaya–cherry tomato–jalapeño

Kale-tomato-avocado

Mango-scallion-cilantro

Mung bean–zucchini-carrot

Orange-arugula-fig

Pear-beet-jicama

Pear-cabbage-pineapple

Persimmon–pomegranate seed–watercress

Pineapple-jicama-carrot

Pineapple-pecan-radicchio

Portobello mushroom–avocado-endive

Radicchio-fennel-mushroom

Radish-cucumber–red onion

Red bell pepper–red leaf lettuce–Vidalia onion

(continued)

Spinach–Vidalia onion–radish

Spinach–sunflower seed–orange

Spinach–cherry tomato–celery

Spinach–pine nut–garlic

Strawberry-arugula-watermelon

Tomato–button mushroom–basil

Tomato–yellow bell pepper–portobello mushroom

Turnip-apple-parsley

Wakame-cucumber-scallion

Wakame–button mushroom–zucchini

Watercress–zucchini–red bell pepper

Zucchini-cauliflower-carrot

WEDGE SALAD

For a while, iceberg was considered a less-than-elegant lettuce, not seen in fine restaurants. But there's nothing better than a wedge of crisp, fresh-from-the-market iceberg with the right dressing and some toppings.

• • • Makes 2 servings • • •

1 small head iceberg lettuce, quartered

2 tablespoons freshly chopped herbs, such as parsley, dill, and/or basil

½ cup Croutons (page 381)

Sea salt and freshly ground black pepper

¼ cup Pickled Pink Onions (page 150)

½ cup Lemon-Dulse Vinaigrette (page 278)

2 to 3 shards Pine Nut Romano (page 147)

8 strips Eggplant Bacon (page 115)

Lemon wedges

1. Arrange the iceberg quarters on a large plate. Sprinkle on the herbs and croutons and season to taste with salt and pepper. Add the onions. Drizzle on the vinaigrette.
2. Place the cheese and bacon strips on top. Serve with lemon wedges and salt and pepper. Serve immediately.

BIG HOUSE SALAD

When we say big, we mean big. This salad has a bit of everything—lettuce, sprouts, marinated and pickled vegetables, herbed cheese, and croutons—all dressed with a red wine vinaigrette. Use this recipe as a blueprint, adding seasonal vegetables and whatever you have on hand, increasing the amount for more servings. No radicchio? Use Belgian endive instead. Substitute pickled carrots for marinated radishes. And here's where all those pickles and marinated vegetables come in handy. You can toss the ingredients all together or arrange them like a classic composed salad.

• • • Makes 1 serving • • •

Big handful of mixed lettuce

½ cup sunflower sprouts

6 radicchio leaves

½ cup sprouted chickpeas

6 cucumber strips

6 carrot strips

4 black olives

2 jalapeño-stuffed green olives

2 tablespoons freshly chopped herbs, such as parsley, dill, thyme, and/or mint

¼ cup Red Wine Vinaigrette (page 281)

4 to 6 pieces Marinated Watermelon Radishes (page 165)

4 to 6 pieces Pickled Cauliflower (page 152)

4 to 6 pieces Marinated Red Beets (page 162)

8 to 10 Croutons (page 381)

Cheese (optional)

Sea salt and freshly ground black pepper

1. Combine the lettuces, sunflower sprouts, radicchio, chickpeas, cucumbers, carrots, olives, and herbs in a large bowl and toss with half of the vinaigrette.
2. Pile the dressed salad in the middle of a large plate. Place the marinated and pickled vegetables around the edges. Top with the croutons and dollops of cheese, if using. Add additional dressing and season with salt and pepper to taste.

. . . .

GREEK SALAD

Ground macadamia nuts give this the texture of feta cheese, so you don't have to make a separate cheese.

• • • Makes 2 servings • • •

½ **pound baby spinach**

1 **large tomato, diced**

1 **cucumber, peeled and diced**

10 **cured black olives, minced**

4 **red radishes, thinly sliced**

¼ **cup fresh flat-leaf parsley leaves**

¼ **cup macadamia nuts, finely ground**

2 **tablespoons extra virgin olive oil**

2 **tablespoons freshly squeezed lemon juice**

2 **garlic cloves, grated on a Microplane rasp**

1 **teaspoon sea salt**

⅛ **teaspoon freshly ground black pepper**

1. Put the baby spinach, tomato, cucumber, olives, radishes, parsley, and macadamia nuts in a large bowl. Toss and set aside.
2. Whisk together the oil, lemon juice, garlic, salt, and pepper in a bowl to make a vinaigrette.
3. Toss the salad with vinaigrette. Allow to marinate for 30 minutes, then serve immediately.

PINK PAPAYA AND ENDIVE SALAD

There's a nice balance of sweet and spicy in this salad. Tossing the hazelnuts with coriander and agave nectar gives them a candy-like flavor.

• • • Makes 2 servings • • •

2 pink papayas, peeled and cubed

2 Belgian endives, leaves separated

1 cup watercress

2 tablespoons extra virgin olive oil

3 tablespoons freshly squeezed lime juice

1 tablespoon minced jalapeño chile

Sea salt

Freshly ground black pepper

1 tablespoon agave nectar

½ teaspoon ground coriander

¼ cup hazelnuts

1. Put the papaya, endive, and watercress in a bowl. Set aside.
2. Whisk together the olive oil, lime juice, jalapeño, and a pinch of salt and pepper to make a vinaigrette. Set aside.
3. Put the agave, coriander, and hazelnuts in a bowl and toss.
4. Arrange the papaya and greens on 2 plates. Top with the hazelnuts. Whisk the vinaigrette again and drizzle over the salad. Serve immediately.

LOBSTER MUSHROOM SALAD

A raw take on the classic New England lobster salad.

• • • Makes 4 servings • • •

1 cup Grezzo Mayonnaise (page 294)

1½ teaspoons Salad Seasoning (page 124)

2 cups diced lobster mushrooms

½ cup minced celery

¼ cup minced red bell pepper

2 tablespoons minced shallots

2 tablespoons ground kelp, rehydrated

¼ cup corn kernels from the cob

4 large tomatoes

2 cups arugula leaves

Splash of extra virgin olive oil, plus more for drizzling

Splash of apple cider vinegar

Sea salt

4 large Corn Chips (page 373)

1. Whisk together the mayonnaise and salad seasoning in a large bowl. Add the mushrooms, celery, bell pepper, shallots, kelp, and corn to the mayonnaise and stir well to combine. Set aside.

2. To make tomato bowls, use a paring knife to carve out a little hat and remove the top of the tomato, as if you are carving a jack-o'-lantern. Use a spoon to scrape out the seeds and pulp.

3. Toss the arugula in a bowl with the olive oil, vinegar, and salt. Arrange the greens on 4 plates.
4. Fill each tomato with the mushroom salad and place on the greens. Drizzle olive oil over the tomatoes, sprinkle on a bit of salt, add the chips, and serve immediately.

. . . .

ARUGULA-GRAPEFRUIT SALAD

This refreshing winter salad is garnished with candied walnuts and macerated super-berries, but you can use whatever is on hand. Sliced avocado makes a nice addition, or substitute blood oranges for the grapefruit. Add croutons, breadsticks, or cheese.

• • • Makes 4 servings • • •

1 pink grapefruit, sections reserved and pulped squeezed into a small bowl (about ¼ cup juice)

¼ cup extra virgin olive oil

Sea salt and freshly ground black pepper

1 pound arugula

½ cup Macerated Super Berries (page 169)

20 Pickled Pink Onions (page 150)

20 Sweet Pickled Asparagus spears (page 158)

½ cup Rawcona Almonds (page 217)

1. Whisk the grapefruit juice and olive oil together in a small bowl with salt and pepper to taste.
2. Combine the arugula, berries, and onions together in a large bowl. Add the dressing and toss well to combine. Arrange 5 pickled asparagus spears on each of 4 plates. Place the dressed salad atop the asparagus, sprinkle on the almonds, and serve.

WORCESTERSHIRE PORTOBELLO DANDELION SALAD

Bright green dandelion leaves, thick ripe tomatoes, and marinated portobellos are layered in an authentic raw Worcestershire sauce.

• • • Makes 4 servings • • •

4 large portobello mushroom caps

½ cup Worcestershire Sauce (page 289)

½ pound dandelion leaves, arugula, or other bitter greens

2 large tomatoes, thickly sliced

¼ cup basil leaves

Sea salt

½ cup Feta Cheese (page 137), optional

1. Marinate the mushroom caps in the Worcestershire sauce in a bowl for 6 hours. Strain off excess marinade and set aside. Slice each cap into 4 or 5 slices.
2. Divide the dandelion leaves among 4 plates. Top with the mushrooms and tomatoes. Garnish with the basil leaves, a pinch of salt, and a drizzle of the remaining marinade including the shallots. Sprinkle with the feta, if using.

SEA VEGETABLE SALAD

Nori, the wrapping around Japanese hand rolls, is just one of the many kinds of sea vegetables (also called seaweed) available. There's dulse, kelp, kombu, wakame, kelp—see page 37 for a complete list. Sea vegetables make refreshing salads, especially when combined with crunchy cucumbers and daikon radishes. Soak dried sea vegetables in cool water as directed on the package before using. Dried sea vegetables are easy to cut with scissors; wet sea vegetables can be cut with a knife. One ounce of dried seaweed equals about one cup rehydrated.

Shiso, also known as perilla, is a jagged-edged herb used in Japanese cooking. It's becoming more available here and can easily be grown in any herb garden. If you can't find it, substitute cilantro, mint, or basil.

• • • Makes 6 servings • • •

1 medium daikon, peeled

1 medium European cucumber

1 yellow bell pepper, seeded and thinly sliced into long strips

4 scallions, green and white parts, thinly sliced

¼ cup chopped fresh cilantro leaves

4 shiso or basil leaves, coarsely chopped

4 mint leaves

1 cup rehydrated kelp

1 cup rehydrated dulse

½ cup Horseradish Vinaigrette (page 285)

1 cup well-rinsed Pickled Ginger (page 153), optional

1 sheet nori, cut into small strips, optional

1. Cut the daikon and cucumber into julienne using a julienne peeler or mandoline. Place the daikon, cucumber, bell pepper, and scallions in a large bowl with the cilantro, shiso, and mint.
2. Just before serving, add the sea vegetables and toss with the vinaigrette. Garnish with the pickled ginger and nori, if using. Serve immediately.

. . . .

MARINATED SHIITAKE–CUCUMBER SALAD

A lovely salad to start off any Asian-themed meal. Take the time to make the Thai Chile Sauce (page 306)—it adds a lot to this salad.

• • • Makes 6 servings • • •

½ cup Nama Shoyu

2 tablespoons freshly squeezed lemon juice

2 tablespoons apple cider vinegar

½ cup extra virgin olive oil

¼ cup freshly grated ginger

6 garlic cloves, grated on a Microplane rasp

½ cup chopped mixed fresh herbs, such as Thai basil, cilantro,
   and/or mint

1 pound shiitakes, stems reserved for Mushroom Tea (page 310)

6 cucumbers, peeled but left whole

1 cup fresh peas, such as snap peas, snow peas, or
   English peas

2 heads radicchio, leaves torn from the core to make cups

1. Whisk together the Nama Shoyu, lemon juice, vinegar, olive oil, ginger, garlic, and herbs in a large bowl. Add the mushrooms and toss well to combine. Let the mushrooms marinate for 15 minutes.

2. Using a vegetable peeler, peel the cucumbers, rotating them, to make thin ribbons of the sliced cucumbers. When you get to the seeds, discard them.
3. Toss the cucumber ribbons and peas with the mushrooms.
4. Arrange the radicchio leaves on 6 plates and fill each leaf with some of the salad. Serve immediately.

. . . .

WALDORF SALAD

Homemade Quick Mayonnaise (page 293) makes it possible to enjoy this classic salad. Use candied nuts if you have some on hand.

• • • Makes 2 to 4 servings • • •

4 apples, cored and diced

2 celery stalks, diced

1 cup raisins

½ cup walnuts

½ cup Quick Mayonnaise (page 293)

1. Put the apples, celery, raisins, and walnuts in a serving bowl and toss with the mayonnaise to coat.

2. Cover and refrigerate the salad for 2 to 4 hours before serving.

ASIAN CUCUMBER SALAD

A refreshing accompaniment that goes well with just about anything—burgers, Sliders (page 240), Falafel (page 338), and maki rolls (pages 242 and 245).

• • • Makes 2 servings • • •

⅓ **cup apple cider vinegar**

1 **teaspoon agave nectar**

½ **teaspoon sea salt**

1 **large cucumber, unpeeled and cut into spirals on a spiral slicer**

1 **plum tomato, diced**

1 **red bell pepper, seeded and diced**

2 **tablespoons sesame seeds**

1. Whisk the vinegar, agave, and salt together in a serving bowl.
2. Add the cucumber, tomato, and bell pepper and toss well. Sprinkle on the sesame seeds. Let the salad sit for an hour or so before serving.

POMEGRANATE SALAD

A colorful winter salad that can go in many directions. Add sliced persimmons or blood oranges. Replace some of the mixed greens with sliced fennel or escarole.

• • • Makes 2 servings • • •

¼ cup freshly squeezed pomegranate juice

1½ tablespoons apple cider vinegar

1½ teaspoons minced shallots

2 teaspoons extra virgin olive oil

¼ teaspoon sea salt

¼ teaspoon freshly ground black pepper

6 cups mixed greens

½ cup pomegranate seeds

2 tablespoons finely chopped pecans

1. Whisk together the pomegranate juice, vinegar, shallots, olive oil, salt, and pepper in a large bowl.
2. Add the salad greens, pomegranate seeds, and pecans. Toss well to combine and serve immediately.

Raw on the Road

With some planning before leaving home and the following tips, you'll have no problem eating raw on the road.

- When dining out, an Italian restaurant is always a good choice. Order a double salad as a main course. Scan the menu to see what other raw ingredients are available—such as mushrooms, pine nuts, and escarole— and ask to have them added raw to the salad.
- Good chefs love a challenge. If possible, call ahead to the restaurant where you will be dining, and ask to speak to the chef to see if she can accommodate your needs.
- Use the Internet to find raw food/vegan restaurants, juice bars, farmers' markets, and health food stores at your destination.
- When traveling overseas, you'll find the most amazing stores and markets wherever you go. Visit the Sunday morning organic (*biologique*) market at Boulevard Raspail in Paris. Barcelona's Boqueria is one of Europe's best, selling all sorts of produce and fresh orange, pomegranate, and other juices. Neighborhood fruit and vegetable purveyors are found in cities and villages throughout the world.
- If you're staying in a hotel for a stretch of time, take some seeds and a sprouting container along. Two teaspoons alfalfa sprouts makes two pounds of sprouts. Add them to salads and other dishes.
- Order organic produce online and have it delivered to your hotel.
- Pack dehydrated crackers, chips, and cookies. Crumbled flax crackers add crunch to salads. Take along some dried fruit and nuts or homemade Strawberry-Apricot Fudge Balls (page 412) or Brownies (page 416).
- Stow a travel blender in your suitcase to whip up morning smoothies. Use the blender to purée greens for juices, then strain them through a nut bag.

FREE-RANGE CHICKENLESS SALAD

This looks like classic chicken salad with grapes and apples, but without the chicken. Choose the freshest summer zucchini with no blemishes.

• • • Makes 2 servings • • •

1 small zucchini, coarsely chopped

1 celery stalk, coarsely chopped

½ cup Quick Cheese (page 129) *or* Grezzo Cheese (page 132), made with cashews

2 tablespoons apple cider vinegar

2½ teaspoons Salad Seasoning (page 124)

Sea salt and freshly ground black pepper

1 shallot, minced

10 to 12 grapes, halved

6 to 8 radicchio leaves

1 apple, cored and sliced

Paprika

1. Put the zucchini and celery in a food processor. Pulse until it is finely chopped but not puréed and watery. Remove to a bowl and set aside.
2. Whisk together the cheese, vinegar, salad seasoning, and salt and pepper to taste in a bowl until combined.
3. Add the zucchini and celery, shallot, and grapes to the cheese mixture and toss to combine.
4. To assemble, arrange the radicchio leaves on each of 2 salad plates in the shape of a bowl and fill with the zucchini salad. Garnish with the apple slices and a sprinkling of paprika. Serve immediately.

CONFETTI WILD RICE SALAD

Diced vegetables combined with the dark wild rice make this a very colorful dish. It travels well, making it ideal to bring to a potluck.

• • • Makes 6 servings • • •

2 cups sprouted wild rice

2 red bell peppers, seeded and diced

2 carrots, diced

2 zucchinis, diced

2 celery stalks, diced

½ cup agave nectar

¼ cup miso

½ tablespoon apple cider vinegar

2 tablespoons extra virgin olive oil

1. Combine the wild rice, bell peppers, carrots, zucchini, and celery in a serving bowl.
2. Whisk the agave, miso, vinegar, and olive oil together in a small bowl. Pour the dressing over the vegetables and mix well. Cover and let the salad sit at room temperature for 2 to 3 hours before serving.

AUTUMN NAPOLEON SALAD

This salad mimics a traditional arugula, goat cheese, and walnut salad.

• • • Makes 2 large salads • • •

1 pound arugula

1 large Belgian endive, separated into leaves

1 Bosc pear, thinly sliced on a mandoline

1 Anjou pear, thinly sliced on a mandoline

1 tart apple, thinly sliced on a mandoline

1 cup Feta Cheese (page 137)

½ cup Red Wine Vinaigrette (page 281)

Sea salt and freshly ground black pepper

1 cup Candied Nuts (page 216)

1. Toss the arugula, endive, pears, apple, and feta in a large bowl. Toss well to combine. Add the vinaigrette with some salt and pepper.
2. Divide between 2 large plates, sprinkle on the nuts, and serve immediately.

EASY SLAW

Simple to put together, this slaw goes with sliders and burgers. If you don't like raisins in your slaw, omit them.

• • • Makes 4 to 6 servings • • •

4 cups shredded green cabbage

1 cup shredded carrots

½ cup raisins

½ red onion, diced

1 tablespoon apple cider vinegar

2 tablespoons agave nectar

½ tablespoon caraway seeds

⅛ teaspoon sea salt

1. Put the cabbage, carrots, raisins, and onion in a large bowl.
2. Whisk together the vinegar, agave, caraway seeds, and salt in a small bowl. Toss all the dressing with the vegetables and let sit at room temperature for 4 hours before serving.

SWEET AND SOUR COLESLAW

There are endless variations for coleslaw. This one is a bit sweeter than our other version.

• • • Makes 4 to 6 servings • • •

1 medium cabbage, shredded

2 large carrots, shredded

⅓ cup finely chopped dried apricots

⅓ cup extra virgin olive oil

2 tablespoons agave nectar

3 tablespoons apple cider vinegar

½ teaspoon sea salt

Pinch of ground allspice

½ cup raisins

1. Place the cabbage, carrots, and apricots in a large bowl.
2. Whisk together the olive oil, agave, vinegar, salt, and allspice in a small bowl. Toss the dressing with the cabbage mixture. Let sit for 1 hour. Stir in the raisins just before serving. Cover and store in the refrigerator for up to 2 days.

JICAMA, GREEN APPLE, AND CORN SLAW

A crunchy slaw that goes well with burgers, Sliders (page 240) and Hawaiian Pizzas (page 333). Once you slice off the kernels from the corn cobs, there's still plenty of good flavor in those cobs, called milk or corn milk. Stand a cob in a bowl and scrape it with the back of a large knife to push out the milk. Fennel thinly sliced on a mandoline makes a nice addition to this slaw.

• • • Makes 4 servings • • •

1 small jicama, peeled and cut into matchstick pieces

1 Granny Smith apple, cut into matchstick pieces

Corn kernels and milk from 2 ears corn

1 red onion, halved and thinly sliced

1 cup Quick Mayonnaise (page 293)

Pinch of sea salt and freshly ground black pepper

1 teaspoon poppy seeds

Put the jicama, apple, corn, corn milk, and onion in a serving bowl. Toss with the mayonnaise to coat. Season with salt and pepper to taste and sprinkle with the poppy seeds.

BROCCOLI SALAD

The simplest salad but always the first to go at any party. The broccoli is made sweet with agave nectar and raisins.

• • • Makes 4 servings • • •

1 recipe Quick Mayonnaise (page 293)

2 tablespoons agave nectar

8 cups bite-size broccoli pieces

½ cup finely chopped onion

1 cup pine nuts or sunflower seeds

1 cup raisins

1. Whisk the mayonnaise and agave together in a small bowl until blended.
2. Combine the broccoli, onion, pine nuts, and raisins in a large bowl. Toss the salad and the dressing together. Cover and let sit at room temperature for 1 hour before serving or up to 8 hours to let the flavors meld.

A homemade, flavor-layered dressing can perk up even the most basic salads. The right salad dressing makes a world of difference in taste and gets you to eat more fresh vegetables and fruits by making them more appealing. Our dressings can be made when you make your salad ahead of time to make your raw food preparation even speedier. And most keep very well in the fridge for several days.

A few tablespoons of a sauce adds new dimensions to many dishes. A lettuce wrap, a plate of spiral-cut zucchini, or a falafel sandwich can be greatly enhanced by a raw sauce. There are many different flavor combinations listed here. Keep a few on hand; a sauce can turn a vegetable-filled cabbage leaf into something special.

LEMON-DULSE VINAIGRETTE

Caesar salad dressing is traditionally made with anchovy, egg, and Parmesan—all ingredients not used in raw foods. Substituting dulse, a sea vegetable, for the anchovy imparts a briny/salty flavor to this creamy dressing. Use it on romaine lettuce à la Caesar salad or crisp wedges of iceberg.

• • • Makes 2 cups • • •

2 cups loosely packed dulse, soaked for 20 minutes and drained

1 large garlic clove

Juice of 1 lemon

½ cup extra virgin olive oil

1. Combine the dulse, garlic, lemon juice, and ¼ cup water in a Vita-Mix. Blend until completely smooth.
2. With the machine on, slowly drizzle in the olive oil and blend until a thick, mayonnaise-like emulsion forms. If the dressing is too thick, add 1 tablespoon water at a time until it becomes the desired consistency.
3. Use immediately or store in a covered container in the refrigerator for up to 5 days.

BLUE CHEESE DRESSING

Serve with Sliders (page 240), as a dip for raw vegetables, or whenever a creamy-style dressing is called for. The texture will be like a blue cheese dressing. Since this recipe yields 3 cups dressing, there will leftovers for salads and other uses.

• • • Makes 3 cups • • •

1 cup macadamia nuts

4 scallions, cut into 2-inch pieces

¼ cup chopped red onion

3 garlic cloves, smashed

1 cup Quick Cheese (page 129)
   or Grezzo Cheese (page 132),
   made with cashews

½ cup apple cider vinegar

1 tablespoon sea salt

1 tablespoon freshly ground black
   pepper

2 tablespoons chopped fresh herbs,
   such as parsley, rosemary, thyme,
   and/or tarragon

1. Put the macadamia nuts, scallions, onion, and garlic in a food processor. Blend until the mixture is coarsely chopped.
2. With the machine running, add the cheese, vinegar, and ½ cup water through the hole in the top. Stop the food processor and scrape down the sides. Continue to pulse until the sauce is well incorporated.
3. Transfer to a bowl. Using a spatula, fold in the salt, pepper, and herbs. The dressing may look thin but will thicken up once chilled.
4. Use immediately or cover and refrigerate for up to 5 days.

GREEN GODDESS DRESSING

Try this lovely, pale green dressing with soft, buttery lettuce or as a dipping sauce with crudités.

• • • Makes 4 cups • • •

1 large cucumber, juiced

Juice of 2 lemons

3 garlic cloves, grated on a Microplane rasp

½ cup apple cider vinegar

1 teaspoon sea salt

1½ teaspoons freshly ground black pepper

2 cups extra virgin olive oil

2 ripe avocados, peeled, pitted, and diced

1 red onion, thinly sliced

1. Whisk the cucumber and lemon juices, garlic, vinegar, salt, and pepper together in a bowl. Slowly drizzle in the olive oil while continuing to whisk.
2. Add the avocado and onion, then stir well to combine. Store in a covered container in the refrigerator for up to 2 days. Whisk the dressing before serving.

RED WINE VINAIGRETTE

Keep a jar of this classic dressing in the fridge to drizzle on salads, especially those with bitter greens like radicchio, endive, and arugula.

• • • Makes 2 cups • • •

1 shallot, minced

2 garlic cloves, grated on a Microplane rasp

½ teaspoon sea salt

½ teaspoon freshly ground black pepper

1½ teaspoons agave nectar

½ teaspoon crushed red pepper flakes

¾ cup raw red wine vinegar

1¼ cups extra virgin olive oil

Combine all the ingredients a glass jar with a lid and shake well before using. The dressing will keep in the refrigerator for several days. Bring to room temperature and shake well before using.

BASIL VINAIGRETTE

Drizzle this over the summer's finest tomatoes and other salads.

• • • Makes 1 cup • • •

1 cup chopped fresh basil

⅓ cup extra virgin olive oil

Juice of 1 lemon

1 garlic clove, grated on a Microplane rasp

2 tablespoons apple cider vinegar

2 to 3 tablespoons agave nectar

1½ teaspoons sea salt

Whisk together all the ingredients in a bowl. Use immediately or cover and store in the refrigerator for 2 days. Whisk again before using.

ORANGE-HEMP VINAIGRETTE

A light dressing that goes well with red and green leaf, Boston, Bibb, and other soft lettuce varieties.

• • • Makes 3 cups • • •

1½ cups extra virgin olive oil

½ cup hemp oil

½ cup apple cider vinegar

½ cup freshly squeezed orange juice

Zest of 1 orange

1 large shallot, diced

½ cup hemp seeds

1 teaspoon sea salt

1 teaspoon freshly ground black pepper

Whisk together all the ingredients in a bowl. Use immediately or cover and store in the refrigerator for up to 2 days. Whisk again before using.

RUSSIAN DRESSING

Spoon over a wedge of iceberg lettuce or use as a sandwich spread.

• • • Makes 1 cup • • •

1 cup Quick Cheese (page 129) *or* Rawmesan (page 292)

¼ cup diced Pickled Cucumbers (page 156)

1½ teaspoons agave nectar

1 teaspoon paprika

Pinch of salt

Whisk together all the ingredients in a bowl. Use immediately or store in the refrigerator for up to 3 days.

HORSERADISH VINAIGRETTE

Nice and pungent, this vinaigrette is perfect with the Sea Vegetable Salad (page 262).

• • • Makes 2 cups • • •

¼ cup freshly grated horseradish

5 large garlic cloves, grated on a Microplane rasp

¼ cup apple cider vinegar

¼ cup Nama Shoyu

¼ cup freshly squeezed lemon juice

1¼ cups extra virgin olive oil

Whisk together all the ingredients in a bowl until combined. This makes more than needed for the salad, but keeps for several days in the refrigerator. Shake well before using.

SPICY CASHEW SAUCE

• • • Makes 1½ cups • • •

1 cup cashews

2 tablespoons Nama Shoyu

2 tablespoons freshly squeezed lime juice

1½ tablespoons agave nectar

1 tablespoon freshly grated ginger

1 jalapeño chile, chopped

Put all of the ingredients and ½ cup water in a Vita-Mix. Blend until the sauce is creamy. Cover and refrigerate for up to 3 days.

SWEET CHILE SAUCE

• • • Makes ¾ cup • • •

½ **cup agave nectar**

¼ **cup apple cider vinegar**

1½ **teaspoons crushed red pepper flakes**

Whisk together all the ingredients in a bowl. Cover and refrigerate for up to 1 week.

SWEET AND SOUR SAUCE

Serve as a dipping sauce with the Buffalo Lentil Tenders (page 239), or marinate broccoli, red bell peppers, mushrooms, and other vegetables in this sauce.

• • • Makes 2 cups • • •

1 cup Nama Shoyu

1 cup agave nectar

2 garlic cloves

2 tablespoons coconut oil, melted

1 tablespoon extra virgin olive oil

½ teaspoon crushed red pepper flakes

Put all the ingredients in a Vita-Mix. Blend until smooth. Use immediately or cover and store in the refrigerator for up to 4 to 5 days.

WORCESTERSHIRE SAUCE

Commercial Worcestershire sauce is made with anchovies and other ingredients that aren't raw. Use this to marinate mushrooms or as a vinaigrette.

• • • Makes 1 cup • • •

½ **cup apple cider vinegar**

½ **cup Nama Shoyu**

1 **tablespoon paprika**

½ **teaspoon cayenne pepper**

1 **large shallot, thinly sliced**

Whisk together all the ingredients in a bowl. Cover and refrigerate for up to 3 weeks.

ASIAN DIPPING SAUCE

Accompany cabbage rolls and lettuce wraps with this tangy and sweet sauce. While this recipe makes more than you will need for one batch of Cabbage Wraps (page 248), it keeps well in the refrigerator for up to a week.

• • • Makes 1½ cups • • •

½ **cup agave nectar**

½ **cup freshly squeezed lemon juice**

3 tablespoons freshly squeezed orange juice

2 tablespoons extra virgin olive oil

2 tablespoons Nama Shoyu

1 tablespoon freshly grated ginger

1 teaspoon apple cider vinegar

½ **teaspoon dry mustard**

Combine all the ingredients in a blender or food processor and process until mixed. Serve immediately or store covered in the refrigerator for up to 1 week.

MUSTARD

Homemade mustard is easy to make. This version is somewhat spicy; for a more mellow version, add a few more dates. Add a teaspoon or so to the Red Wine Vinaigrette (page 281), schmear on sandwiches, or combine with Rawmesan (page 292) for a mustard-flavored cream sauce.

• • • Makes 1 cup • • •

1 tablespoon black mustard seeds

1 tablespoon yellow mustard seeds

¼ cup apple cider vinegar

½ teaspoon salt

3 pitted dates

½ cup extra virgin olive oil

1. Combine the mustard seeds, vinegar, salt, dates, and ¼ cup water in a Vita-Mix. Blend the ingredients in quick pulses, stopping the machine to scrape down the sides as necessary. Mixture should be completely smooth.

2. With the machine on, drizzle in the olive oil until the mixture is emulsified and well blended. Store the mustard in a covered container in the refrigerator for up to 2 weeks.

RAWMESAN

This is our go-to cream sauce used in many of our recipes. It's the basis for Creamy Horseradish-Dill Sauce (page 301) and Grezzo Mayonnaise (page 294). Blend some of this with tomatoes for a quick, creamy soup. You can cut the recipe in half, but once you make it, you'll find so many ways to use it.

• • • Makes 6 cups • • •

2 cups cashews

2 cups pine nuts

4 cups coconut milk (page 108)

3 large garlic cloves

1 teaspoon sea salt

1 teaspoon freshly ground black pepper

Put all the ingredients in a Vita-Mix. Blend thoroughly, using the tamper to continuously move the sauce. Cover and refrigerate for up to 3 days.

QUICK MAYONNAISE

Although thinner than mayonnaise made with eggs, this tastes very much like the genuine article. For a thicker spread, cover and refrigerator for 2 to 3 hours.

• • • Makes 1 cup • • •

¾ **cup almond milk (page 104)**

2 **tablespoons avocado**

1½ **tablespoons apple cider vinegar**

¾ **teaspoon sea salt**

¾ **cup extra virgin olive oil**

1. Put the almond milk, avocado, vinegar, and salt in a blender. Blend until combined.
2. With the machine running, slowly drizzle in the oil through the hole in the top and blend until smooth.
3. Cover and refrigerate for up to 3 days.

GREZZO MAYONNAISE

Another great mayonnaise to make when you have Rawmesan (page 292) on hand.

• • • Makes 2 cups • • •

2 cups Rawmesan (page 292)

3 tablespoons apple cider vinegar

3 tablespoons agave nectar

1 tablespoon chopped fresh parsley, rosemary, or thyme

Pinch of sea salt

Whisk together all the ingredients in a bowl until fluffy. Cover and refrigerate for up to 3 days.

> **SPICY MAYONNAISE** • Add 1 tablespoon Chile Oil (page 112) to 1 cup of either mayonnaise.

TZATZIKI

A multipurpose sauce to accompany falafel, use as salad dressing, or as a dip with a platter of bright vegetables.

• • • Makes 1½ cups • • •

1 cup Quick Cheese (page 129)

1 small cucumber, seeded and diced

¼ cup chopped fresh dill

Squeeze of lemon juice

2 garlic cloves, grated on a Microplane rasp

Pinch of sea salt

Put all the ingredients in a bowl. Stir to combine. Serve immediately or cover and store in the refrigerator for up to 3 days. Taste for seasoning before serving.

TAHINI DRESSING

Tart and tangy—perfect for salads and Falafel (page 338).

• • • Makes 2 cups • • •

½ **cup extra virgin olive oil**

½ **cup Nama Shoyu**

1 **garlic clove**

¼ **cup apple cider vinegar**

¼ **cup freshly squeezed lemon juice**

⅜ **cup tahini**

Put all the ingredients in a Vita-Mix. Blend until smooth and creamy. Use immediately or cover and store in the refrigerator for up to 3 to 4 weeks.

POMODORO SAUCE

A hearty sauce with plenty of depth and flavor that can be used with lasagna, zucchini strands cut on a spiral slicer, or as a dip with breadsticks.

• • • Makes 4 cups • • •

1 cup chopped Unroasted Peppers (page 116)

3 garlic cloves

½ fennel bulb, coarsely chopped

5 to 6 tomatoes, quartered

10 basil leaves

¼ cup fresh oregano leaves *or* 1 tablespoon dried oregano

2 tablespoons extra virgin olive oil

1 teaspoon sea salt

1 teaspoon freshly ground black pepper

1. Combine the peppers, garlic, and fennel in a food processor and process until coarsely chopped. Add the tomatoes, basil, oregano, olive oil, salt, and pepper and blend. The sauce should have texture but not be chunky.
2. Store in a covered container in the refrigerator for up to 3 to 4 days.

MARINARA SAUCE

A simple tomato sauce for topping vegetable noodles and pizzas that is complex and rich in flavor. This will rival any traditional Italian "gravy." Adjust the consistency and flavor to your own taste—if you like a thinner sauce, add fewer sun-dried tomatoes; for a less sweet sauce, use fewer dates.

• • • Makes 3 cups • • •

2½ cups coarsely chopped tomatoes

12 sun-dried tomatoes, soaked in water for 15 minutes

3 dates, pitted and soaked in water for 15 minutes

¼ cup extra virgin olive oil

4 garlic cloves

2 tablespoons chopped fresh parsley

1 teaspoon sea salt

⅛ teaspoon cayenne pepper

Place all of the ingredients in a food processor and blend until smooth. Use immediately, or cover and refrigerate for up to 3 days.

MOLE

Mole, a thick Mexican sauce, is traditionally made with thirty or more ingredients, including chocolate and various chiles. Our streamlined version can garnish nachos or top pizzas.

• • • Makes 2 cups • • •

3 red bell peppers, quartered and seeded

2 jalapeño chiles

1 teaspoon crushed red pepper flakes

1 tablespoon ground cumin

1 cup cacao powder

Juice of 1 lime

Juice of 1 orange

1 tablespoon apple cider vinegar

4 pitted dates

1 mango, peeled and pulp removed

1. Process the bell pepper and jalapeños in a food processor until finely chopped. Add the red pepper flakes, cumin, cacao, lime and orange juices, vinegar, dates, and mango and process until smooth.
2. Use immediately or refrigerate for up to 3 days, bringing the mole back to room temperature before using. If the sauce is too thick, thin it with a tablespoon or so of water.

SAFFRON SAUCE

Yes, saffron is expensive, but a little bit goes a long way. Quality saffron is dark orange or red, not yellow. Saffron needs to bloom overnight before using to release its flavor and vibrant color. This sauce goes with the Wild Mushroom Fettuccine (page 355).

• • • Makes 6 cups • • •

.5 gram Spanish saffron threads

2 cups cashews

2 cups pine nuts

3 large garlic cloves

1 teaspoon sea salt

1 teaspoon freshly ground black pepper

1. Combine the saffron and 4 cups water in a bowl and let sit at room temperature overnight.
2. The next day, combine the saffron water, cashews, pine nuts, garlic, salt, and pepper in a Vita-Mix. Blend until completely smooth; there should be no lumps. Once the ingredients are blended, carefully remove the lid while the machine is running. As long as the machine is not too full, taking the lid off while the machine is running will not result in splatter. Using a spatula, push the mixture around to make sure it's smooth. Replace the top before turning the machine off. Use immediately or cover and store in the refrigerator for up 5 days.

CREAMY HORSERADISH-DILL SAUCE

We serve this sauce with the Star Anise Papaya Steak (page 358), but try it with shredded cabbage and other vegetables for a spicy coleslaw, too.

• • • Makes 1 cup • • •

1 cup Rawmesan (page 292)

3 tablespoons freshly grated horseradish

2 garlic cloves, grated on a Microplane rasp

¼ cup chopped fresh dill

½ teaspoon sea salt

½ teaspoon freshly ground black pepper

Combine all the ingredients in a large bowl and whisk together by hand. This sauce should be made just before using.

PINK SAUCE

A raw version of penne alla vodka with a pretty-in-pink sauce over spiral-cut zucchini. If there's no Bloody Mary mix on hand, use Pomodoro Sauce (page 297).

• • • Makes 4 cups • • •

2 cups Rawmesan (page 292)
2 cups Bloody Mary mix (page 402)

Whisk together Rawmesan and Bloody Mary mix until combined. Cover and refrigerate for up to 3 days.

SAUCE RÉMOULADE

A companion sauce for Calamari (page 219) or Onion Rings (page 236).

• • • Makes 1 cup • • •

**1 cup Quick Cheese (page 129) *or* Grezzo Cheese (page 132), made with
    macadamia nuts**

1 Pickled Cucumber (page 156), diced

2 tablespoons pickle brine

1 tablespoon chopped fresh herbs, such as parsley, tarragon, and/or thyme

Pinch of sea salt

Whisk together all the ingredients to combine. Use immediately or cover and refrigerate for up to 3 days.

COCONUT-CURRY SAUCE #1

Try this Indian-inspired sauce with pumpkin or butternut ravioli or on top of burgers.

• • • Makes 1½ cups • • •

1 cup tightly packed coconut meat

½ cup coconut water

½ teaspoon ground coriander

1 teaspoon ground turmeric

½ teaspoon Sichuan peppercorns

¼ teaspoon ground cloves

¼ teaspoon anise seeds

¼ teaspoon ground star anise

Combine all the ingredients in a Vita-Mix and blend until smooth. Serve immediately or store in a covered container in the refrigerator for up to 2 days.

COCONUT-CURRY SAUCE #2

Toss this with kelp noodles or long strips of daikon to fill your Thai lettuce wraps.

• • • Makes 1½ cups • • •

1 cup tightly packed coconut meat

½ cup almond milk (page 104)

1 teaspoon turmeric

1 teaspoon garam masala (page 121)

1 tablespoon grated ginger

Pinch of salt

Combine all the ingredients in a Vita-Mix and blend until smooth. Serve immediately or store in a covered container in the refrigerator for up to 2 days.

THAI CHILE SAUCE

• • • Makes 2 cups • • •

2 cups tightly packed coconut meat

½ cup coconut water

2 Thai chiles *or* **1 jalapeño chile**

½ cup chopped lemongrass

1. Put the coconut meat and water, chiles, and lemongrass in a Vita-Mix. Blend until combined.
2. Pass the sauce through a fine-mesh strainer or a nut bag. Pour the strained sauce into a covered jar and store in the refrigerator for up to 2 days. Bring the sauce to room temperature before using.

BARBECUE SAUCE

While any plum variety can be used in this sauce, we prefer black plums for this sweet-and-spicy sauce. This is a quick barbecue sauce. For more intense flavors, cold-smoke (page 207) the plums, garlic, and jalapeño.

• • • Makes 4 cups • • •

5 black plums, pitted and quartered

1 apple, quartered and cored

1 cup pitted dates

1 large beet, peeled and diced

3 garlic cloves

1 jalapeño chile

½ cup apple cider vinegar

3 tablespoons paprika

1 teaspoon sea salt

1½ teaspoons freshly ground black pepper

Combine all of the ingredients in a Vita-Mix. Blend until smooth, stopping the machine to scrape down the sides as necessary. Use immediately or cover and refrigerator for up to 5 days.

MUSHROOM GRAVY

A rich mushroom sauce to serve with Root Vegetable Purée (page 221) and Un-roasted Vegetables (page 117).

• • • Makes 2 cups • • •

5 large portobello mushrooms caps, chopped

¼ cup mixed coarsely chopped celery, carrot, and onion

1 small garlic clove

2 tablespoons Nama Shoyu

1 teaspoon chopped fresh rosemary or sage leaves

Pinch of sea salt

Splash of extra virgin olive oil

1. Put the mushrooms, vegetables, garlic, and Nama Shoyu in a food processor. With machine running, drizzle in a tablespoon of water at a time through the hole in the top to create a creamy and rich gravy.
2. Add the rosemary, salt, and olive oil. Cover and refrigerate for up to 2 days.

SOUPS: BOWLS of BIG FLAVORS

Shouldn't soups be served hot? Not really. Especially when they're made with lots of seasonings and spices that bring out the inherent flavors of fruits and vegetables. At room temperature, you can really taste the soup. These soups are perfect for brown-bag lunches, as they don't have to be reheated.

Soups are simple to make. Adding a drizzle of olive or nut oil, some chopped herbs, or some diced avocado or tomato can personalize these recipes.

Put soup bowls in the dehydrator for 15 minutes before ladling in the soup to warm them a bit.

MUSHROOM TEA

A soothing broth that can be enjoyed on its own or used as a base for other soups and sauces. The vegetables are dehydrated to intensify their flavors. Keep a bag or two of the dehydrated vegetables on hand so the broth can be made. Whenever using mushrooms like shiitakes, toss the unused stems into a plastic bag and freeze them until you're ready to make this broth. We're known to drink the tea as is, but at Grezzo we plate the broth with chopped pineapple, vegetables, and herbs. You could add a scattering of whatever you have on hand, such as peas or diced vegetables.

• • • Makes 4 cups • • •

1 carrot, coarsely chopped

1 celery stalk, coarsely chopped

1 large onion, coarsely chopped

1 cup or more mushroom stems

1 cup portobello, button, or shiitake mushrooms

2 garlic cloves, grated on a Microplane rasp

Sea salt

Freshly ground black pepper

¼ cup Nama Shoyu

2 tablespoons agave nectar

½ teaspoon crushed red pepper flakes

1 cup soaked dulse

½ cup chopped pineapple

1 chopped scallion, green and white parts

1 teaspoon chopped fresh flat-leaf parsley

Extra virgin olive oil

1. Arrange the carrots, celery, onion, and mushroom stems on dehydrator trays. Dehydrate for 12 hours.

2. Combine the dehydrated ingredients in a large jar and cover with 4 cups water. Add the grated garlic. Season with salt and pepper, cover, and allow the broth to infuse for 2 hours.

3. Marinate the mushrooms in a bowl with the Nama Shoyu, agave, and red pepper flakes for 10 minutes.

4. To serve, divide the dulse, mushrooms, pineapple, and scallion between 2 soup bowls. Strain the broth through a strainer into the bowls. Sprinkle with parsley and add a drizzle of olive oil before serving.

. . . .

MISO SOUP

Although any sea vegetable can be used in this soup, we prefer the texture and flavor of kelp.

• • • Makes 4 servings • • •

¼ cup Nama Shoyu

2 tablespoons miso

½ cup coarsely chopped dried kelp

4 scallions, green and white parts, coarsely chopped

4 red radishes, thinly sliced

¼ cup torn fresh basil leaves

1 avocado, peeled, pitted, and diced

Sea salt

1. Whisk the Nama Shoyu, miso, and 7 cups water together in a bowl.
2. Add the kelp to the miso mixture and let sit for 30 minutes so the kelp rehydrates.
3. Divide the soup among 4 bowls. Garnish with scallions, radishes, basil, and avocado. Season to taste. Serve immediately.

AJO BLANCO

This chilled Spanish soup, often called white gazpacho, is made with almonds and plenty of garlic.

• • • Makes 3 servings • • •

4 cups almond milk (page 104)

1½ cups almonds

4 large garlic cloves

½ cup red, green, or black grapes, sliced

1 tablespoon extra virgin olive oil

2 tablespoons chopped fresh parsley

Sea salt

Paprika

1. Put the almond milk, almonds, and garlic in a Vita-Mix. Blend until very smooth. The soup can be covered and refrigerated for up to 3 days.
2. Divide the soup into 3 bowls. Garnish each with grapes, olive oil, parsley, a sprinkle of sea salt, and a dash of paprika.

MAROON CARROT BISQUE

Who says carrots have to be orange? They come in a riot of colors—from the traditional orange and yellow to parsnip-white and deep maroon. Maroon carrots are earthy rose-red on the outside and deep orange on the inside. Nutritionally, they have 40 percent more beta-carotene and are crisper and sweeter than orange carrots, making them good for snacking, too. Make this in the autumn when parsnips, pears, and horseradish root are in season. Best of all, they hold their vibrant colors in this spicy soup. You can, of course, prepare this soup with any variety of carrots. Top the soup with thin maroon carrot shavings, diced avocado or pear, and a drizzle of olive oil for a sophisticated presentation.

• • • Makes 4 servings • • •

3 cups maroon carrot juice
   (from about 15 large carrots)
½ pound parsnips, peeled and
   coarsely chopped
2 Bosc pears, cored
1 avocado, peeled and pitted
1 tablespoon freshly grated horseradish

1 tablespoon freshly grated ginger
1 tablespoon caraway seeds
1 tablespoon coriander seeds
2½ tablespoons Nama Shoyu
Pinch of sea salt and freshly ground
   black pepper

1. Combine all the ingredients in a Vita-Mix. Blend for five 1-minute intervals until the mixture is puréed. Use the tamper to push down the ingredients and thoroughly incorporate.
2. Divide the soup among warm bowls and garnish as desired.

CREAMY MUSHROOM SOUP

With its creamy texture and intense fresh-and-dried mushroom flavor, this is the perfect first course for a Thanksgiving or Christmas dinner. (Of course, it can be doubled.) There's no need to rehydrate the dried mushrooms before preparing this dish; they'll rehydrate as they are blended.

• • • Makes 4 servings • • •

8 ounces cremini mushrooms

½ cup dried porcini mushrooms

1 red bell pepper, quartered and seeded

1 carrot, chopped

2 garlic cloves

1 cup almonds

1 tablespoon Nama Shoyu

½ teaspoon sea salt

½ teaspoon freshly ground black pepper

1 tablespoon chopped fresh herbs, such as rosemary, parsley, and thyme

1. Put the mushrooms, bell pepper, carrot, garlic, almonds, Nama Shoyu, 4 cups water, the salt, pepper, and half the herbs in a Vita-Mix. Blend until completely smooth. For a smoother soup, pour the mixture through a fine-mesh strainer.

2. Divide the soup among 4 bowls, garnish with the remaining herbs, and serve immediately, as this soup doesn't keep.

CREAMY BROCCOLI SOUP

The cumin and sea salt are essential for bringing out the soup's flavors. Add more salt if needed. Rich, creamy, and thick, this is the perfect soup for cold winter nights.

• • • Makes 4 servings • • •

1 cup almonds

1 teaspoon agave nectar

2 cups chopped broccoli

1 avocado, peeled, pitted, and chopped

1 small garlic clove

1 tablespoon extra virgin olive oil

1 teaspoon chopped onion

1 teaspoon sea salt

⅛ teaspoon ground cumin

⅛ teaspoon freshly ground black pepper

1. Put 3 cups water, the almonds, and agave in a Vita-Mix. Blend until smooth.
2. Add the broccoli, avocado, garlic, olive oil, onion, salt, cumin, and pepper. Blend until the soup is smooth and creamy.
3. Serve immediately or cover and refrigerate for up to 2 days.

CREAMY FENNEL-ORANGE SOUP

Fennel and orange are often paired in salads, so why not soup? Float a few drops of neroli or orange blossom water on each serving.

• • • Makes 4 servings • • •

1 cup cashews

1 large fennel bulb, coarsely chopped

1 avocado, peeled, pitted, and chopped

1 celery stalk, coarsely chopped

Juice of 1 orange

2 garlic cloves

1 avocado, peeled, pitted, and diced

½ fennel bulb, thinly sliced

1 red jalapeño chile, thinly sliced in rings

Zest and sections of 1 orange

2 tablespoons extra virgin olive oil

1 teaspoon sea salt

1 teaspoon freshly ground black pepper

1. Put the cashews and 4 cups water in a Vita-Mix. Blend until smooth.
2. Add the chopped fennel, chopped avocado, celery, orange juice, and garlic and blend until smooth.
3. Transfer to a large bowl and stir in the diced avocado, thinly sliced fennel, jalapeño, orange zest and segments, olive oil, salt, and pepper.
4. Let the soup stand for 15 minutes so the flavors have the opportunity to meld before serving. Cover and refrigerate for up to 1 day.

VANILLA-SCENTED PARSNIP SOUP

East (vanilla and a heady spice blend) meets West (parsnips) in this velvety, Asian-inspired soup. Buy parsnips as you would carrots—firm, not flabby. Don't peel the apples, as so much of their tart flavor comes from the skins. Marinated black trumpets are the preferred mushrooms here, but portobellos or cremini can be substituted. Pungent grains of paradise come from West Africa and look like peppercorns. Look for them online or on spice shelves at some markets.

Have all the ingredients ready and make this soup just before serving as a first course at a late fall or early spring dinner party.

• • • Makes 8 cups • • •

1 cup black trumpet or other mushrooms

2 tablespoons extra virgin olive oil, plus more for finishing

Sea salt

4 to 5 parsnips, peeled and coarsely chopped

2 tart apples, such as Granny Smith, cored, seeded, and chopped

4 cups almond milk (page 104)

½ teaspoon whole cloves

1 whole star anise

1 teaspoon grains of paradise, optional

½ teaspoon Sichuan peppercorns

Seeds from 1 vanilla bean

1 Granny Smith apple, diced

Flat-leaf parsley or chervil leaves

1. Put the mushrooms in a bowl and toss with the olive oil and a dash of sea salt. Set aside to marinate.
2. Put the parsnips, apples, almond milk, cloves, star anise, grains of paradise, if using, Sichuan peppercorns, and vanilla seeds in a Vita-Mix. Blend for five 1-minute intervals until the mixture is puréed. Use a spatula to keep the soup in constant motion.
3. Pour the soup through a fine-mesh strainer into a clean bowl. Season with salt and pepper to taste.
4. Divide the soup among warm bowls and garnish with the marinated mushrooms, diced apple, parsley, and olive oil.

. . . .

CORN CHOWDER

A thick soup made with fresh corn and creamy avocado that can be ready in minutes.

• • • Makes 2 servings • • •

Kernels from 5 ears corn

2½ cups almond milk (page 104)

1 small avocado, peeled and pitted

1 teaspoon sea salt

1. Reserve ¼ cup of the corn kernels. Put the almond milk, remaining corn, avocado, and salt in a blender or a Vita-Mix. Blend until the soup is smooth and creamy; it will have bits of corn in it.
2. Divide the soup between 2 bowls, garnish with the reserved corn, and serve.

AVOCADO-CUCUMBER SOUP

Perfect for a steamy summer night, when all you want is something cool and refreshing. If you wish, garnish with some chopped cucumber and avocado.

• • • Makes 2 servings • • •

2 avocados, peeled and pitted

2 cucumbers, coarsely chopped

½ cup chopped fresh dill

1 tablespoon freshly squeezed lemon juice

½ teaspoon sea salt

1. Put all the ingredients in a blender or Vita-Mix. Blend until the soup is smooth and creamy.
2. Serve at room temperature or refrigerate for 1 hour. Stir before serving.

SUMMER MELON STEW

Although this summer-perfect soup can be made with a single type of melon—in addition to the watermelon—we prefer a variety. Honeydew and cantaloupe are fine, but search out Canary, Crenshaw, Galia, Persian, and Santa Claus as well. Blend this just before serving; it doesn't keep well.

• • • Makes 4 servings • • •

2 cups melon balls, scooped with a melon baller

¼ cup chopped fresh herbs, such as mint, basil, and cilantro

Juice of 2 limes

7 cups chopped watermelon

2 ripe mangoes, peeled and pitted

1 teaspoon culinary lavender *or* 2 fresh sprigs lavender

½-inch piece ginger, peeled

3 cardamom pods

1. Put the melon balls, herbs, and lime juice in a bowl. Toss and set aside.
2. Put the watermelon, mangoes, lavender, ginger, and cardamom in a Vita-Mix and blend until smooth, using the tamper as necessary. Add the broth to the fruit and stir well.
3. Serve immediately or cover and refrigerate for up to 2 days.

VIETNAMESE COCONUT SOUP

Once all the ingredients are prepped, this soup is easy to put together. Serve it immediately—it doesn't keep—with a choice of Asian garnishes.

• • • Makes 4 servings • • •

2 cups tightly packed coconut meat

4 cups coconut milk

3 Thai chiles *or* 1 jalapeño chile

3 garlic cloves

½ lemongrass stalk, peeled

1 carrot, halved

½-inch piece ginger, peeled

1 tablespoon ground turmeric

1 tablespoon ground star anise or Sichuan peppercorns

3 tablespoons Nama Shoyu

1. Put all the ingredients in a Vita-Mix and blend until smooth.
2. Pass the mixture through a fine-mesh strainer or a nut bag. Discard the solids. The soup will have a creamy but not-too-thick consistency. Divide the soup among 4 bowls and serve immediately.

TOMATO-BASIL BISQUE WITH GREMOLATA

The Rawmesan imparts a creaminess to the soup, much like the consistency of a bisque. Gremolata, a fresh Italian garnish of chopped parsley, lemon zest, and garlic, is sprinkled over the top of the soup with a drizzle of olive oil. The tomatoes add another layer of texture.

• • • Makes 4 servings • • •

5 to 6 large ripe tomatoes, quartered

4 cups Rawmesan (page 292)

5 garlic cloves, grated on a Microplane rasp

Quarter-size piece fresh horseradish, grated on a Microplane rasp

½ cup mixed chopped herbs, such as tarragon, Thai basil,
    and/or flat-leaf parsley

1½ teaspoons sea salt

1½ teaspoons freshly ground black pepper

1 teaspoon ground cumin

½ teaspoon cayenne pepper

1 teaspoon paprika

Gremolata (recipe follows)

Extra virgin olive oil

1. Put the tomatoes into a food processor and blend until coarsely chopped and juicy.
2. Whisk together the Rawmesan and puréed tomatoes in a large bowl until well

combined. Add the garlic, horseradish, tarragon, salt, pepper, cumin, cayenne, and paprika. Stir well to combine. Let the soup sit for an hour or so, so the flavors can meld.

3. Divide the soup among 4 bowls. Pass the gremolata and the olive oil at the table. The soup can be made ahead and refrigerated for up to 2 days. Stir well before serving.

GREMOLATA

Zest of 1 lemon
¼ cup chopped fresh flat-leaf parsley
2 large garlic cloves, grated on a Microplane rasp
¼ cup minced olives

Stir all the ingredients together in a small bowl.

SWEET POTATO–GRAPEFRUIT SOUP

An unusual pairing, but this creamy but light soup is bright in flavor and in color. It's perfect during the winter when sweet potatoes and grapefruit are abundant. Chiles add a little kick.

Two good-size sweet potatoes put through a juicer will yield approximately 2 cups juice. There's no need to peel the potatoes before juicing them.

Garnish with some jalapeño rings or grapefruit segments if you like.

• • • Makes 4 servings • • •

2 cups sweet potato juice (from about 2 sweet potatoes)

2 cups coarsely chopped sweet potatoes (from about 1 sweet potato)

3 cups coconut milk

2 cups freshly squeezed grapefruit juice

2 jalapeño chiles

8 basil leaves, torn

1. Put the sweet potato juice, chopped sweet potatoes, coconut milk, grapefruit juice, and chiles in a Vita-Mix. Blend to a purée.
2. Divide the soup among 4 bowls, garnish with the basil, and serve immediately. Cover and refrigerate for up to 1 to 2 days.

MAIN COURSES:

THE BIG EVENT

R aw food is not just about eating carrot sticks and apple slices, as these main courses show. They have all the choices you want from a section on entrees—from a light meal made entirely of papaya or hearty gnocchi to vegetable pasta with marinara sauce or burgers with an endless choice of toppings. These dishes can be garnished or embellished with other recipes to dress them up for special occasions.

BACON-LETTUCE-
TOMATO-AVOCADO WRAP

Any classic sandwich like this one deserves to be accompanied by Salt and Vinegar Potato Chips (page 370) and some pickles of your choosing.

• • • Makes 1 serving • • •

3 butter lettuce leaves

2 tomato slices

2 avocado slices

3 thin carrot strips

3 thin cucumber strips

1 tablespoon Red Wine Vinaigrette (page 281)

1½ tablespoons Quick Cheese (page 129) *or* Grezzo Cheese (page 132),
    any flavor

1 Italian Bread Wrap (page 386)

4 strips Eggplant Bacon (page 115)

1. Put the lettuce, tomato and avocado slices, carrots, and cucumbers in bowl. Toss gently with the vinaigrette and set aside.
2. Carefully spread the cheese onto the wrap. Layer the vegetables on top of the cheese and add the bacon. Gently roll up the wrap and serve immediately.

Making Pizza

Our pizzas are small, six-inch pies. The crusts can be made ahead in the dehydrator. Once topped, they spend another two hours in the dehydrator. Be generous with your sauces and toppings, as the pizzas will shrink a bit as they dehydrate.

We offer some ideas for pizza toppings, but the possibilities are endless. You can use any kind of cheese and toppings. One favorite is with Marinara Sauce (page 298) spread on a crust, then topped with spinach, mushrooms, and onions or with onions and red and green peppers. For a super-quick pizza, pulse two tomatoes in the food processor, add some grated garlic and sea salt, and pour on top of a pizza crust with some torn basil leaves and black olives. Topped and dehydrated pizzas can be eaten immediately or covered and refrigerated for two days. Bring them to room temperature or warm in the dehydrator before serving.

PIZZA CRUSTS

These crusts stay fresh for up to a week, making them convenient to assemble any time of day. They are chewy and flavorful and make a perfect thin-crust pizza.

• • • Makes 8 to 10 crusts • • •

2 medium carrots

3 celery stalks

¼ fennel bulb

2 garlic cloves

½ small red onion

4 jalapeño-stuffed green olives

½ cup chopped tomatoes

1 tablespoon extra virgin olive oil

1 tablespoon chopped fresh flat-leaf parsley

1 tablespoon chopped fresh rosemary leaves

1 teaspoon sea salt

1 teaspoon freshly ground black pepper

2 cups flax meal

1. Put the carrots, celery, fennel, garlic, onion, olives, and tomatoes in food processor. Blend to a smooth consistency.
2. Add the olive oil, parsley, rosemary, salt, and pepper. Pulse to incorporate.
3. Add the flax meal and pulse to create a spreadable but firm batter. Add up to ½ cup more flax meal if the dough is too wet.

4. Pour 8 to 10 ½-cup measures of batter onto Teflex-lined dehydrator racks. Use an offset spatula to spread the batter into rounds that are 6 inches in diameter and ¼ to ½ inch thick. Dehydrate for 8 hours. Remove the racks, turn the crusts over, peel off the Teflex sheets, and dehydrate for another 2 hours, until the crusts are firm but not too crisp.
5. Use as directed immediately in the pizza recipes or cover and refrigerate for up to 4 to 5 days.

. . . .

GREEK PIZZAS

Redolent with Mediterranean flavors and sage, a favorite Greek herb. Sage leaves can be crisped in the dehydrator by laying them out on a mesh rash, then topping them with another mesh rack so they don't blow around. Dehydrate for 24 hours and store in a covered container on the countertop for up to a week. The same method can be used for drying any fresh herbs.

• • • Makes 2 pizzas • • •

½ cup Quick Cheese (page 129) *or* Grezzo Cheese (page 132)

2 Pizza Crusts (page 330)

2 cups spinach leaves

Sea salt

Extra virgin olive oil

1 large tomato, thinly sliced

½ small red onion, thinly sliced

8 black olives, pitted and minced

1 tablespoon crisp sage leaves

Pinch of crushed red pepper flakes

1. Spread the cheese over the crusts.
2. Toss the spinach with a pinch of salt and splash of olive oil. Arrange the spinach on the pizzas, followed by the tomato, onion, and olives. Add the sage leaves, a pinch of sea salt, the red pepper flakes, and a drizzle of olive oil.
3. Place the pizzas on dehydrator racks and dehydrate for 2 hours. Serve immediately.

HAWAIIAN PIZZAS

Think about doubling the recipe. They're that good!

• • • Makes 2 pizzas • • •

¼ **cup Barbecue Sauce (page 307)**

¼ **cup Blue Cheese Dressing (page 279)**

2 Pizza Crusts (page 330)

12 fresh cilantro leaves

½ **cup diced pineapple**

8 strips of Eggplant Bacon (page 115), crumbled

¼ **cup Feta Cheese (page 137)**

Extra virgin olive oil

Sea salt

1. Spread the sauce and dressing over the pizza crusts. Add the cilantro, pineapple, and bacon.
2. Top each pizza with the feta cheese, a splash of olive oil, and a pinch of salt.
3. Place the pizzas on dehydrator racks and dehydrate for 2 hours. Serve immediately.

PEPPERONI PIZZAS

Pepperoni? Thin slices of Marinated Watermelon Radishes look and taste like pepperoni on this pizza. Pile them on; they'll curl up like pepperoni in the dehydrator.

• • • Makes 2 pizzas • • •

½ cup Pink Sauce (page 302)

2 Pizza Crusts (page 330)

10 thin slices tomato

½ cup fresh basil leaves

½ cup Marinated Watermelon Radishes (page 165) (about 20 slices)

Extra virgin olive oil

Sea salt

1. Spread the sauce over the pizza crusts. Layer on the tomato, then the basil. Top each with radishes. Garnish pizza with a splash of olive oil and a pinch of sea salt.
2. Arrange the pizzas on dehydrator racks and dehydrate for 2 hours. Serve immediately.

SAUSAGE AND ONION PIZZAS

Just like sausage and onions at the ballpark!

• • • Makes 2 pizzas • • •

½ **cup crushed tomatoes**

½ **cup Sauerkraut (page 154)**

2 Sausage Patties (page 208), crumbled

½ **cup thinly sliced white onion**

2 Pizza Crusts (page 330)

Sea salt

Extra virgin olive oil

1. Layer the crushed tomatoes, sauerkraut, sausage, and onion onto the pizza crusts. Sprinkle on some salt and drizzle on some olive oil.

2. Arrange the pizzas on dehydrator racks and dehydrate for 2 hours. Serve immediately.

SUNNY BURGERS

Nestle these simple burgers between tomato slices or tuck into lettuce leaves. Serve with Blue Cheese Dressing (page 279) or another dressing and quick pickles of your choosing.

• • • Makes 6 to 8 burgers • • •

    2 cups Sunflour (page 41)

    4 cups coarsely chopped carrots

    2 celery stalks, chopped

    1 red bell pepper, quartered and seeded

    1 scallion, green and white part, chopped

    1½ teaspoons sea salt

1. Put the Sunflour, carrots, celery, bell pepper, scallion, and salt in a food processor. Blend until the mixture is well combined but not too smooth. It should have some texture.

2. Divide and shape the mixture into 6 to 8 patties, approximately 2 inches round and ½ to ¾ inch thick. Place the burgers on Teflex-lined dehydrator racks and dehydrate for 4 hours. Carefully remove the racks one at a time, turn them over, and peel off the Teflex sheets. Return the racks to the dehydrator and dehydrate for another 4 hours. Cover and store in the refrigerator for up to 1 week.

BISTRO BURGERS

These burgers are earthy, flavorful, and satisfying. Accompany with a scoop of guacamole and Sweet Potato Chips (page 371).

• • • Makes 6 large or 12 small burgers • • •

2 cups hydrated kelp

8 portobello mushroom caps, coarsely
   chopped

3 garlic cloves

½ jalapeño chile, diced

1 shallot, diced

½ fennel bulb, diced

2 tablespoons hemp oil

1 cup Sunflour (page 41)

1 cup hemp seeds

Sea salt and freshly ground
   pepper

1. Put the kelp in the food processor and blend until finely chopped, then transfer to a large bowl. Add the mushrooms, garlic, jalapeño, shallot, fennel, and hemp oil and process until well chopped. The mixture should be the consistency of ground meat. Stop and scrape down the machine as necessary.

2. With a spatula, scrape the mushroom mixture into the bowl with the ground kelp. Stir in the Sunflour and hemp seeds and salt and pepper to taste for a burger-like consistency. Divide and shape the mixture into 6 large or 12 small patties.

3. Place the burgers on olive oil-brushed mesh dehydrator racks and dehydrate for 10 to 12 hours. Bistro burgers should be crisp on the outside and soft in the middle. Cover and store in the refrigerator for up to 1 week.

FALAFEL

Enjoy these with a chopped tomato, cucumber, and red onion salad and Tahini Dressing (page 296). Another serving idea: Remove the tough center stems from a few Swiss chard leaves. Toss them with a little olive oil to soften. Lay a leaf on a work surface, crumble a falafel on top, and add some Tzatziki (page 295), sliced tomato, and pickles. Roll up burrito-style and serve.

• • • Makes 6 pieces • • •

½ cup chopped fresh parsley leaves

¼ cup chopped fresh cilantro leaves

¼ cup chopped fresh mint leaves

1 tablespoon ground cumin

2 tablespoons Nama Shoyu

Juice of 1 lemon

2 garlic cloves, crushed

Pinch of sea salt and freshly ground black pepper

2 cups almond flour (page 106)

1. Put the parsley, cilantro, and mint in a food processor. Blend to chop coarsely. Add the cumin, Nama Shoyu, lemon juice, garlic, and salt and pepper and process to combine. The mixture should be wet.
2. Turn on the food processor and slowly add the almond flour. Stop the machine frequently to scrape down the sides. Drizzle in ¼ to ½ cup water until a dough forms with the consistency of wet sand.
3. Divide the mixture into 6 portions using an ice cream scoop. Place falafel balls on a Teflex-lined dehydrator rack and dehydrate for 10 to 12 hours. Flip and dehydrate on the other side for an additional 2 to 4 hours, until crisp on the outside and soft in the middle. Cover and refrigerate for 2 to 3 days.

CHILI CHICKPEAS

Tex-Mex inspired, this marinade can be used with lentil or adzuki and mung beans in place of the chickpeas. Serve over sprouted quinoa or sprouted wild rice.

• • • Makes 4 servings • • •

1 cup diced tomatoes

1 cup diced red onions

1 cup corn kernels, optional

½ cup freshly squeezed lime juice

2 garlic cloves, grated on a Microplane rasp

1 tablespoon Nama Shoyu

1 tablespoon chili powder

½ teaspoon ground cumin

2 cups sprouted chickpeas

1. Combine the tomatoes, onions, corn, lime juice, garlic, Nama Shoyu, chili powder, and cumin powder in a bowl and toss well to mix. Add the chickpeas and mix well.

2. Marinate for several hours or overnight before serving. Cover and store in the refrigerator for up to 2 to 3 days.

PAPAYA PAPPARDELLE

Wide papaya noodles sliced with a vegetable peeler go well with this creamy mustard sauce.

• • • Makes 4 servings • • •

¼ **pound green beans or haricot vert, trimmed**

Extra virgin olive oil

1 garlic clove, grated

Salt and freshly ground black pepper

1 large ripe Maradol papaya

1½ cups cashews

½ **cup pine nuts**

1 whole garlic clove

1 small shallot

1½ tablespoons yellow mustard seeds

1 tablespoon apple cider vinegar

2 teaspoons freshly squeezed lemon juice

¼ **cup dried currants, soaked for 2 to 4 hours in apple cider vinegar and drained**

2 tablespoons fresh tarragon leaves

Arugula leaves

Sesame seeds

1. Toss the beans with a splash of olive oil, the grated garlic, and salt and pepper to taste. Arrange the beans in a single layer on a Teflex-lined dehydrator rack and "unroast" (page 117) in the dehydrator for 1 hour.

2. Using a knife, peel the thick outer skin from the papaya. Switch to a vegetable peeler, and peel the papaya into long strands so they resemble pappardelle pasta, about 1 inch wide.

3. Combine the cashews, pine nuts, whole garlic clove, shallot, mustard seeds, vinegar, lemon juice, 1 teaspoon salt, and 1 teaspoon pepper in a Vita-Mix. Add 1 cup water and blend until completely smooth. The sauce will stay fresh for 3 days, covered and refrigerated.

4. Gently toss the papaya noodles with the soaked currants (discard the soaking vinegar), green beans, tarragon leaves, and enough sauce to coat. Divide the noodles among 4 plates and top each with a handful of arugula leaves and a pinch of sesame seeds. Serve immediately.

. . . .

PUPUSAS

Pupusas are Salvadoran flatbreads traditionally made with masa harina and stuffed with meat, cheese, or beans. Fill them with any of the following—chopped tomatoes, avocado, cilantro leaves, lettuce, sprouted lentils, and mango slices.

• • • Makes about 12 pupusas • • •

3 cups corn kernels

1 cup flax seeds, soaked in 1 cup water for 4 hours

1 banana

2 jalapeño chiles

¼ cup chopped fresh cilantro

1 teaspoon ground cumin

1 teaspoon sea salt

1 teaspoon freshly ground black pepper

1. Combine all the ingredients in a food processor. Blend until smooth.
2. Using a ladle, drop ½-cup portions of batter onto Teflex-lined dehydrator racks and, using the bottom of the ladle, spread into a circle. The batter should be spread ¼ inch thick. Dehydrate for 6 hours. Remove the rack, turn it over, peel off the Teflex sheets, and return the pupusas to the rack. Dehydrate for another hour. They should be flexible, not too crisp.
3. Select from the fillings above. Serve immediately, or store unfilled and wrapped in the refrigerator for up to 2 to 3 days.

THAI LETTUCE WRAPS

Raw kelp noodles can be purchased in some health food stores and from online sources. Since they take well to all sorts of sauces, we suggest making wraps with lettuce leaves and serving two dipping sauces.

• • • Makes 4 servings • • •

1 cucumber, thinly sliced

2 cups sliced button or cremini mushrooms

1 red bell pepper, seeded and thinly sliced

½ cup Worcestershire Sauce (page 289)

1 pound kelp noodles

1 cup Coconut-Curry Sauce (page 304)

1 head red leaf lettuce, leaves separated

1 large carrot, peeled into strips using a vegetable peeler

1½ cups Spicy Cashew Sauce (page 286)

¾ cup Sweet Chile Sauce (page 287)

1. Marinate the cucumber, mushrooms, and bell pepper in the Worcestershire sauce for 30 minutes.
2. Toss the kelp noodles and curry sauce in a bowl.
3. Put the lettuce leaves, carrot ribbons, marinated mushrooms, and noodles on the table, accompanied by the two sauces. Make wraps using the lettuce leaves and generously dip into the sauces.

WILD MUSHROOM AND FRUIT SALAD TERRINE

Three layers—papaya salad, kelp, and creamy mushrooms—are layered in a 3 x 5-inch rectangular mold and then topped with a selection of unroasted vegetables.

• • • Makes 4 servings • • •

2 cups diced papaya

½ cup Macerated Super Berries (page 169)

¼ cup torn tarragon leaves

2 cups mixed wild mushrooms

1 tablespoon ground mustard seeds (a combination of dark and yellow
    mustard seeds works best)

1 shallot, minced

1 cup Quick Cheese (page 129) *or* 1 cup Rawmesan (page 292)

Pinch of sea salt and freshly ground black pepper

1 cup coarsely ground kelp

Unroasted Vegetables (page 117), such as carrots, green beans, Brussels
    sprouts, broccoli florets, corn kernels, and snap peas, tossed with extra
    virgin olive oil, grated garlic, salt, and pepper and dehydrated for 3 hours

1. Combine the papaya, berries, and tarragon in a bowl. Set aside.
2. Combine the mushrooms, mustard seeds, shallot, cheese, salt, and pepper in a large bowl, using a spatula to make sure the mushrooms are well coated. Set aside.

3. Spread the papaya evenly into the mold, followed by the kelp, then the mushroom mixture.

4. To remove the ring mold, get a good grip on the mold with one hand and use a spoon in the other hand to press down with stability while you gently bring the ring mold straight up. Put 1 terrine on each of 4 plates and surround with warm-from-the-dehydrator vegetables. Serve immediately.

. . . .

ZUCCHINI PRIMAVERA

Here, zucchini ribbons are dressed with a pesto-like sauce and topped with a selection of vegetables.

• • • Makes 4 servings • • •

1 cup cashews

1 cup pine nuts

1 cup fresh basil leaves

4 garlic cloves

½ teaspoon sea salt, plus more for sprinkling

½ teaspoon freshly ground black pepper

4 large zucchinis, peeled into wide strips with a vegetable peeler

4 cups assorted Unroasted Vegetables (page 117), such as broccoli, carrots,
   corn kernels, cherry tomatoes, snap peas, cauliflower, bell peppers, and
   peas, tossed with extra virgin olive oil, grated garlic, salt, and pepper
   and dehydrated for 3 hours

Splash of extra virgin olive oil

Pine Nut Romano (page 147) shavings

1. Put the cashews, pine nuts, basil, 2 of the garlic cloves, the salt, and pepper in a Vita-Mix. Add 2 cups water and blend until very smooth. Cover and refrigerate for up to 3 days.
2. Toss the zucchini pasta and warm-from-the-dehydrator vegetables with about half of the basil cream sauce, adding more as necessary. Divide among 4 plates. Drizzle with olive oil and sprinkle on some salt and cheese shavings. Serve immediately.

BRAZILIAN STEW

A hearty stew made with satisfying sprouted barley and dark leafy greens with a rich and bold broth. It's even better the next day when the flavors have had a chance to meld.

• • • Makes 4 servings • • •

6 large tomatoes, puréed

2 cups coarsely chopped dark
   leafy greens, such as kale,
   Swiss chard, or collard greens

¼ cup Date Paste (page 110)

¼ cup minced onion

½ cup minced carrot

½ cup minced celery

1 jalapeño chile, minced

3 garlic cloves, thinly sliced

1 tablespoon Cajun Seasoning
   (page 120)

1 teaspoon sea salt

2 cups sprouted barley

4 Sausage Patties (page 208), crumbled

½ cup Cashew Shrimp (page 218)

1. Put the puréed tomatoes, greens, date paste, onion, carrot, celery, jalapeño, garlic, Cajun seasoning, salt, and barley in a bowl. Whisk to combine. Let the mixture sit at room temperature for 1 hour. The broth should be flavorful and spicy with a slight sweetness. Add a pinch more salt if needed to bring out the flavors.
2. Fold in the crumbled sausage. Divide among 4 large bowls and garnish with the cashew shrimp.
3. Serve immediately or cover and refrigerate up to 4 days.

GNOCCHI CARBONARA

Rich and decadent best describe these dumplings tossed with a creamy nut cheese. At Grezzo, fresh English peas and their sweet, tender shoots accompany the gnocchi, made with nuts, spices, and lemon juice, but snow peas, snap peas, and arugula are more readily available. While several steps are involved, much of the preparations can be done ahead of time. This recipe yields a lot of gnocchi, but they don't require any dehydrating and stay fresh for at least four days. The cream sauce should be made the day of serving the gnocchi. The crispy eggplant "bacon" needs two days in the dehydrator, but it can be omitted if you don't have time. This is one of our most popular dishes at Grezzo; we can never take it off the menu! Serve 15 to 20 per person as a first course or as a side dish.

• • • Makes about 115 to 125 gnocchi • • •

3½ cups cashews

½ cup pine nuts

3 garlic cloves, grated on a
   Microplane rasp

2 tablespoons ground cumin

3 tablespoons Nama Shoyu

Juice of 2 lemons

1 cup Sunflour (page 41) or 1 cup
   cashew flour (page 106)

¼ cup fresh peas

Rawmesan (page 292)

Fleur de sel

Freshly ground black pepper

Extra virgin olive oil

½ pound arugula or pea shoots

About 30 slices Eggplant Bacon
   (page 115)

1. Put the cashews in a food processor, and blend until they reach a flour-like consistency. Pour into a bowl and set aside. Do not wash out the food processor.

2. Combine the pine nuts, garlic, and cumin in the food processor and process until it has the consistency of nut butter. Cut the pine nut butter into the cashew flour with your hands to make sure it is thoroughly incorporated. Return this mixture to the food processor.

3. Combine ½ cup water, the Nama Shoyu, and lemon juice in a measuring cup. With the machine running, drizzle in the liquid through the hole in the top and blend until the mixture looks like a moist dough. If the dough seems too wet, add a sprinkle of flour and pulse a few times to incorporate. The dough should be wet and sticky, not a stiff ball.

4. Turn out the gnocchi dough—use a spatula to remove every bit—onto a large cutting board dusted with Sunflour. Knead with the flour until ball of dough forms. Divide the dough into 5 or 6 pieces. Using the palms of both hands, gently roll each piece into 1-inch-thick coils. Take note of the dough's consistency. If the dough crumbles as you try to roll it out, then it's too dry. Return the dough to the food processor and add a tablespoon or more of water until it is the right consistency.

5. Diagonally cut the coils of dough into ¹/₂-inch pieces with a knife. Transfer the gnocchi to a sheet tray or large platter and top with a dusting of flour. Cover and refrigerate until needed, up to 4 days in advance.

6. Toss the gnocchi, peas, and some of the Rawmesan in a large bowl. Divide the dressed gnocchi among dinner plates. Sprinkle with a pinch of salt and some pepper. Drizzle on a bit of Rawmesan, if desired, and some olive oil. Arrange the pea shoots and crumbled eggplant bacon on top and serve.

LAND AND SEA

Land and Sea is our raw version of surf and turf. Sea vegetables play the surf role; mushrooms represent the turf. Allow enough time for the mushrooms to marinate and become soft. It may look complicated, but the Herb Oil and Grezzo Ricotta can be prepared ahead. Although we call for a mix of mushrooms, any combination can be used. Finally, the dish is assembled in small ring molds for an elegant presentation. Ring molds are available in kitchenware stores. If you don't have molds, then layer the ingredients in stemmed glasses.

• • • Makes 4 servings • • •

1 cup chopped cremini mushrooms

¼ cup Nama Shoyu

3 cups gently torn mushrooms, such as maitake, oyster, chanterelle,
   or trumpet

½ cup extra virgin olive oil

1 tablespoon freshly squeezed lemon juice

Sea salt

½ teaspoon freshly ground black pepper

2 tablespoon chopped herbs, such as parsley, tarragon, thyme,
   and/or rosemary

1 cup soaked seaweed, such as dulse, kelp, or nori

1 cup Grezzo Ricotta (page 146)

4 cups assorted greens, such as watercress, arugula, and endive

2 red radishes, thinly shaved

1 teaspoon white truffle oil

Herb Oil (page 113), optional

1. Put the cremini mushrooms and Nama Shoyu in a bowl. Toss well and set aside to marinate for 10 minutes.
2. Put the mushroom mixture, olive oil, lemon juice, ½ teaspoon salt, black pepper, and herbs in a bowl. Toss gently, making sure that all the mushrooms are well coated with the oil and other seasonings. Set aside to marinate.
3. Divide the cremini mixture among 3 x 3-inch cylindrical ring molds set on dinner plates. Put equal amounts of the sea vegetables on top of the mushrooms, firmly pushing it down. Put equal amounts of ricotta on top of the sea vegetables, then add the marinated mixed mushrooms. Set aside while assembling the salad.
4. Put the greens and radishes in a bowl and toss with the truffle oil and a pinch of salt.
5. To release the mold, press down on the filling and lift up the mold; everything should slide right through in one tower. Add some salad to each plate and serve immediately, garnishing with herb oil, if using.

MEDITERRANEAN-STYLE PRESSED LASAGNA

This large stacked tower is extremely impressive with layer upon layer of flavor, color, and texture. It's best when served warm from the dehydrator. The shiitake ricotta is creamy, the pasta provides texture, and the flavors all complement each other.

• • • Makes 8 servings • • •

5 medium zucchini, sliced lengthwise into long thin strips on a mandoline

½ cup Herb Oil (page 113)

Sea salt and freshly ground black pepper

2 tomatoes, quartered

½ cup pitted olives

2 cups Quick Cheese (page 129) *or* Grezzo Cheese (page 132), made with macadamia nuts

3 garlic cloves, grated on a Microplane rasp

2 tablespoons chopped fresh rosemary leaves

1 teaspoon crushed red pepper flakes

Sea salt

1 teaspoon freshly ground black pepper

1 pound shiitake mushroom caps, torn

2 tablespoons Garlic Oil (page 114)

1 pound baby spinach

2 tomatoes, thinly sliced

1. Lay the zucchini strips out on baking sheets. Using a pastry brush, brush each layer of zucchini with the herb oil. Lightly salt and pepper each layer and set aside.
2. Put the tomato quarters and olives in a food processor and blend until smooth. Add the cheese, garlic, rosemary, red pepper, 1 teaspoon salt, and the black pepper. Pulse until the mixture is creamy. Transfer to a bowl. Using a spatula, fold in the shiitakes until thoroughly coated. Set aside.
3. Whisk the garlic oil and a pinch of salt together in a bowl. Add the spinach and toss to coat.
4. To layer the lasagna, you'll need an 8-inch square pan. Cut the zucchini slices into 8-inch lengths. Layer the lasagna as follows: zucchini, spinach, shiitake cheese, and tomato slices, then repeat.
5. Cover the pan with parchment paper and using water-filled jars, weight down the lasagna and refrigerate for 3 to 4 hours. To serve, cut pieces and garnish with any remaining herb oil. Cover any leftovers and refrigerate for up to 5 days.

ANGEL HAIR PASTA AND MARINARA SAUCE

Use a spiral slicer to make the thinnest possible strands of pasta for this dish. The sauce can be made a few hours ahead—the sooner it's served the better, but the zucchini should be sliced just before tossing it with the sauce.

• • • Makes 2 servings • • •

2 medium zucchini, cut into angel hair on a spiral slicer

Marinara Sauce (page 298)

1. Put the angel hair pasta in a large serving bowl and set aside.
2. Pour the sauce over the angel hair zucchini pasta and serve.

WILD MUSHROOM FETTUCCINE

A rich, creamy pasta dish that can be made with a variety of mushrooms. If desired, garnish with some arugula and Pickled Garlic (page 160). Shaved Brazil nuts on top look like Parmesan.

• • • Makes 4 servings • • •

2 cups chopped mushrooms, such as cremini, shiitake, oyster, or chanterelle

2 garlic cloves, grated on a Microplane rasp

1 Anaheim chile, sliced into thin rings

1 shallot, minced

3 tablespoons extra virgin olive oil

3 tablespoons apple cider vinegar

1 tablespoon paprika

2 teaspoons Mushroom Seasoning (page 123)

½ teaspoon plus a pinch of sea salt

½ teaspoon plus a pinch of freshly ground black pepper

5 large zucchini, peeled into long strands using a vegetable peeler

2 cups Saffron Sauce (page 300)

1. Put the mushrooms, garlic, chile, shallot, olive oil, vinegar, paprika, seasoning, ½ teaspoon salt, and ½ teaspoon pepper in a bowl. Toss to combine thoroughly. Set aside.
2. Season the zucchini with a pinch of salt and pepper and toss with the mushroom mixture.
3. Toss with the saffron sauce to coat. Divide among 4 plates and serve immediately.

BUTTERNUT SQUASH RAVIOLI

A delicious seasonal entree that can be made nut-free. Choose the ripest, most flavorful pumpkin or squash available.

• • • Makes 4 servings • • •

½ cup coconut oil, melted

½ cup extra virgin olive oil

5 vanilla bean pods

2 large turnips, thinly sliced on a mandoline

4 cups chopped pumpkin, butternut squash, or other winter squash

Juice of 1 orange

¼ cup agave nectar *or* 4 to 5 dates, plus more if needed

1 cardamom pod

1 whole allspice berry

Coconut water if needed

4 cups baby spinach

2 garlic cloves, grated on a Microplane rasp

Sea salt and freshly ground black pepper

1 cup Coconut-Curry Sauce (page 304)

1 teaspoon black sesame seeds

1 cup Candied Pecans (page 216)

¼ cup mixed chopped fresh sage, basil, and/or cilantro

1. Put the olive and coconut oils in a jar, add the vanilla pods, and store in the dehydrator overnight to infuse.

2. Generously brush baking sheets with the oil. Arrange the turnips on the oiled sheets in a single layer. Generously brush the turnip slices with the oil.

3. Combine the pumpkin, orange juice, agave, cardamom, and allspice in a Vita-Mix. Cover the Vita-Mix and, using a tamper, blend to a smooth and fluffy consistency. Add a splash of coconut water if necessary to reach the desired creamy and rich consistency. Some squashes and pumpkins are naturally sweeter than others. If necessary, add a little more sweetener.

4. Toss the spinach with the grated garlic cloves, salt and pepper to taste, and ½ cup of the curry sauce to coat the leaves. Divide among 4 plates. One by one, put a small dollop of filling in the center of the round turnip wrappers. Gently fold in half, pressing around the edges, allowing the oil to seal the ravioli. Arrange the ravioli on the plates. Drizzle on more curry sauce and sprinkle with the sesame seeds, pecans, and herbs. Serve immediately, or the wrappers, filling, and sauce can be individually covered and refrigerated for up to 3 days.

. . . .

STAR ANISE PAPAYA STEAK

A stunning dish with three components—spice-rubbed and glazed papaya slices, vegetable vermicelli in a creamy dill sauce, and a salad of cucumber, green olive, and radish.

• • • Makes 4 servings • • •

1 papaya, peeled, seeded, and carved (see Cold Smoked Papaya, page 206)

¼ cup Nama Shoyu

¼ cup agave nectar

1 tablespoon Sichuan peppercorns, ground

1 tablespoon ground star anise

4 carrots, peeled into strips

4 parsnips, peeled into strips

1 cup shredded radicchio

1 cup shredded fennel

1 cup Creamy Horseradish-Dill Sauce (page 301)

1 cucumber, preferably seedless, sliced into thin rounds

3 red radishes, thinly sliced

12 jalapeño-stuffed olives, sliced

¼ cup olive brine

1 tablespoon mustard seeds, ground

1 tablespoon caraway seeds, ground

1. Arrange the carved papaya steaks on a platter. Whisk together the Nama Shoyu and agave to create a teriyaki sauce. Brush the sauce all over papaya steaks and allow to pool in the platter so the marinade has a chance to reduce and the steaks can be basted. Combine the Sichuan peppercorns and star anise in a bowl. Dust the papaya steaks with the spice blend.
2. Dehydrate for 3 hours, basting with the teriyaki sauce every 30 minutes.
3. Put the carrots, parsnips, radicchio, and fennel in a bowl. Add the dill horseradish sauce, toss, and set aside.
4. Put the cucumbers, radishes, olives, brine, and mustard and caraway seeds in a bowl. Toss well and let marinate for 10 to 15 minutes.
5. Slice the papaya steaks into 4 pieces, place on plates, and drizzle with remaining sauce. Add some vegetable vermicelli and cucumber salad to each plate.
6. Refrigerate the papaya steaks for up to 2 days after they have been dehydrated.

. . . .

RED CURRY IN COCONUT

This spicy red curry dish is slurped right out of the baby Thai coconut. Scrape the coconut meat right from the shell as you indulge. Fun and impressive.

• • • Makes 3 servings • • •

For the Red Curry Paste

1 shallot

1 stalk lemongrass, chopped fine

2 Thai chilis

4 cloves garlic

1 thumb-size piece ginger

¼ cup chopped tomato

1½ teaspoons agave nectar

1 teaspoon coriander seeds

¼ teaspoon black pepper

3 tablespoons Nama Shoyu

2 tablespoons cayenne pepper

½ cup coconut milk (page 108)

Juice of 1 lime

½ teaspoon ground cinnamon

Blend all ingredients in a food processor until thoroughly combined. Store covered and airtight for up to 1 week.

For the Red Curry in Coconut

4 tablespoons Red Curry Paste

4 cups coconut milk (page 108)

1 cup tightly packed coconut meat

2 carrots, shredded

1 cup snow peas

1 cup diced pineapple

¼ cup chopped fresh herbs, such as mint, cilantro, and basil

1 cup whole cashews

1 red bell pepper, sliced thin

1 tablespoon Nama Shoyu

3 young Thai coconuts, tops lopped off, water reserved for a different use

3 tablespoons dried shredded coconut

1. Put the curry paste, coconut milk, and coconut meat in a Vita-Mix. Blend to a purée. Pour into a large bowl.
2. Stir in the carrots, snow peas, pineapple, herbs, cashews, pepper, and Nama Shoyu.
3. Ladle the curry concoction into the coconuts. Garnish with dried coconut and a few drops of Nama Shoyu.

ENCHILADAS

When fresh corn is in season, scrape the kernels off the cobs, put them in plastic bags, and freeze so you can enjoy these enchiladas on a cold winter night. In fact, frozen corn works best; fresh imparts an odd flavor to the tortilla batter. Serve with Guacamole (page 226) and Confetti Wild Rice Salad (page 271). Prepare them in the morning for that evening's dinner.

• • • Makes 2 enchiladas • • •

4 cups frozen corn kernels, thawed

½ cup ground flax meal

½ cup freshly squeezed orange juice

1 garlic clove

Sea salt

3 to 4 cups finely diced mixed vegetables, such as red peppers, spinach, mushrooms, and/or zucchini

¼ cup extra virgin olive oil

Dash of cumin

Dash of chili powder

1. Put the corn, flax seeds, orange juice, garlic, and ¼ teaspoon salt in a food processor. Blend into a thick batter.
2. Using a ladle, drop the tortilla batter onto Teflex-lined dehydrator sheets and spread about ⅛ inch thick to make one large square. Dehydrate for 3 hours, remove the Teflex, and dehydrate on the other side for 1 to 2 hours. The tortilla may still be soft at this point, but it will be returned to the dehydrator after it is filled.

3. Toss the mixed vegetables, olive oil, ⅛ teaspoon salt, the cumin, and chili powder together in a large bowl. Let the vegetable mixture marinate for 30 minutes to 1 hour before assembling the enchiladas.

4. Slice the tortilla in half so you have two large pieces. Place one quarter of the vegetable mixture down the center of each tortilla half in a long thick strip. Roll up the tortillas. Seal the "seam" with your fingers and a little water if necessary. (The ends will still be open; that's fine.)

5. Return the tortillas to the dehydrator for 1 to 2 hours, until soft and pliable as tortillas should be. Don't let them get too crisp. Serve immediately or cover and refrigerate for up to 2 days.

. . . .

BUDDHA BOWL

Buddha means "the awakened one." With its bright, spicy flavors, this fruit-and-vegetable dish awakens the palate. This intense broth can also be enjoyed on its own.

• • • Makes 4 servings • • •

2 pitted dates

2 tablespoons chopped fresh ginger

3 scallions, halved

1 large jalapeño chile

2 garlic cloves

3 cups coconut water, coconut milk, or Mushroom Tea (page 310)

1 mango, peeled, pitted, and sliced in thin strips

1 avocado, peeled, pitted, and sliced into thin strips

1 small daikon radish, cut into matchstick pieces

2 large carrots, peeled into long strips using a vegetable peeler

2 cups sprouted mung beans

4 small bok choy leaves, horizontally sliced into long strips

1 cup snow peas

¼ cup torn fresh herbs, such as basil, cilantro, and/or mint

1. Put the dates, ginger, scallions, jalapeño, and garlic in a food processor. Blend until finely chopped.

2. Add the coconut water and blend until combined, about 30 seconds. If not using immediately, cover and store in the refrigerator for up to 3 days.

3. Toss the mango, avocado, daikon, carrots, sprouts, bok choy, and snow peas together in a large bowl. Add the broth and herbs and toss everything together.

4. Divide the mixture among 4 bowls and serve immediately.

TOMATO RAVIOLI

A simple but elegant dish that requires the freshest of ingredients—ripe summer tomatoes, bright fresh herbs, and soft greens. Garnish with some edible flowers and chile and truffle oil, if you wish. We provide instructions for creating just one serving, but make as many as you wish. Olive oil is used below, but any infused oil adds a nice touch. A platter of these accompanied with Breadsticks (page 382) makes a quick dinner or good first course for a party. Although this dish is light, it is quite satisfying and filling without leaving you feeling heavy or stuffed.

• • • Makes 1 serving • • •

1 tablespoon extra virgin olive oil, plus more for serving

1 small garlic clove

1 large tomato, cut into 10 thin slices on a mandoline

6 tablespoons Grezzo Cheese (page 132) *or* cheese of your choice

Sea salt and freshly ground black pepper to taste

1 tablespoon chopped fresh basil

1 cup Bibb, butter, baby arugula, or other soft lettuce leaves *or* sprouts

1. Drizzle the olive oil onto a serving plate. Using a Microplane rasp, grate the garlic onto the oil and spread with the back of a spoon to make a quick garlic oil.
2. Arrange 5 tomato slices on the garlic oil. Top each tomato slice with a dab of cheese, then add another tomato slice to create a tomato ravioli. Sprinkle with salt, pepper, and basil.
3. Add the lettuce to the plate and serve with additional olive oil for drizzling.

JAMBALAYA

Here's our raw version of the Creole classic using wild rather than white rice. Since wild rice doesn't sprout as much as other grains (it's actually a grass), you'll need 3½ cups to yield 4 sprouted cups. For added flavor, leftover Bloody Mary mix (page 402) can be substituted for the tomato sauce. An arugula salad and Breadsticks (page 382) make nice accompaniments.

• • • Makes 4 servings • • •

1 cup diced onion

1 cup diced green pepper

1 cup diced celery

4 garlic cloves, grated on a Microplane rasp

1 tablespoon Cajun Seasoning (page 120)

1 teaspoon sea salt

1 teaspoon freshly ground black pepper

3 tablespoons extra virgin olive oil

4 cups sprouted and drained wild rice

2 cups Pomodoro Sauce (page 297) or Marinara Sauce (page 298)

1. Put the onion, bell pepper, celery, garlic, Cajun seasoning, ½ teaspoon of the salt, ½ teaspoon of the pepper, and the olive oil in bowl. Toss to combine. Arrange the vegetables on Teflex-lined dehydrator sheets. Dehydrate for 2 hours, or until the vegetables become translucent and soft.

2. Put the wild rice in a food processor. Pulse until the rice is broken up into small pieces. Transfer to a serving bowl.

3. Add the vegetables and sauce to the rice and let sit for 15 minutes so the flavors can combine and the rice has a chance to soften. Season with the remaining ½ teaspoon salt and ½ teaspoon pepper and serve.

. . . .

CRACKERS and WRAPS: THE BREADBASKET

Those who embark on a raw foods lifestyle often say that they miss crusty bread, crunchy crackers, or thin wraps for favorite fillings. The recipes in this chapter provide those much-missed textures.

The breads and crackers are quickly put together in a food processor or Vita-Mix, and then dried in a dehydrator. Make large batches of crackers; they last for several weeks.

An offset spatula will help when spreading the batter to make paper-thin crackers and consistent wraps and dough. All chips and crackers may be stored in the dehydrator until ready to be served.

SALT AND VINEGAR POTATO CHIPS

The longer these are left in the dehydrator, the crispier they will become. The potatoes must be rinsed and soaked to remove the starch.

• • • Makes 1 good-size bowl of chips • • •

4 large russet potatoes, thinly sliced on a mandoline

6 cups apple cider vinegar

¼ cup sea salt

1. Thoroughly rinse the potatoes in cold water several times to remove excess starch. Drain well in a colander.
2. Whisk together the vinegar, salt, and 2 cups water in large bowl. Add the potatoes, making sure they're all covered by the brine, and soak overnight.
3. Remove from the brine and arrange the chips in single layers on dehydrator racks and dehydrate for 18 to 24 hours, until crisp. Store in a sealed container at room temperature.

SWEET POTATO CHIPS

This is a crunchy accompaniment to cocktails and sandwiches. Increase the amount as you wish. For delicious chips, it's important to rinse the sweet potatoes to remove the starch.

• • • Makes 1 good-size bowl of chips • • •

3 sweet potatoes, peeled and thinly sliced on a mandoline
4 to 5 vanilla bean pods
Sea salt and freshly ground black pepper

1. Rinse the sweet potatoes slices with cold water several times and drain to remove the starch.
2. Soak the sweet potatoes and vanilla pods in a large bowl with fresh water for 3 hours.
3. Remove from the water and arrange the chips in single layers without touching on dehydrator racks. Sprinkle with salt and pepper.
4. Dehydrate for 18 to 24 hours; the longer the better. Store the crisp chips in sealed containers at room temperature.

NORI CHIPS

Keep a batch of these on hand in your car or your desk for nibbling.

• • • Makes 1 tray of chips • • •

1 cup Sunflour (page 41)

¼ cup freshly squeezed lemon juice

2 teaspoons curry powder

⅛ teaspoon cayenne pepper

¼ teaspoon ground cumin

½ teaspoon freshly grated ginger

2 tablespoons chopped scallions

¼ teaspoon paprika

½ cup coarsely chopped carrots

Sesame seeds

3 nori sheets

1. Put the Sunflour, lemon juice, curry powder, cayenne, cumin, ginger, scallions, paprika, carrots, and sesame seeds in a food processor. Blend well until the mixture is the consistency of oatmeal cookie batter.

3. Divide and spread the mixture ¼ inch thick on the nori sheets. Place the nori on Teflex-lined dehydrator racks.

4. Dehydrate for 5 to 7 hours. Carefully remove the racks one at a time, turn them over, and peel off the Teflex sheets. Return the racks to the dehydrator and dehydrate for another 5 to 7 hours, depending on the degree of crispness desired. Cut or break the chips into small squares and store at room temperature in a covered container for up to 2 weeks.

Greek Pizza

Gnocchi Carbonara

Land and Sea

Mediterranean-Style Pressed Lasagna

Wild Mushroom Fettuccine

Star Anise Papaya Steak

Chocolate Torte

New York–Style Cheesecake

CORN CHIPS

Scoop up Guacamole (page 226) or Tomato Salsa (page 223) with these homemade corn chips.

• • • Makes 2 to 2½ trays of chips • • •

4 cups fresh corn and corn milk
   scraped from cobs

4 celery stalks, chopped

2 jalapeño chiles, halved

1 red bell pepper, quartered and
   seeded

¼ cup chopped fresh cilantro

2 tablespoons freshly squeezed lime juice

1 tablespoon ground cumin

1 teaspoon sea salt

1 teaspoon freshly ground black pepper

1 cup almond flour (page 106)

1 cup flax meal

1. Put the corn kernels and milk, celery, chiles, bell pepper, cilantro, lime juice, cumin, salt, and pepper in a food processor. Blend until all the ingredients are well combined. Add the almond flour and flax meal; blend to combine. The batter should have the consistency of wet cornmeal. If the batter is too thick to spread, add water, 1 tablespoon at a time.

2. Using an offset spatula, spread the batter ¼ inch thick on Teflex-lined dehydrator racks. Dehydrate for 12 hours. Carefully remove the racks one at a time, turn them over, and peel off the Teflex sheets. Return the racks to the dehydrator and dehydrate for another 2 to 4 hours, depending on degree of crispness desired. Break the chips into small pieces and store at room temperature in a covered container for up to 3 weeks.

KALE CHIPS

To say these are good is an understatement. Be careful when tasting them to see if they're done, or you might not have any left.

• • • Makes 1 huge bowl of chips • • •

½ cup extra virgin olive oil
½ cup Nama Shoyu
⅓ cup apple cider vinegar
⅓ cup freshly squeezed lemon juice
⅓ cup Tahini Dressing (page 296)
2 garlic cloves, crushed
2 large bunches of kale, torn into large pieces

1. Combine the olive oil, Nama Shoyu, vinegar, lemon juice, tahini dressing, and garlic in a Vita-Mix. Blend until smooth.
2. Tear the leaves from the large stems in the center of each kale leaf. Soak the leaves in a large bowl of cool water, swishing the kale around several times to remove any sand or dirt. You may have to do this several times. Once the kale is clean, shake off any excess water, but the leaves should be damp.
3. Toss the kale leaves with the tahini mixture until all the leaves are coated.
4. Arrange the kale leaves in single layers on Teflex-lined dehydrator racks. Dehydrate for 3 to 4 hours, until crisp.
5. Store in a covered container at room temperature for 2 to 3 days. These chips don't hold up well in humid weather.

SUNFLOWER AND PUMPKIN SEED CRACKERS

Made with sunflower and pumpkin seeds instead of the usual flax, these crackers are thicker in texture and more likely to crumble than flax-based crackers. Serve them alone or with dips and cheeses.

• • • Makes one 12- x 15-inch sheet that can • • •
be broken up into crackers

1 cup chopped spinach leaves

2 carrots, coarsely chopped

1 cup sun-dried tomatoes, soaked
    in water for 2 to 3 hours

½ cup seeded and chopped red
    bell pepper

½ cup chopped fresh parsley

1 cup chopped red onion

2 teaspoons Nama Shoyu

2 garlic cloves

1 cup sunflower seeds, soaked in water
    for 8 hours

1 cup pumpkin seeds, soaked in water
    for 8 hours

1. Combine the spinach, carrots, tomatoes, bell pepper, parsley, onion, Nama Shoyu, and garlic in a food processor and blend until it resembles oatmeal cookie batter.
2. Add the soaked seeds and blend until smooth.
3. Spread the batter ¼ inch thick on Teflex-lined dehydrator racks. Dehydrate for 5 to 7 hours. Turn the crackers over, peel off the Teflex sheets, and dehydrate for another 5 to 7 hours, depending on the degree of crispness desired. Break them into random pieces. Store the crackers in a covered container at room temperature.

Making Crackers

It's hard to say just how many crackers each recipe will yield, because the batter isn't scored before going into the dehydrator. Instead, the batter is thinly spread in layers on Teflex-lined dehydrator racks. Dehydrate as instructed in each recipe, remove the racks, flip the crackers over, and peel off the Teflex. Return the racks to the dehydrator and continue to dry. Once the cracker sheets are crisp, remove them from the dehydrator and break them into random pieces. Store the crackers in a covered container at room temperature.

VEGETABLE CRACKERS

Keep these crisp flax seed crackers packed with vegetables on hand for nibbling and serving with cheese, salsas, and dips.

• • • Makes two 12- x 15-inch sheets that can • • •
be broken up into crackers

2 cups whole flax seeds, soaked in 2 cups water for at least
    4 hours or overnight
1 head red leaf lettuce
1 head green leaf lettuce
4 whole baby bok choy
4 celery stalks, cut into large pieces
1 cucumber, peeled
1 cup seeded and chopped green bell pepper
Juice of 3 limes
1 tablespoon sea salt

1. Put all the ingredients in a food processor. Blend until well mixed. (This may have to be done in two stages if your processor isn't large enough.)
2. Spread the batter about ½ inch thick on 2 Telfex-lined dehydrator racks.
3. Dehydrate for 5 to 7 hours. Turn the crackers over, peel off the Teflex sheets, and dehydrate for another 5 to 7 hours, depending on degree of crispness desired. Break them into random pieces. Store the crackers in a covered container at room temperature.

RED ONION AND DILL CRACKERS

Crisp crackers packed with vegetables and dill.

• • • Makes two 12- x 15-inch sheets that can • • •
be broken up into crackers

2 cups whole flax seeds, soaked in 2 cups water for at least
    4 hours or overnight
2 carrots, shredded
¼ cup thinly sliced red onion
½ cup chopped fresh dill
¼ teaspoon sea salt

1. Combine all the ingredients in a bowl and stir until well mixed.
2. Spread the batter about ⅛ inch thick on 2 Teflex-lined dehydrator racks.
3. Dehydrate for 5 to 7 hours. Turn the crackers over, peel off the Teflex sheets, and dehydrate for another 5 to 7 hours, depending on the degree of crispness desired. Break up the sheets into crackers. Crisp crackers will keep indefinitely in a covered container at room temperature.

HORSERADISH-SCALLION CRACKERS

The horseradish gives these a slight bite. They're great with smoked papaya and dill scallion cheese.

• • • Makes two to three 12- x 15-inch sheets that can • • •
be broken up into crackers

3 pitted dates

4 garlic cloves, grated on a Microplane rasp

5 scallions, chopped

¼ cup freshly grated horseradish

1 tablespoon ground caraway seeds

1 teaspoon sea salt, plus more for sprinkling

1 teaspoon freshly ground black pepper

2 cups flax seeds, soaked in 2 cups water for 4 hours or overnight

1. Put the dates in a food processor and chop finely. Add the garlic, scallions, horseradish, caraway seeds, salt, and pepper and process until incorporated. Add the flax seeds and pulse to incorporate.

2. Spread the batter as thinly as possible on Teflex-lined dehydrator racks and sprinkle with salt. Dehydrate for 10 to 12 hours. Turn the crackers over, peel off the Teflex sheets, and dehydrate for another 2 to 4 hours, until crisp.

3. Remove from the dehydrator and break up the sheets into random pieces. Store the crackers in a covered container at room temperature.

CARAWAY CRACKERS

Spread with Cream Cheese Dip (page 229) and some sliced radishes, scallions, and sesame seeds.

• • • Makes two 12- x 15-inch sheets that can • • •
be broken up into crackers

2 cups flax seeds, soaked in 2 cups water for at least 4 hours or overnight

½ tablespoon minced garlic

1 tablespoon freshly squeezed lemon juice

1 teaspoon sea salt

1½ tablespoons caraway seeds

1. Combine the flax seeds, garlic, lemon juice, and salt in a blender. Blend until combined. Add the caraway seeds and blend for 2 or 3 seconds, just until they're mixed in.

2. Spread the batter about ⅛ inch thick on Teflex-lined dehydrator racks. Dehydrate for 5 to 7 hours. Turn the crackers over, peel off the Teflex sheets, and dehydrate for another 5 to 7 hours, depending on the degree of crispness desired. Break them into random pieces. Store the crackers in a covered container at room temperature.

CROUTONS

We make croutons using a piping bag, but you can also smear the batter ½ inch thick on a Teflex-lined dehydrator rack and score the top with a knife before dehydrating.

• • • Makes about 3 cups • • •

2 cups almonds

1 teaspoon sea salt

1 teaspoon freshly ground black pepper

8 garlic cloves, grated on a Microplane rasp

½ cup chopped mixed fresh herbs, such as parsley, rosemary, and/or thyme

1. Grind the almonds in a food processor to a fine powder. Add the salt and pepper and pulse for 30 seconds. Add the grated garlic and herbs and pulse until well incorporated.

2. Scrape down the sides of the machine. Turn on the food processor and add ½ cup water in a steady stream through the hole in the top. Stop the machine and scrape the sides again. Pulse the mixture until it is thick.

3. Fill a piping bag halfway with the batter and twist the top closed. Pipe ½-inch or 1-inch dollops onto Teflex-lined dehydrator racks.

4. Dehydrate the croutons for 24 to 48 hours. The longer they're in the dehydrator, the crispier they will be. Store in a covered container.

BREADSTICKS

These breadsticks go like hotcakes. It makes sense to prepare a large quantity of them at one time. Plan ahead, as the flax seeds have to soak and the buckwheat needs time to sprout. If you don't have a piping bag to pipe out the breadsticks, make a cone out of parchment paper and snip off the end.

• • • Makes about 60 breadsticks • • •

1 cup Unroasted Peppers (page 116)

5 jalapeño-stuffed olives

1 tomato, quartered

4 garlic cloves, grated on a Microplane rasp

4 cups sprouted buckwheat

2 cups flax seeds, soaked in 2 cups water for at least 4 hours or overnight

2 tablespoons chopped fresh herbs, such as parsley, basil, thyme,
   and/or mint

2 teaspoons sea salt

2 teaspoons freshly ground black pepper

3 tablespoons hemp oil

1. Combine the peppers, olives, tomato, and garlic in a food processor. Blend until the mixture is coarse, like salsa. Add the sprouts and blend until well incorporated. Add the flax seeds and blend until well incorporated. Add the herbs, salt, pepper, and oil and blend to combine until it has the consistency of a thick batter. Taste the batter and adjust for seasoning.

2. Transfer the mixture into a disposable piping bag. Pipe the dough into 12-inch-long breadsticks onto Teflex-lined dehydrator racks, about 20 to each rack. The breadsticks can be close together but should not touch one another.

3. Allow to dehydrate for 12 to 15 hours, until crisp. Store the breadsticks in a covered container at room temperature.

. . . .

RYE ROUNDS

We usually make these round, like burger buns, but the batter can also be spread into a large square, and once dehydrated cut into smaller squares to look like bread. Rye rounds replace English muffins in Lobster Mushrooms Benedict (page 205). To make them, wheat and rye berries should be sprouted for one to two days, just until they show the first signs of tails. Sprouting any longer will give them a fermented flavor.

• • • Makes 8 to 10 bread rounds, about 5 inches in diameter • • •

1 cup wheat berries

1 cup rye berries

¼ cup carob powder

1½ tablespoons ground caraway seeds

1 teaspoon ground coriander

1 teaspoon ground cumin

2 teaspoons sea salt

2 teaspoons freshly ground black pepper

3 tablespoons extra virgin olive oil

½ tablespoon caraway seeds

1. Sprout the wheat and rye berries for 1 to 2 days, just until tails start to emerge.
2. Combine the sprouted berries, ¼ cup water, the carob powder, caraway seeds, coriander, cumin, salt, pepper, and olive oil in a food processor. Process until the mixture is somewhat smooth. There will be some texture.
3. Using an ice cream scoop or a large spoon, drop ½-cup balls of dough on Teflex-lined dehydrator racks. Moisten your hands with water and flatten the dough balls into rounds like hamburger buns about 3 inches in diameter and ¼ inch thick using a circular motion. Sprinkle the rounds with the caraway seeds. Dehydrate for 4 hours, turn them, and dehydrate another 2 hours, until firm but not crisp. Wrap in plastic wrap and store in the refrigerator for up to 3 days.

. . . .

ITALIAN BREAD WRAPS

These wraps are ideal for ALTs—avocado, lettuce, and tomato sandwiches—or spread with cheese.

• • • Makes 6 wraps; 12 servings • • •

2 cups coarsely chopped carrots

½ cup sun-dried tomatoes, soaked in 1 cup water

1 red bell pepper, seeded and diced

3 celery stalks

3 garlic cloves

¼ cup pitted black olives

¼ cup chopped mixed herbs, such as parsley, basil, and/or oregano

1 tablespoon apple cider vinegar

1½ teaspoons sea salt

2 cups ground flax meal

1 cup almond flour (page 106)

1. Put the carrots in food processor. Process to a fine pulp, then transfer to a large bowl.

2. Put the tomatoes and a few tablespoons of soaking water into the food processor. Blend to the consistency of tomato paste. Add the bell pepper, celery, garlic, olives, herbs, vinegar, and salt to the food processor and process until finely chopped. Transfer to the bowl with carrot pulp.

3. Fold the flax meal and almond flour into the vegetables, using a spatula to blend well.

4. Drop the batter in heaping 1-cup measures onto Teflex-lined dehydrator racks. Using an offset spatula dipped in water, spread the batter into six 12-inch circles about ¼ inch thick. Dehydrate for 6 hours, or until the wraps are dry but not hard. Remove the racks from the dehydrator, turn them over, and remove the Teflex. Dehydrate for an additional 2 hours, or until pliable and not too crisp. They need to be flexible enough to fold into wraps. Wrap and store at room temperature for up to 5 days. The wraps should be cut in half before assembling the sandwiches.

. . . .

HOLIDAY STUFFING

This stuffing is moist and comforting—like the real thing. For best results, the vegetables should be coarsely chopped in a food processor.

· · · Makes 4 servings · · ·

3 large carrots, chopped

1 large onion, chopped

4 celery stalks, chopped

1 cup coarsely ground cashews

¼ cup coconut oil

1 teaspoon sea salt

1 teaspoon freshly ground black pepper

½ cup chopped mixed fresh herbs, such as sage, thyme, parsley,
    and/or rosemary

1. Put the carrots, onion, and celery in a food processor. Blend until coarsely chopped. Transfer to a large bowl. Add the cashews and remaining ingredients; toss to combine. The mixture should be crumbly and moist but not wet.
2. Spread the mixture ½ inch thick on a Teflex-lined dehydrator rack. Dehydrate for 8 hours, or until the stuffing reaches the desired consistency. Once dehydrated, serve warm or cover and refrigerate for up to 3 days.

MOCKTAILS, COCKTAILS, *and* OTHER BEVERAGES: GET THE PARTY STARTED

These sophisticated mocktails and cocktails are ideal for all kinds of occasions—brunches and dinner and cocktail parties. Sake infusions are designed to taste like vodka, tequila, rum, and other liquors people are familiar with. Even though they're called bourbon or gin, they are made with sake, a filtered fermented rice wine. And for bubbly nonalcoholic mocktails, kombucha adds a nice fizz.

Our sake infusions are made with apples, figs, cinnamon sticks, vanilla beans, lavender sprigs, tomatoes, and other vegetables, fruits, herbs, and spices. The results are robust infusions bursting with flavor. Combine the infusion ingredients with sake in a large decorative glass container with a lid; they look as fabulous as they taste.

ALMOND JOY

Like a date shake for grown-ups; for a nonalcoholic version, omit the sake.

• • • Makes 1 drink • • •

3 ounces almond milk (page 104)

3 ounces sake

½ vanilla bean pod

1½ tablespoons agave nectar

2 or 3 Rawcona Almonds (page 217)

Fill a tall glass with ice. Put the almond milk, sake, vanilla pod, and agave in a shaker. Shake well and pour into the glass. Garnish with Rawcona Almonds.

BLACKBERRY-SAGE SPRITZER

No blackberries? Create your own combinations with other fruit or try one of the variations. Kombucha adds fizz.

• • • Makes 1 drink • • •

4 sage leaves, torn

4 blackberries

1 teaspoon agave nectar

6 ounces kombucha or sake

Cover the bottom of a tall glass with the sage leaves. Add the blackberries and agave. Use a muddler or a wooden spoon to muddle or mash the ingredients. Add ice and the kombucha or sake and stir.

> **STRAWBERRY-THAI BASIL SPARKLER** • Follow the directions above using 4 Thai basil leaves and 2 mint leaves and 4 ripe strawberries in place of the sage and blackberries.
>
> **RASPBERRY-THYME SPARKLER** • Follow the directions above using 2 sprigs thyme and 2 tablespoons puréed raspberries in place of the sage and blackberries.

PROSECCO COCKTAIL

A Mimosa is traditionally made with sparkling wine and orange juice. We prefer a combination of various citrus juices—orange, grapefruit, blood orange, Meyer lemon, tangerine—with Prosecco, a much underrated and inexpensive sparkling wine from Italy's Veneto region. Freshly squeezed juice is essential.

• • • Makes 1 drink • • •

5 ounces Prosecco or other sparkling wine

4 ounces freshly squeezed citrus juice

Fill a chilled champagne glass about two-thirds full with Prosecco. Once the bubbles settle, fill the glass with juice.

Sake and Sake Infusions

Although often referred to as "Japanese rice wine," sake is made from rice, which is a grain, so it's technically a liquor. At our restaurants, we use Oregon-made Momokawa Organic Ginjo Sake because it's smooth, has hints of tropical fruits and coconut, and can be infused with an endless variety of fruits, vegetables, herbs, and spices for making cocktails.

If you're going to drink wine or other forms of alcohol, sake is the best choice. It's not raw, but it's not distilled or processed. There is so much tradition, spirituality, and dedication that goes into sake production that we serve it at our restaurants for this reason, as we do wines that are bio-dynamically, organically, and consciously produced.

When making infusions, cut the fruits and vegetables into 1-inch chunks. Put the ingredients in a large, clean glass jar and cover with sake. Store in the refrigerator or in a cool basement. Infusions take anywhere from one day to one week, depending on the ingredients and how intensely flavored you like them. Once infused to your satisfaction, strain the sake into another clean jar and discard the solids. (The infused fruit will be so potent that only the strong of heart will be able to handle them.) Infused sakes will keep up to three months.

We offer recipes (and they can all be doubled) for several infusions, but we encourage you to experiment with your own combinations or the ones suggested here.

Pear-Vanilla	Raspberry-Lime	Plum-Rosemary
Lemongrass–Thai Basil	Cranberry-Clove	Watermelon-Mint
Cucumber–Lemon Thyme	Cold-Smoked Cherry	Green Apple–Ginger
Pineapple-Ginger		

"BOURBON" SAKE INFUSION

• • • Makes 1 quart • • •

3 to 4 apples

4 crushed cinnamon sticks

5 vanilla bean pods

5 bay leaves

1 (750-ml) bottle sake

Combine all the ingredients in a large jar, cover, and infuse to your desired taste, then strain into a clean jar and cover. Store in the refrigerator.

LAVENDER-JUNIPER SAKE INFUSION

• • • Makes 1 quart • • •

4 fresh lavender sprigs *or* 2 tablespoons culinary lavender

2 tablespoons juniper berries

1 (750-ml) bottle sake

Tie the lavender and juniper in a sachet and submerge in the sake. Cover and infuse to taste, then strain into a clean jar and cover. Store in the refrigerator.

PEACH-SAGE SAKE INFUSION

· · · Makes 1 quart · · ·

5 ripe peaches
20 to 25 sage leaves, torn
1 (750-ml) bottle sake

Combine the peaches, sage, and sake in a large, clean jar. Cover and allow to infuse to taste, then strain into a clean jar and cover. Store in the refrigerator.

MINT SAKE INFUSION

· · · Makes 2 cups · · ·

2 cups sake
½ cup fresh mint leaves

Combine the sake and mint in a glass jar. Let infuse overnight at room temperature. Strain the mint into a clean jar so the infusion doesn't become bitter. Cover.

GREZZO RUM

4 cups sake

1 cup dry figs, roughly torn up so insides are exposed

1 cup medjool dates, pitted

¼ cup yakon syrup

4 leftover vanilla bean pods

Put all ingredients in a covered glass jar. Shake really well to combine. Let infuse for at least 24 hours before using. Store in refrigerator for up to 2 weeks. Do not strain.

SAKEQUILA INFUSION

· · · Makes 1 quart · · ·

15 fresh thyme sprigs

3 lemongrass stalks, root ends smashed

3 jalapeño chiles, halved

1 (750-mi) bottle sake

Combine the thyme, lemongrass, jalapeños, and sake in a large clean jar. Cover and allow to infuse to taste, then strain into a clean jar and cover.

DIRTY TOMATO INFUSION

Save all those tomato odds and ends from making salads, soups, and sauces and make this infusion at the height of tomato season.

• • • Makes 1 quart • • •

4 cups chopped tomatoes and/or tomato scraps

2 tablespoons black peppercorns

1 (750-ml) bottle sake

Combine the tomatoes, peppercorns, and sake in a large clean jar. Cover and allow to infuse to taste, then strain into a clean jar and cover.

LYNCHBURG LEMONADE

This cocktail is traditionally made with Jack Daniel's whiskey, which is distilled in Lynchburg, Tennessee. We created a bourbon-like sake infusion and added some fresh herbs for our version of this Southern classic.

• • • Makes 1 drink • • •

Squeeze of 1 lemon wedge

2 thyme sprigs

3 mint leaves

1 tablespoon agave nectar

6 ounces "Bourbon" Sake Infusion (page 394)

Lemon twist

Put the lemon juice in a shaker. Add the thyme and mint, and use a muddler or a wooden spoon to muddle or mash the herbs. Add the agave and "Bourbon," fill with ice, and shake well. Pour into a tall glass, garnish with the lemon twist, and serve.

PEACH-SAGE BELLINI

Bellinis are traditionally served in champagne flutes, but we prefer a 10-ounce highball glass so the chunks of peaches may also be enjoyed.

• • • Makes 1 drink • • •

6 ounces Peach-Sage Sake Infusion (page 396)
2 ounces Prosecco or other sparkling wine

Combine the infusion and Prosecco in a glass of your choice and serve.

BLOODY MARYS

Weekend brunch doesn't seem complete unless Bloody (with sake) or Virgin (without) Marys are included. Keep a pitcher of this homemade mix in the fridge to enjoy—without the sake—anytime as a savory breakfast drink or afternoon pick-me-up. It is important to blend the tomatoes separately and quickly as not to overprocess them and lose their bright red color. At Grezzo, we add a hearty measure of sake, but when serving at home, 2 ounces is standard.

• • • Makes 4 quarts • • •

5 large tomatoes, sliced

2 garlic cloves

1 carrot, coarsely chopped

1 jalapeño chile, chopped

1 shallot, chopped

4 celery stalks, coarsely chopped

1 red bell pepper, seeded and coarsely chopped

½ English cucumber, chopped

1 tablespoon yacón syrup *or* 3 tablespoons Date Paste (page 110)

3 jalapeño-stuffed green olives

¼ cup Nama Shoyu

3 teaspoons freshly grated horseradish

¼ cup freshly squeezed lemon juice

1 teaspoon sea salt

1 teaspoon freshly ground black pepper

1 tablespoon ground celery seed

1 tablespoon sea salt

Lime wedges

2 ounces sake per serving, optional

Vegetable skewers

1. Place the tomatoes in a Vita-Mix and purée on high, using the tamper as necessary. Pour the puréed tomatoes into a pitcher.

2. Put the next fourteen ingredients (from garlic to black pepper) in the Vita-Mix and blend. Pour the mixture into a bowl and stir in the tomatoes. Cover and re-frigerate for up to 3 days.

3. Combine the celery seed and sea salt in small saucer. Wipe the rims of tall glasses with the lime wedges and then dip rims into the celery salt mixture. Stir the juice mixture, then pour into the rimmed glass. Add the sake, if using, to each glass, and garnish with a vegetable skewer.

Vegetable Skewers

Bloody Marys are traditionally garnished with a tall celery stalk for stirring, but a bamboo or metal skewer with some colorful pickled vegetables adds variety. Try pickled carrots, cauliflower, mushrooms, sea vegetables, olives, and folded-over radish or daikon slices.

ORANGARITA

Strong, citrusy, and salty—just like a margarita. You can use any sea salt on the rim of the glass, but pink Himalayan looks particularly nice with the citrus juices.

• • • Makes 1 drink • • •

Orange or grapefruit wedge

Ground Himalayan pink salt

4 ounces Sakequila Infusion (page 398)

1 tablespoon Rosemary-Infused Agave (page 437)

1 ounce freshly squeezed grapefruit juice

1 ounce freshly squeezed orange juice

Orange twist, optional

1. Wipe the rim of a wine glass with the orange or grapefruit wedge. Dip the glass in a saucer with pink salt. Wipe the inside of the rim so salt doesn't get into the drink.
2. Fill a shaker with ice. Add the Sakequila, agave, and grapefruit and orange juices. Shake the mixture and pour into a glass. Garnish with an orange twist if you like.

WATERMELON-MINT SAKE COOLER

The perfect cocktail on a hot summer's night.

• • • Makes 1 drink • • •

Himalayan pink salt

½ cup Mint Sake Infusion (page 396)

⅓ cup fresh watermelon juice

Fresh mint leaves

1. Dip the rim of a wet glass in a saucer with pink salt. Wipe the inside of the glass so the drink isn't salty. Fill with ice and set aside.
2. Put the infused sake, watermelon juice, and some ice into a cocktail shaker. Shake well and strain in salt-rimmed glass. Garnish with mint.

GREEN APPLE-GINGER SAKETINI

This subtle cocktail goes well with big-flavored, spicy appetizers like Habanero-Cilantro Cheese (page 140) and Corn Chips (page 373). For a more pronounced apple flavor, cover quartered apples with sake in a jar and infuse overnight.

• • • Makes 1 drink • • •

1 tablespoon freshly grated ginger

6 thin slices Granny Smith apple

5 ounces sake

Use a muddler or a wooden spoon to muddle or mash the ginger and 3 apples slices in the bottom of a cocktail shaker. Fill with ice and the sake. Cover the shaker and shake to combine. Strain into a martini glass, garnish with the remaining 3 apple slices, and serve.

MOJITO

Cuban mojitos go well with Tex-Mex dishes such as Nopales Nachos (page 230) and a jicama-orange salad.

• • • Makes 1 drink • • •

8 large fresh mint leaves, torn

1½ tablespoons freshly squeezed lime juice

2 tablespoons agave nectar

6 ounces kombucha or sake

Thin slice of lime

Put the mint, lime juice, and agave in a tall glass and muddle using a muddler or wooden spoon. Fill the glass with ice and add the kombucha or sake and stir well to combine. Garnish with a slice of lime.

DIRTY TOMATO MARTINI

This is one of our most popular cocktails at Grezzo. To put a spin on the classic dirty vodka Martini, we add sun-dried tomato water, which is made by soaking some sulfite-free sun-dried tomatoes in water overnight. The olive juice is from the jar of jalapeño-stuffed olives.

• • • Makes 1 drink • • •

4 ounces Dirty Tomato Infusion (page 399)

1½ tablespoons sun-dried tomato water

1½ tablespoons olive brine

2 jalapeño-stuffed olives

Fill a cocktail shaker with ice. Add the sake infusion, tomato water, and olive brine. Taste for desired saltiness, adding more tomato water or brine as desired. Shake and strain into a martini glass. Add a toothpick with the jalapeño-stuffed olives to the glass.

LAVENDER AND JUNIPER "GIN" GIMLET

Juniper berries and other botanicals are the primary flavorings in gin, so we make an infused sake version with juniper and lavender. Try your own blend using caraway seeds, cinnamon, citrus zest, or other herbs and spices.

• • • Makes 1 drink • • •

4 ounces Lavender-Juniper Sake Infusion (page 395)

½ tablespoon freshly squeezed lime juice

1 tablespoon freshly squeezed lemon juice

¾ tablespoon agave nectar

Crushed fresh lavender buds

Fill a cocktail shaker with ice. Add the sake infusion, lime and lemon juices, and agave. Cover and shake well. Strain into a chilled martini glass and float a few crushed lavender buds on the top.

LEMON DROP

Bubbly, fresh, and perky, this is a good brunch drink.

• • • Makes 1 drink • • •

5 ounces sake

2½ tablespoons freshly squeezed lemon juice

2 tablespoons agave nectar

Raw cane sugar

1 ounce Prosecco or other sparkling wine

Thin slice of lemon

Fill a cocktail shaker with ice. Add the sake, lemon juice, and agave and shake well. Wipe the rim of a martini glass with lemon and dip the rim into the raw sugar. Strain the mixture into the glass, top with the Prosecco, and garnish with the lemon slice.

DESSERTS:

HOW SWEET IT IS

magine eating dessert every day without guilt? The quickest way to turn someone on to raw foods is to serve them one of these. You won't have to say a word. They speak for themselves, loudly saying "decadent." And no one will even know they are raw. A slice of chocolate or date nut torte, a few biscotti, or coconut meringue will make them speechless. And since they're made with fruits, vegetables, nuts, and seeds, you can eat these any time of day, every day—even for breakfast.

. . . .

STRAWBERRY-APRICOT FUDGE BALLS

Carry these with you for when a craving for something sweet hits. Soaking the dates and apricots for more than 8 hours will cause them to fall apart.

• • • Makes 30 fudge balls • • •

2 cups dates, pitted and soaked in water for 2 to 8 hours

1 cup dried apricots, soaked in water for 2 to 8 hours

1 cup almond butter

½ cup carob power

¾ cup strawberries

1. Put the dates and apricots in a food processor and blend to a smooth paste.
2. Add the almond butter, carob powder, and strawberries and process until smooth.
3. Remove from processor and form into 1-inch balls. They will keep for several weeks in the refrigerator, but they're so good they most likely won't last that long.

CHOCOLATE TRUFFLES

For best results and accuracy, the ingredients for making these truffles must be weighed on a kitchen scale, which can be found in housewares stores. (Note that these are weight, not volume, measurements.)

• • • Makes twenty-four 1-inch truffles • • •

4 ounces cacao butter, melted

4 ounces coconut oil, melted

9 ounces agave nectar

7 ounces cacao powder, sifted

1. Whisk together the cacao butter, coconut oil, and agave in a bowl to combine.
2. Add the cacao powder and vigorously whisk to combine.
3. Using a melon baller, your hands, or a small scoop, roll the mixture into 1-inch balls (allowing this mixture to sit for 15 minutes first will make this step easier). Pressing the mixture into plastic candy molds will work, too. You may then choose to roll the balls in more cacao as a garnish. Allow to set in refrigerator for 1 hour before serving. Cover and refrigerate for up to 2 weeks.

PEPPERMINT TRUFFLES • Add 8 drops essential mint oil in Step 1.

ALMOND BUTTER TRUFFLES • Whisk 1 cup almond butter and a pinch of sea salt into the batter in Step 2.

COCONUT MOUNDS

The easiest dessert in the world—dates filled with coconut, then dipped in chocolate. Make as many as you want.

10 dates, pitted and sliced in half

½ cup dried coconut flakes

½ cup Chocolate Sauce (page 434)

1. Fill each date with a teaspoon of coconut, then dip each date into the chocolate sauce.
2. Arrange the dipped dates on a parchment-paper-lined tray and freeze for 1 hour to firm up. The dates will keep at room temperature for several days.

YOUNG THAI COCONUT MERINGUE

Soften the coconut oil and butter for a few hours before making this spin on a classic French dessert. We suggest layering the meringue with blackberry salsa, but sliced peaches or other fruit work, too.

• • • Makes 6 cups • • •

3 cups tightly packed coconut meat

¾ cup coconut water

Seeds from 2 vanilla beans

¼ cup agave nectar

¾ cup melted coconut oil

¾ cup coconut butter

Blackberry Salsa (page 438)

1. Put the coconut meat and water, vanilla seeds, and agave in a Vita-Mix. Blend until completely smooth in texture. With the machine running, remove the Vita-Mix lid and use a rubber spatula to help the mixture become smooth. As long as the machine is not too full, taking the lid off while the machine is running will not result in splatters. Always replace the cover before stopping the Vita-Mix. Start and stop the machine frequently so as not to let it become too hot and to scrape down the sides as necessary.

2. Add the coconut oil and coconut butter last and blend until well incorporated.

3. Transfer to a container. Cover and let the meringue set in the refrigerator for 8 to 10 hours, or overnight.

4. Alternate layers of blackberry salsa and meringue in martini or parfait glasses and serve immediately.

BROWNIES

Delicious on their own, better with the accompaniments!

• • • Makes 20 brownies • • •

2 cups pecans	4 cups cacao powder
2 cups walnuts	4 cups pitted dates
2 cups hazelnuts	1½ cups agave nectar

1. Put 1 cup each of the pecans, walnuts, and hazelnuts in a food processor. Blend until finely ground. Remove the ground nuts and transfer to a bowl, then repeat with remaining nuts. Put the cacao powder into the food processor and pulse a few times to get rid of any lumps. Add the cacao to the ground nuts and stir to combine.

2. Put the dates and agave in the food processor (no need to wash it). Blend until a coarse paste forms. Remove to another bowl.

3. Put one third of the nut mixture and one third of the date mixture in a food processor (again, no need to wash it). Pulse for about 30 seconds, until the mixture is crumbly and moist. Transfer a bowl. Repeat two more times. When there are three batches in the bowl, mix to combine.

4. Evenly spread the brownie batter into an 11 x 7-inch pan. You can cut the brownies immediately into large or small pieces, or cover and store at room temperature for up to 3 days. If kept for more than 3 days, brownies may begin to dry out. To bring them back to their moist state, rebuzz them in the food processor with a few tablespoons of agave.

RICH BROWNIE SUNDAE

• • • Makes 1 sundae • • •

1 Brownie (page 416)

1 large scoop Vanilla Chip Ice Cream (page 451)

3 tablespoons Chocolate Sauce (page 434)

1 Brazil nut

2 tablespoons macerated fruit, fruit sauce, or fresh fruit

Place a brownie square on a plate and top with large scoop of ice cream. Pour the chocolate sauce over the ice cream and shave the Brazil nut on top, using a Microplane rasp. Add the fruit or sauce.

SUPER COOKIES

Chocolaty and minty, these look and taste like a double-rich peppermint cookie. What makes them super is the addition of blue-green algae. Buy a good-quality blue-green algae at any health food store or online. Whole oats should be made into a flour using the same technique as making a nut flour. Choose the Vita-Mix over the food processor to make oat flour. Just a few quick bursts of the Vita-Mix will yield a light and fluffy flour that can be stored, covered, on the countertop for up to a week. Raw oats should be floured first for this recipe, then measured.

• • • Makes 12 cookies • • •

2½ cups cashew flour (page 106)

1¾ cups oat flour

¾ cup cacao powder

1 tablespoon blue-green algae

1½ teaspoons sea salt

¾ cup agave nectar

8 drops mint essential oil

2 cups Chocolate Frosting (page 435)

1. Combine the cashew and oat flours, cacao powder, algae, and salt in a bowl. In another bowl, mix together ¼ cup water, the agave, and mint oil.

2. Using a spatula, fold the wet ingredients into the dry ingredients. Fold in 1 cup of the frosting.

3. Drop ½-cup circles of batter about 1 inch apart onto Teflex-lined dehydrator racks. With wet hands, press into 4-inch cookies about ½ inch thick. Dehydrate for 8 hours, remove the Teflex, flip the cookies over, and dehydrate for 4 more hours.

4. Spread each cookie with the remaining frosting. Cover and store at room temperature for as long as they last.

OATMEAL COOKIES

Soft and chewy oatmeal cookies, perfect for a bake sale or cookie platter or as a gift.

• • • Makes 8 to 10 cookies • • •

1¾ cups oat flakes

1 banana

½ cup agave nectar

Seeds from 1 vanilla bean

2 tablespoons ground cinnamon

1 cup pecans

1 cup raisins

⅛ teaspoon sea salt

1. Combine 1 cup of the oats, the banana, agave, vanilla seeds, and cinnamon in a food processor. Blend until the ingredients are smooth.
2. Add the pecans and the remaining ¾ cup oats and pulse-chop until the pecans and remaining oats are coarsely chopped. Add the raisins and pulse-chop again until everything is combined to make a batter.
3. Drop ½ cup measures of the batter onto Teflex-lined dehydrator racks. Moisten the palm of your hand with water and press slightly. They should not be perfect circles, and pieces of raisins and nuts will stick out.
4. Dehydrate the cookies 6 hours, remove the racks and turn them over, and peel off the Teflex. Dehydrate for an additional 6 hours. The cookies should be moist but still hold their shape. Store covered at room temperature for up to 5 days.

VANILLA MACAROONS

A classic cookie!

• • • Makes 14 to 16 macaroons • • •

2 cups dried coconut flakes

1 cup almond flour (page 106)

3 tablespoons melted coconut butter

Seeds from 1 vanilla bean

⅔ cup agave nectar

½ teaspoon sea salt

1. Put all the ingredients in a food processor. Process to form a batter.
2. Drop ¼-cup measures of the batter onto Teflex-lined dehydrator racks. Moisten the palm of your hand with water, and press down on each round to make circles approximately ¼ inch thick.
3. Dehydrate the cookies for 6 hours, then turn them and dehydrate an additional 6 hours. The cookies should be moist but still hold their shape. Cover and store at room temperature for up to 5 days.

BISCOTTI

The almonds and buckwheat can be soaked, sprouted, and dehydrated together. Enjoy with a glass of nut milk.

• • • Makes about 24 biscotti • • •

2 cups almonds, soaked, then
  dehydrated for 12 hours

2 cups buckwheat, soaked and sprouted,
  then dehydrated for 12 hours

½ cup agave nectar

½ cup pistachios, coarsely chopped

½ cup dried cranberries, coarsely chopped

½ cup pitted dates, soaked in
  1 cup water for 1 hour, then
  puréed, reserving
  ½ cup soaking water

¼ cup freshly grated ginger

2 teaspoons ground anise seeds

1 teaspoon sea salt

1. Put the almonds and buckwheat in a food processor and blend to a smooth consistency. Transfer the mixture to a large bowl.

2. Add the agave, pistachios, cranberries, date purée, ginger, anise, and salt to the bowl and mix well. Put the dough on a work surface. Using your hands, work into a smooth dough, adding a little of the reserved soaking water if necessary.

3. Shape the dough into a log about 12 inches long and 5 inches wide. Transfer the log to a Teflex-lined dehydrator rack and dehydrate for 8 hours. Remove the log to a cutting board and, using a serrated knife, slice into ½-inch biscotti. Place the cookies ½ inch apart on the dehydrator rack and dehydrate for another 4 hours, until firm but not too hard.

4. Cover and store at room temperature for up to 1 week.

BOSTON MERINGUES

A dried fruit-and-nut base (we call this a doughnut crust because it has the scent and flavor of freshly baked doughnuts) is layered with a creamy coconut and banana filling. Serve in stemmed martini glasses or use ring molds for a more professional look.

• • • Make 8 individual pies • • •

¾ cup hazelnuts

½ cup pecans

½ cup walnuts

1 cup cacao powder

¼ cup pitted dates (about 6 dates)

½ cup agave nectar

1 teaspoon ground nutmeg

Pinch of sea salt

3½ cups tightly packed coconut meat

Seeds from 3 vanilla beans

2 bananas

½ cup Thai coconut water

¾ cup coconut butter

¾ cup coconut oil, melted

1 banana, thinly sliced

1. Reserve ¼ cup of the hazelnuts and set aside. Combine the pecans, walnuts, and remaining ½ cup hazelnuts with the cacao powder in a food processor. Pulse until the nuts are finely chopped but not a powder. Stop the machine as necessary and scrape down the sides so all the nuts are incorporated.

2. Turn on the food processor and add the dates one at a time, again stopping to scrape down the sides.

3. Once all the dates are added, drizzle in ¼ cup of the agave through the hole in the lid. Remove the chocolate dough to a mixing bowl. Put the ¼ cup reserved hazelnuts, the nutmeg, and salt in the food processor (no need to wash it out) and pulse

until finely chopped. Return the chocolate dough to the food processor with the hazelnuts and pulse until the mixture is crumbly.

4. Divide the dough into 8 pieces. Press a piece of dough into the bottoms of eight 3½-inch-tall x 2-inch-wide ring molds to form a base for the meringue. If you don't have ring molds, press the dough into martini glasses. Set aside.

5. Combine the coconut meat, vanilla seeds, banana, remaining ¼ cup agave, and coconut water in a Vita-Mix and blend until the meringue is of a smooth consistency. Blend in the coconut butter and oil. Use the tamper as necessary to make sure all the ingredients are combined and the mixture is as smooth as possible. Scrape the meringue into a large piping bag or bowl and refrigerate for at least 12 hours.

6. About 1 or 2 hours before serving, either spoon or pipe meringue on top of the chocolate doughnut crusts. Return to the refrigerator to set. If using molds, sweep a paring knife around the edges to loosen, and carefully lift the mold up and off the meringue. Serve on plates garnished with banana slices.

MOCHA CREAM PIE • Omit the bananas in the meringue. Add 2 tablespoons cacao powder when making the meringue.

DARK CHOCOLATE MERINGUE • Omit the bananas in the meringue. Add 1 cup cacao powder, an additional ½ cup coconut water, and ½ cup agave when making the meringue.

CHOCOLATE TORTE

A rich, dense chocolate fudge-like filling is poured into a graham cracker crust.

Graham Cracker Crust (page 445)

2 cups cashews, soaked in coconut water
   for 6 hours

¼ cup coconut water

1¼ cups agave nectar

1¼ cups cacao powder

¼ cup coconut meat

1 cup coconut butter, softened

1. Press the crust into the bottom of an 8-inch springform pan and set aside.

2. Put the soaked cashews, coconut water, and agave in a Vita-Mix. Blend until completely smooth, stopping the machine to scrape down the sides with a spatula. Add the cacao powder, coconut meat, and coconut butter and blend until thoroughly combined and the mixture is as smooth as possible. While the Vita-Mix is running, carefully remove the lid and using a spatula, "row" the mixture along to be sure it is in constant motion. This will help the torte become smoother more quickly without the batter becoming too hot. Replace the lid before turning off the machine.

3. Pour the batter into the crust-lined pan. Cover with plastic wrap and chill for at least 8 hours. Remove the springform before slicing. Store in the refrigerator for up to 5 days or freeze for up to 2 weeks.

MEXICAN CHOCOLATE TORTE · Add 1 teaspoon ground cinnamon and 1 teaspoon Puréed Chiles (page 111) with the other ingredients in Step 2.

DATE NUT TORTE

When asked to bring dessert for an occasion, make this quick-and-easy torte. No one will believe it's raw.

• • • Makes 12 to 14 servings • • •

2 cups raisins

2 cups walnuts

1 cup pitted dates, soaked for 2 hours

Juice of ½ lemon

1. Combine the raisins and walnuts in a food processor and blend well until moist. (This will take a few minutes. A ball will form.)
2. Put the raisin-walnut mixture in a 9-inch pie plate. Using your hand, press down.
3. Combine the dates and lemon juice in a food processor and blend until smooth and creamy. Using a butter knife, spread the date-lemon frosting on top of the torte. Serve slices at room temperature when the torte is still sticky. For a firmer texture that's easier to slice, refrigerate the torte for 2 to 3 hours before serving.

ANGEL FOOD CAKE

Satisfying with a morning cup of tea or with a Burdock-Shilajit Latte (page 173) or Muira Puama Cappuccino (page 174). The raspberry jam becomes sticky and syrupy in the dehydrator. This cake is light and fluffy in texture with a bright citrus finish. This recipe is a good way to use up leftover nut and coconut pulp.

• • • Makes 4 servings • • •

1 cup pitted dates

1 cup dried coconut pulp (left over from making coconut milk)

1 cup almond pulp (left over from making almond milk)

½ teaspoon sea salt

1 cup raspberries

½ cup plus 3 tablespoons agave nectar

½ cup cashews

½ cup almond milk (page 104)

2 tablespoons coconut butter

½ teaspoon freshly squeezed lemon juice

1. Put the dates, ¼ cup water, the coconut and almond pulps, and salt in a food processor. Blend until combined.
2. Using your hands, divide and shape the batter into two 5-inch-square cakes about ¾ inch to 1 inch thick on Teflex-lined dehydrator racks. Dehydrate the cakes for 12 hours, or until firm.
3. Combine the raspberries, 1 cup water, and ½ cup of the agave in a shallow dish. Dehydrate for 2 to 3 days. Stir the jam daily. The jam's volume will decrease by

approximately one third. When it's thick and jam-like, transfer to an airtight container refrigerate for up to 1 week.

4. Soak the cashews in the almond milk for 2 hours. Blend the soaked cashews, the remaining 3 tablespoons of agave, the coconut butter, and lemon juice in a Vita-Mix until smooth. Use a little of the almond milk if necessary, but not too much, as you want this to be thick, like frosting.

5. Assemble the cake by generously spreading jam on one cake layer. Top with the other layer and frost generously. Slice the cake into 4 pieces. Serve immediately or cover and refrigerate for up to 3 days.

. . . .

NEW YORK–STYLE CHEESECAKE

Although adding Grezzo Cheese to the batter is optional, it does make this creamy cheesecake even creamier and more authentic in flavor.

• • • Makes one 8-inch cake • • •

2 cups Graham Cracker Crust (page 445)

2 cups macadamia nuts

2 cups cashews

2½ cups coconut water

½ cup agave nectar

¼ cup freshly squeezed lemon juice

Seeds from 3 vanilla beans

2 ripe bananas

¼ cup tightly packed coconut meat

½ cup coconut oil, melted

1 cup Grezzo Cheese (page 132) made with cashews or macadamias, optional

1. Line an 8-inch springform cake pan with the graham cracker crust. Set aside.
2. Soak the macadamias and cashews in the coconut water in a bowl for 8 hours.
3. Put the soaked nuts and any remaining soaking liquid, the agave, lemon juice, and vanilla seeds in a Vita-Mix and blend until smooth. With the machine on, carefully remove the lid. Using a spatula, stir the mixture in a rowing motion to keep it continuously turning over to make sure it's smooth. Replace the lid before turning the machine off. Periodically turn the machine off and scrape down the sides. Do not allow the batter to get hot.

4. Add the banana and coconut meat to the batter and process until smooth.
5. With the machine running, drizzle in the coconut oil. The batter should have a smooth, silky texture. Add the cheese, if desired, to the Vita-Mix and process to incorporate, making sure there are no lumps. Remove the lid while the machine is running and use a spatula to help the batter along.
6. Pour the batter into the prepared pan, cover, and refrigerate for 8 hours before serving. For a quicker set, freeze the cake for 2 hours and then transfer to the refrigerator for 1 hour for the cake to thaw. Serve or cover and refrigerate for up to 1 week.

· · · · · · · · · · · · · · · · ·

LUCUMA CARAMEL CHEESECAKE • Substitute 3 coarsely chopped apples for the bananas. Once the cake is set, frost with 1½ cups Lucuma Caramel Sauce (page 440), allowing the caramel to dribble down the sides.

MARBLE CHEESECAKE • Omit the bananas. Increase the vanilla beans to 5 and the coconut meat to 1 cup. Once the batter is in the pan, but not yet set, swirl in 1 cup Chocolate Sauce (page 434), using a chopstick.

SUGAR PUMPKIN CHEESECAKE • Omit the lemon juice and banana. Once the coconut oil has been incorporated, fold in 4 cups pumpkin purée, ½ teaspoon sea salt, and ¼ teaspoon *each* ground cloves, nutmeg, and cinnamon. (To make pumpkin purée, put 6 cups cubed pumpkin meat, ½ cup coconut water, 2 tablespoons freshly squeezed lime juice, and the seeds from 1 vanilla bean in a Vita-Mix.) Blend until puréed using the tamper, stopping the machine to scrape down the sides. Use as directed in recipes or cover and refrigerate for up to 2 days. Process to make sure all the ingredients are incorporated. If using Grezzo cheese, opt for the cashew variety. Taste to be sure cheesecake is sweet enough, as some pumpkins have a higher sugar content than others. Add more agave if necessary.

RASPBERRY MACADAMIA MASCARPONE CHEESECAKE • Once the batter is in the pan but not set, swirl in 1 cup muddled fresh raspberries or 1 cup raspberry jam from the Angel Food Cake (page 426), using a chopstick. If using Grezzo cheese, opt for the macadamia variety.

APPLE PAVÉ

Pavé translates to "paving stone" in French, which is what these layered apple slices look like when sliced. A mixture of tart (Granny Smith) and sweet (McIntosh) apples are macerated in citrus juices and zest and agave to soften them. To dress up this dessert, line the pan with Shortbread Crumble (page 444) and accompany each serving with a scoop of Clove Ice Cream (page 456) and a drizzle of Lucuma Caramel Sauce (page 440).

• • • Makes 4 servings • • •

Juice of 1 grapefruit

Juice of 1 orange

Juice of 1 lemon

Juice of 1 lime

A few grates of grapefruit, orange, lemon, and lime zest

2 tablespoons agave nectar

Seeds from 2 vanilla beans

6 apples, unpeeled and sliced paper-thin on a mandoline (discard the seeds)

1. Whisk the citrus juices and zests, agave, and vanilla seeds together in a bowl.
2. Add the apple slices and toss to coat. Let apple slices macerate for 1 hour at room temperature.
3. Layer the apples evenly in a 6-cup dish, slightly overlapping each slice a bit. The goal is make the pavé uniform with no peaks in the middle or sides. Pour any leftover citrus juices over the apples to cover.
4. Put a piece of wax paper over the apples, then weight down the pavé with glass jars filled with water and refrigerate for 2 to 3 hours before slicing. To serve, slice into 4 pieces. Cover and refrigerate for up to 4 days.

CHOCOLATE PUDDING

This is the best chocolate pudding. Ever. Cooked or raw. It even develops a thin skin on the surface like the cooked version.

• • • Makes 4 servings • • •

5 avocados, peeled and pitted

1 cup agave nectar

¼ cup cacao powder

Pinch of sea salt

Seeds from 1 vanilla bean

1. Put all the ingredients in a Vita-Mix. Blend the ingredients to a creamy consistency. Stop and start the machine, scraping down the sides as necessary.
2. Pour the mixture into a bowl. You can eat this warm right away or refrigerate to thicken for 1 hour. Cover and refrigerate for 2 to 3 days.

DESSERT SAUCES and TOPPINGS: FINISHING TOUCHES

These dessert toppings and sauces are literally the "icing on the cake"! A basic brownie, simple banana whip, or a quick cookie can be turned into the most decadent of desserts by topping them with a rich, creamy chocolate frosting, Coconut Cream, or sweet agave or pumpkin sauce. Mix and match desserts and toppings to create new taste sensations.

· · · · · · · · · · · · · · · · ·

CHOCOLATE SAUCE

A go-to sauce for desserts of all kinds—from brownie to ice cream sundaes.

• • • Makes 3 cups • • •

1 cup cacao powder

1 cup agave nectar

1 cup coconut oil, melted

1. Blend the cacao powder and agave together in a Vita-Mix.
2. With the machine on, drizzle in the coconut oil, stopping the machine every so often to scrape down the sides. Blend until smooth and, with the machine still on, slowly add ¼ cup water. The sauce should be smooth and thick. Store in a covered container at room temperature; it will keep for up to 10 days.

CHOCOLATE FROSTING

Our go-to frosting for cookies, brownies, and cakes.

• • • Makes 3 cups • • •

1¾ cup cashews, soaked in water for 8 hours

1 cup agave nectar

1 cup cacao powder

½ teaspoon sea salt

1. Put all the ingredients in a Vita-Mix. Blend to a smooth consistency. Add a tablespoon of water if the frosting is too thick to blend.
2. Cover and store in the refrigerator for up to 1 week. Bring to room temperature before using.

LAVENDER AGAVE SAUCE

Drizzle a spoonful over a bowl of ice cream or berries or a slice of cheesecake.

• • • Makes 2 cups • • •

2 cups agave nectar

3 fresh lavender wands, greens, and flowers *or* 1 tablespoon culinary lavender

1. Combine the agave and lavender in a Vita-Mix and blend. Pour the mixture through a strainer to remove any stems or rough bits.
2. Store in a covered container at room temperature for up to 10 days.

CINNAMON AGAVE SAUCE • Use two 3-inch cinnamon sticks in place of the lavender. Pour the mixture through a strainer to remove any bits of cinnamon sticks.

ROSEMARY-INFUSED AGAVE

• • • Makes 1 cup • • •

¼ cup chopped fresh rosemary leaves

1 cup agave nectar

1. Combine the rosemary and agave in a Vita-Mix and blend for 1 minute. Pour the mixture into a container through a strainer to remove any stems or rough bits.
2. Cover and refrigerate for up to 3 weeks.

BLACKBERRY SALSA

A combination of berries is nice and colorful, but if you only have one type available, that's fine. Use as a topping for desserts and on cereals. Substitute regular basil or mint if Thai basil isn't available.

• • • Makes about 2 cups • • •

½ **pint (about 1 cup) blackberries**
½ **pint (about 1 cup) raspberries**
10 Thai basil leaves, thinly sliced into strips
Pinch of fleur de sel
Pinch of dried stevia

Combine all the ingredients together in a bowl. Using a wooden spoon, crush some of the berries to release their juices. Allow the sauce to sit for an hour or so before using.

CRANBERRY COULIS

This thick sauce is not only good for desserts but can also garnish arugula salads or be folded into juices and smoothies.

• • • Makes 2 cups • • •

3 cups (12-ounce bag) fresh cranberries

1 cup dried cranberries

¼ cup freshly squeezed grapefruit juice

¾ cup freshly squeezed orange juice

Zest of 1 lime

½ cup agave nectar

1. Put all the ingredients in a Vita-Mix. Blend until puréed.
2. Pass the mixture through a fine-mesh strainer or a nut bag. Whisk half of the solids into the sauce; discard the rest. Store the sauce in a covered jar in the refrigerator for up to 1 week.

LUCUMA CARAMEL SAUCE

The lucuma gives this sauce an authentic butterscotch flavor and texture.

• • • Makes 2 cups • • •

1 cup agave nectar

½ cup lucuma powder

1. Put the agave and ½ cup water in a Vita-Mix. Blend until combined.
2. With the machine running, pour the lucuma in through the top. The sauce should be thick, creamy, and smooth. Blend thoroughly, as lucuma tends to be a bit gritty.
3. Cover and store at room temperature for up to 1 week.

COCONUT CREAM

Don't be afraid to crack a coconut and get the meat out! Once you get the hang of it, you'll find cracking a few coconuts very therapeutic. We use the variety known as young Thai coconuts for their soft, almost gelatinous and creamy consistency. Start by selecting heavy coconuts. A light one indicates that there may be cracks and the coconut may be dried out or the coconut water has leaked out. One young Thai coconut yields ½ cup to 1 cup fresh coconut meat.

• • • Makes 2½ cups • • •

2 cups fresh coconut meat

1 cup coconut water

1. Put the coconut meat and coconut water in a Vita-Mix. Blend until the mixture is thick and creamy, like heavy cream.
2. Pour into a glass jar with a lid, refrigerate, and shake before using. It will stay fresh for 2 days.

PUMPKIN COULIS

A bright, seasonal sauce to garnish desserts.

• • • Makes 3½ cups • • •

6 cups coarsely chopped sugar pumpkin meat

1 cup agave nectar

½ cup fresh squeezed grapefruit juice

Seeds from 1 vanilla bean

Pinch of sea salt

1. Put all the ingredients in a Vita-Mix. Blend until puréed using the tamper.
2. Pass the mixture through a fine-mesh strainer or a nut bag. Whisk half of the solids into the sauce; discard the rest. Store the sauce in a covered jar in the refrigerator for up to 1 week.

STRAWBERRY-VANILLA SAUCE

Drizzle over ice cream or add to sparkling beverages and lemonade.

• • • Makes 2 cups • • •

2½ cups coarsely chopped strawberries

2 tablespoons agave nectar

1 vanilla bean pod

1. Combine the strawberries and agave in a food processor. Using the pulse button, process to coarsely chop the fruit.
2. Transfer the mixture to a bowl. Submerge the vanilla pod in the sauce, cover, and let infuse for 4 hours before using. Store, covered, in the refrigerator for 1 week.

SHORTBREAD CRUMBLE

An easy-to-make crumble that can be used as a dessert crust or with ice cream.

• • • Makes 2 cups • • •

2 cups cashews

¼ teaspoon ground nutmeg

¼ teaspoon ground cinnamon

¼ teaspoon sea salt

½ cup pitted dates

1. Put the cashews, nutmeg, cinnamon, and salt in a food processor. Pulse to make a coarse flour. Don't overprocess the nuts into a butter.

2. One by one, quickly feed the dates into machine through the hole in the top while it's running. As soon as they are incorporated, the shortbread is done. The crumble will be light and airy. Cover and store in an airtight container at room temperature for up to 2 weeks.

GRAHAM CRACKER CRUST

Dried goji berries combined with the spices give the crust a graham cracker–like flavor. If you can't get them, substitute dried apricots or figs.

• • • Makes 8 to 10 servings • • •

2 cups walnuts

1 cup dried goji berries

½ teaspoon ground nutmeg

½ teaspoon ground cinnamon

½ teaspoon sea salt

1. Put all the ingredients in a food processor.
2. Blend until the mixture is coarsely ground. The crust can be covered and stored at room temperature for up to 1 week.

ICE CREAMS and SORBETS: CHILL OUT

The rich, creamy ice cream served at Grezzo has become so popular that we now ship it all over the country. But it's so easy to make these gluten-free, dairy-free, wheat-free, soy-free treats at home. They contain no processed sugars or chemicals and no preservatives or fillers of any kind. Unlike dairy-based ice cream, there's no custard to cook and cool down, so these treats can be ready in an hour or two. Making raw vegan ice cream is easy; use the basic techniques and recipes to create your own innovations.

You will need an ice cream maker, and once you try these recipes, you'll want to keep your freezer filled with different flavors. The ingredients blend easily in the Vita-Mix, then they get spun like authentic dairy ice cream in your ice cream machine.

One important technique: Whenever blending ingredients in a Vita-Mix to achieve a super-smooth consistency, removing the lid while the machine is running and using a spatula to move the ingredients around is a must. Once ingredients start to blend and the mixture has settled, carefully remove the lid and use a spatula to "row" the mixture along, front to back and side to side. This guarantees that the mixture is being processed entirely, and not just the bottom half is being blended. Also, be sure to taste the ice cream base before putting it into the ice cream machine to make sure it is sweet and flavorful enough. Feel free to add an extra drop of essential oil, a splash more of agave, or an extra date as desired.

. . . .

QUICK BANANA WHIP

• • • Makes 2 servings • • •

If you have too many overripe bananas, peel them, put them in a plastic bag, and freeze them to make whip similar to soft-serve ice cream. Use a juicer that homogenizes or a food processor.

2 to 3 frozen bananas

1. Feed the frozen bananas through the juicer with the homogenizing attachment in place, or place the bananas in a food processor and blend until super-smooth. If using a food processor, the bananas may look gritty. Continue to blend until whipped.
2. Enjoy right away as is or add a topping of your choice.

Making Raw Ice Cream

- All recipes make two quarts, except when specified.
- The ice cream will be soft and custardy right out of the machine. If you prefer firmer ice cream, scrape it from the machine into a plastic container and freeze it for an hour. If you're not going to serve (or eat) it immediately, then store in the freezer for up to one month.

VANILLA ICE CREAM

For purists who prefer their ice cream plain, simple, and all vanilla. For those who need something more, see the variations that follow or top with some Lucuma Caramel Sauce (page 440) or puréed strawberries.

• • • Makes 2 quarts • • •

2 cups cashews

2 cups tightly packed coconut meat

4 cups coconut water

Seeds from 4 vanilla beans

1 cup agave nectar

1. Combine all of the ingredients in a Vita-Mix. Blend until completely smooth; there should be no lumps. Once the ingredients are blended, carefully remove the lid while the machine is running. The ingredients won't splatter. Using a spatula, push the mixture around to make sure it's smooth. Replace the top before turning the machine off.

2. Pour into an ice cream maker and freeze according to the manufacturer's directions. Serve immediately or freeze.

BROWNIE SUNDAE • Add 2 cups Brownie (page 416) chunks during the last 10 minutes of the ice cream machine's cycle.

MINT TRUFFLE VANILLA • Add 10 Peppermint Truffles (page 413) cut into quarters during the last 10 minutes of the ice cream machine's cycle.

STRAWBERRY BREEZE • Add 3 cups smashed strawberries during the last 10 minutes of the ice cream machine's cycle.

VANILLA CHIP • Add ¼ cup cacao nibs during the last 10 minutes of the ice cream machine's cycle.

VANILLA PEACH • Add 2 cups coarsely chopped peach during the last 10 minutes of the ice cream machine's cycle.

CHOCOLATE ICE CREAM

The most popular flavor. Raw cacao and agave nectar balance the bitter and sweet perfectly.

Top with Lucuma Caramel Sauce (page 440) or Chocolate Sauce (page 434) or try the variations that follow.

• • • Makes 2 quarts • • •

2 cups cashews

2 cups tightly packed coconut meat

4 cups coconut water

1 cup cacao powder

1 cup agave nectar

1. Combine all the ingredients in a Vita-Mix. Blend until completely smooth; there should be no lumps. Once the ingredients are blended, carefully remove the lid while the machine is running. The ingredients won't splatter. Using a spatula, push the mixture around to make sure it's smooth. Replace the top before turning the machine off.

2. Pour into an ice cream maker and freeze according to the manufacturer's directions. Serve immediately or freeze.

ALMOND BUTTERCUP • Drop in 1 cup almond butter (page 105) during the last 10 minutes of the ice cream machine's cycle.

CHOCOLATE ALLSPICE • Grind 2 whole pieces allspice in a spice grinder or Vita-Mix, then combine with the other ingredients in the Vita-Mix.

CHOCOLATE CHOCOLATE CHIP • Add ¼ cup cacao chips during the last 10 minutes of the ice cream machine's cycle.

DARK CHOCOLATE • Increase the cacao powder and agave to 1½ cups and use 1½ cups cashews.

MINT FUDGE • Add 8 drops high-quality peppermint essential oil and fold in 1 cup Chocolate Sauce (page 434) during the last 5 minutes of the ice cream machine's cycle. Or fold in 10 Chocolate Truffles (page 413).

MOCHA BROWNIE • Reduce the cacao powder to 2 tablespoons and add 2 cups Brownie (page 416) chunks during the last 10 minutes of the ice cream machine's cycle.

MOCHA FUDGE RIPPLE • Add 2 tablespoons cacao powder and the seeds from 2 vanilla beans to the Vita-Mix, and add 1 cup Chocolate Sauce (page 434) during the last 5 minutes of the ice cream machine's cycle.

CHOCOLATE MALT ICE CREAM

Maca, a powder made from a South American tuber, imparts a malt-like flavor to this frozen confection. Sprinkle some Graham Cracker Crust (page 445) crumble on top for a crunchy contrast.

• • • Makes 2 quarts • • •

2 cups cashews

2 cups tightly packed coconut meat

4 cups coconut water

¼ cup maca powder

1 cup agave nectar

¾ cup cacao powder

1. Combine all the ingredients in a Vita-Mix. Blend until completely smooth; there should be no lumps. Once the ingredients are blended, carefully remove the lid while the machine is running. The ingredients won't splatter. Using a spatula, push the mixture around to make sure it's smooth. Replace the top before turning the machine off.

2. Pour into ice cream maker and freeze according to the manufacturer's instructions. Serve immediately or freeze.

RUM RAISIN–PISTACHIO ICE CREAM

Unlike the other ice cream recipes in this chapter, this one takes some planning ahead, soaking the raisins in rum and dehydrating the pistachios overnight. Dehydrating the nuts makes them crunchier. Fresh stevia is preferred if you can find it, or use dried green stevia. White stevia is processed and not raw.

• • • Makes 2 quarts • • •

2 cups raisins

1 cup Grezzo Rum (page 397)

1 tablespoon dried stevia *or*

   1 cup fresh stevia leaves

4 cups coconut water

2 cups cashews

2 cups tightly packed coconut meat

Seeds from 3 vanilla beans

1 cup pistachios, dehydrated for 8 hours

1. Combine the raisins and rum in a bowl and soak overnight.
2. Combine the stevia and coconut water in a Vita-Mix and blend. Strain through a fine-mesh strainer or nut bag.
3. Rinse out the Vita-Mix. Put the sweetened coconut water, cashews, coconut meat, and vanilla seeds in the Vita-Mix. Blend until completely smooth; there should be no lumps. Once the ingredients are blended, carefully remove the lid while the machine is running. The ingredients won't splatter. Using a spatula, push the mixture around to make sure it's smooth. Replace the top before turning the machine off.
4. Pour into an ice cream maker and freeze according to the manufacturer's directions. Add the rum-soaked raisins and pistachios during the last 10 minutes. Serve immediately or freeze.

CLOVE ICE CREAM

Spicy and exotic, this ice cream pairs well with tart fruit. Drizzle on some Cinnamon Agave Sauce (page 436) before serving.

• • • Makes 2 quarts • • •

2 teaspoons ground cloves

2 cups cashews

2 cups tightly packed coconut meat

4 cups coconut water

1 cup agave nectar

1. Combine all the ingredients in a Vita-Mix. Blend until completely smooth; there should be no lumps. Once the ingredients are blended, carefully remove the lid while the machine is running. The ingredients won't splatter. Using a spatula, push the mixture around to make sure it's smooth. Replace the top before turning the machine off.

2. Pour into an ice cream maker and freeze according to the manufacturer's instructions. Serve immediately or freeze.

CINNAMON ICE CREAM • Substitute 2 teaspoons ground cinnamon for the cloves.

CAROB-CANDIED WALNUT ICE CREAM

When using carob in ice cream, pass the mixture through a nut bag or fine-mesh strainer so the grainy bits are left behind.

• • • Makes 2 quarts • • •

2 cups cashews

2 cups tightly packed coconut meat

4 cups coconut water

1 cup agave nectar

¾ cup carob powder

¼ cacao powder

1 or 2 ripe bananas

1 cup Candied Walnuts (page 216)

1. Combine all ingredients except for candied walnuts in a Vita-Mix. Blend until completely smooth; there should be no lumps. Once the ingredients are blended, carefully remove the lid while the machine is running. The ingredients won't splatter. Using a spatula, push the mixture around to make sure it's smooth. Replace the top before turning the machine off.
2. Squeeze the ice cream base through a nut bag.
3. Pour into an ice cream maker and freeze according to the manufacturer's directions. Add the candied walnuts during the last 10 minutes. Serve immediately or freeze.

SALTY ALMOND ICE CREAM

A little salt brings out the sweet flavor of this nutty confection. The mouth feel is incredibly creamy and rich. Top it with Chocolate Sauce (page 434), Strawberry-Vanilla Sauce (page 443), Coconut Cream (page 441), or Blackberry Salsa (page 438).

• • • Makes 2 quarts • • •

2 cups cashews

2 cups tightly packed coconut meat

4 cups almond milk (page 104)

½ cup coconut water

10 pitted dates

1 teaspoon fleur de sel

1. Combine the cashews, coconut meat, almond milk, coconut water, and dates in a Vita-Mix. Blend until completely smooth; there should be no lumps. Once the ingredients are blended, carefully remove the lid while the machine is running. The ingredients won't splatter. Using a spatula, push the mixture around to make sure it's smooth. Replace the top before turning the machine off.

2. Pour into an ice cream maker and freeze according to the manufacturer's directions. Add the salt during the last 10 minutes of the machine's cycle. Serve immediately or freeze.

CANDY APPLE ICE CREAM

A spin on an autumn caramel candied apple.

• • • Makes 2 quarts • • •

2 cups cashews

2 cups tightly packed coconut meat

3 cups coconut water

4 apples

1 cup agave nectar

Juice of ½ lemon

1 cup Lucuma Caramel Sauce (page 440)

1. Combine all ingredients except the caramel in a Vita-Mix. Blend until completely smooth; there should be no lumps. Once the ingredients are blended, carefully remove the lid while the machine is running. The ingredients won't splatter. Using a spatula, push the mixture around to make sure it's smooth. Replace the top before turning the machine off.

2. Pour into an ice cream maker and freeze according to the manufacturer's directions. Add the caramel during the last 10 minutes of the machine's cycle. Serve immediately or freeze.

LAVENDER BLUE ICE CREAM

A stunningly beautiful ice cream made with midsummer fruit and flowers. Use fresh lavender flowers that have not been sprayed with pesticides. (Culinary lavender is available in some stores. You can also dry your own in the dehydrator for year-round use.) A little lavender goes a long way; don't overdo it.

• • • Makes 2 quarts • • •

2 cups cashews

2 cups tightly packed coconut meat

4 cups coconut water

3 lavender sprigs *or* 1 tablespoon dried edible lavender flowers

1 cup agave nectar

1 cup blueberries, lightly crushed

1. Combine the cashews, coconut meat and water, ¼ cup blueberries, lavender, and agave in a Vita-Mix. Blend until completely smooth; there should be no lumps. Once the ingredients are blended, carefully remove the lid while the machine is running. The ingredients won't splatter. Using a spatula, push the mixture around to make sure it's smooth. Replace the top before turning machine off.

2. Pour into an ice cream maker and freeze according to the manufacturer's directions. Add the remaining crushed blueberries during the last 10 minutes. Serve immediately or freeze.

PUMPKIN PATCH ICE CREAM

The perfect dessert for a Thanksgiving or autumn dinner.

• • • Makes 2 quarts • • •

1 cup cashews

2 cups tightly packed coconut meat

5 cups diced pumpkin

3 cups coconut water

Seeds from 1 vanilla bean

1 cup agave nectar

¼ teaspoon ground cinnamon

¼ teaspoon ground nutmeg

¼ teaspoon ground cloves

1. Combine all the ingredients in a Vita-Mix. Blend until completely smooth; there should be no lumps. Once the ingredients are blended, carefully remove the lid while the machine is running. The ingredients won't splatter. Using a spatula, push the mixture around to make sure it's smooth. Replace the top before turning the machine off.

2. Pour into an ice cream maker and freeze according to the manufacturer's directions. Serve immediately.

BLACK RASPBERRY–CARDAMOM ICE CREAM

Top with some chocolate sauce or fresh berries.

• • • Makes 2 quarts • • •

2 cups black raspberries or blackberries

2 cardamom pods

1 cup agave nectar

2 cups cashews

2 cups tightly packed coconut meat

4 cups coconut water

Seeds from 1 vanilla bean

1. Combine the blackberries, cardamom pods, and agave in a Vita-Mix and blend until smooth. Strain the mixture through a nut bag or a fine-mesh strainer over a bowl. (Don't skip this step; it will remove the seeds and any coarse bits from the cardamom.)

2. Rinse out the Vita-Mix and blend the cashews, coconut meat and water, and vanilla seeds. Blend until completely smooth; there should be no lumps. Once the ingredients start to come together, carefully remove the lid while the machine is running. The ingredients won't splatter. Using a spatula, push the mixture around to make sure it's smooth. Replace the top before turning the machine off. Fold in the blackberry agave.

3. Pour into an ice cream maker and freeze according to the manufacturer's directions. Serve immediately or freeze.

GINGER-PEACH ICE CREAM

Break up some Shortbread Crumble (page 444) on top of each serving.

• • • Makes 2 quarts • • •

2 cups cashews

2 cups tightly packed coconut meat

2 cups coconut water

¼ cup freshly grated ginger

6 ripe peaches, pitted and diced

1 cup agave nectar

2 cups Shortbread Crumble (page 444)

1. Combine the cashews, coconut meat and water, ginger, 4 of the diced peaches, and the agave in a Vita-Mix. Blend until completely smooth; there should be no lumps. Once the ingredients are blended, carefully remove the lid while the machine is running. The ingredients won't splatter. Using a spatula, push the mixture around to make sure it's smooth. Replace the top before turning the machine off.

2. Pour into an ice cream maker and freeze according to the manufacturer's directions.

3. Add the remaining 2 diced peaches and the shortbread crumble during the last 10 minutes of the ice cream machine's cycle. Serve immediately or freeze.

TOMATO-BASIL SORBET

Accompany a cup of this savory sorbet with an arugula salad or an antipasto plate or add a scoop to avocado soup.

• • • Makes 1½ quarts • • •

6 cups chopped tomatoes (about 5 to 6 tomatoes)

2 cups tightly packed coconut meat

½ cup tomato water (page 408)

½ cup chopped basil leaves

1. Combine the tomatoes, coconut meat, and tomato water in a Vita-Mix. Blend until completely smooth; there should be no lumps. If necessary, stop the machine and use a rubber spatula to scrape down the sides of the blender.
2. Pour into an ice cream maker and freeze according to the manufacturer's directions, adding the basil during the last 10 minutes. Serve immediately or freeze.

CAPE COD CRANBERRY SORBET

Pass the cranberry mixture through a nut bag or fine-mesh strainer to remove the skins. If using dried cranberries, use just 3 cups dried fruit and 5 cups coconut water. Good accompaniments are Lucuma Caramel Sauce (page 440) or Chocolate Sauce (page 434).

• • • Makes 2 quarts • • •

3 cups tightly packed coconut meat

3 cups coconut water

4 cups fresh cranberries

½ teaspoon orange zest

1 cup agave nectar

1. Combine all the ingredients in a Vita-Mix. Blend until completely smooth; there should be no lumps. If necessary, stop the machine and use a rubber spatula to scrape down the sides of the blender.

2. Pour into an ice cream maker and freeze according to the manufacturer's directions. Serve immediately or freeze.

COCONUT SORBET

Serve with any chocolate dessert or top with diced tropical fruit.

• • • Makes 2 quarts • • •

4 cups tightly packed coconut meat

4 cups coconut water

1 tablespoon dried stevia

1. Combine all the ingredients in a Vita-Mix. Blend until completely smooth; there should be no lumps. If necessary, stop the machine and use a rubber spatula to scrape down the sides of the blender.
2. Pour into an ice cream maker and freeze according to the manufacturer's directions. Serve immediately or freeze.

LIME RICKEY SORBET

See the note at the beginning of the chapter with suggestions for other citrus combinations, such as blood orange and lime.

• • • Makes 2 quarts • • •

4 cups tightly packed coconut meat

4 cups coconut water

¼ cup freshly squeezed lime juice

1 cup agave nectar

2 cups raspberries, muddled

1. Combine all the ingredients except the raspberries in a Vita-Mix. Blend until completely smooth; there should be no lumps. If necessary, stop the machine and use a rubber spatula to scrape down the sides of the blender.

2. Pour into an ice cream maker and freeze according to the manufacturer's directions. Add the raspberries during the last 10 minutes. Serve immediately or freeze.

LEMON-LIME SORBET

Perfect on a hot summer's night.

• • • Makes 2 quarts • • •

2½ cups freshly squeezed lemon juice

2½ cups freshly squeezed lime juice

Zest of 6 lemons

Zest of 6 limes

4 cups tightly packed coconut meat

1½ cups agave nectar

1. Put all the ingredients in a Vita-Mix. Blend until completely smooth; there should be no lumps. If necessary, stop the machine and use a rubber spatula to scrape down the sides of the blender.
2. Pour into an ice cream maker and freeze according to the manufacturer's directions.

SUPER BERRY SORBET

Tangy and tart, this refreshing sorbet is made with antioxidant-rich berries, so it not only tastes great but is good for you, too.

• • • Makes 2 quarts • • •

3 cups tightly packed coconut meat

4 cups coconut water

½ cup golden berries

½ cup goji berries

¼ cup fresh or dried cranberries

¼ cup pitted dates

1. Combine all the ingredients in a Vita-Mix. Blend until completely smooth; there should be no lumps. If necessary, stop the machine and use a rubber spatula to scrape down the sides of the blender.
2. Pour into an ice cream maker and freeze according to the manufacturer's directions.

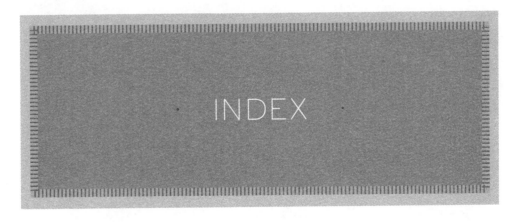

INDEX